NINETEENTH-CENTURY LOCAL GOVERNANCE IN OTTOMAN BULGARIA

Edinburgh Studies on the Ottoman Empire
Series Editor: Kent F. Schull

Published and forthcoming titles

Migrating Texts: Circulating Translations around the Eastern Mediterranean
Marilyn Booth

The Kizilbash-Alevis in Ottoman Anatolia: Sufism, Politics and Community
Ayfer Karakaya-Stump

*Çemberlitaş Hamami in Istanbul: The Biographical Memoir
of a Turkish Bath*
Nina Macaraig

*Nineteenth-Century Local Governance in Ottoman Bulgaria:
Politics in Provincial Councils*
M. Safa Saraçoğlu

Prisons in the Late Ottoman Empire: Microcosms of Modernity
Kent F. Schull

Ruler Visibility and Popular Belonging in the Ottoman Empire
Darin Stephanov

edinburghuniversitypress.com/series/esoe

NINETEENTH-CENTURY LOCAL GOVERNANCE IN OTTOMAN BULGARIA

POLITICS IN PROVINCIAL COUNCILS

M. Safa Saraçoğlu

EDINBURGH
University Press

*To my mother, Nurcan Kaygusuz,
my sister, Nihan Yolsal
and my wife, Heather Almer*

Edinburgh University Press is one of the leading university presses in the UK.
We publish academic books and journals in our selected subject areas across the humanities and social sciences, combining cutting-edge scholarship with high editorial and production values to produce academic works of lasting importance. For more information visit our website: edinburghuniversitypress.com

© M. Safa Saraçoğlu, 2018

Edinburgh University Press Ltd
The Tun – Holyrood Road
12 (2f) Jackson's Entry
Edinburgh EH8 8PJ

Typeset in Jaghbuni by
Servis Filmsetting Ltd, Stockport, Cheshire

A CIP record for this book is available from the British Library

ISBN 978 1 4744 3099 9 (hardback)
ISBN 978 1 4744 3101 9 (webready PDF)
ISBN 978 1 4744 3102 6 (epub)

The right of M. Safa Saraçoğlu to be identified as author of this work has been asserted in accordance with the Copyright, Designs and Patents Act 1988 and the Copyright and Related Rights Regulations 2003 (SI No. 2498).

Contents

List of Maps, Figures and Tables		vii
Abbreviations		viii
Preface		ix
1.	Introduction	1
	The Argument	4
	Vidin	5
	Structure of the Book	8
2.	Contextualising the Nineteenth Century	14
	The Tanzimat Era: Marking a Crisis and a Transition	15
	Means of Production and Ottoman Social Formation	18
	From Tax Farmers to Tax Collectors	22
	The Liberal-capitalist Ottoman Social Formation	26
	Governance, Official Print and Information Flow	31
	Conclusion	35
3.	Sitting Together: Local Councils and the Politics of Election in the County of Vidin	44
	The Many Parts of the Imperial Dominions: the County as an Administrative Unit	46
	The 1871 Regulation: the County as a Reflection of the Province	48
	Councils: Inevitable Dynamism?	49
	Councils: Conveying or Constituting Reality?	54
	Of Permanency and Change: the Politics of Election	58
	Conclusion	72
4.	Once Inside the Chamber . . . Participation in the Politics of Local Administration	81
	Seals: Images of Participation?	82
	Yearbooks: Reflections of the Judicio-administrative Sphere	101
	Conclusion: a Better Vision of the System?	110

5. Writing Politics: Ottoman Governmentality and the
   Language of Reports 116
   'Several Times He Had Been Given Well-intended
   Reminders': a Case of Local Antagonism 117
   Land and Power in Berkofça 122
   Ottoman Governmentality 125
   Utilising Ottoman Governance 130
   Staying Out: Challenging Ottoman Governmentality 136
   Conclusion 140

6. 'Cattle Thieves': Refugee Settlement, Ottoman
   Governmentality and Biopolitics 146
   The Numbers 147
   Cattle as Liquidity 152
   'Security, Territory, Population' in Vidin 156
   From Refugees to Cattle Thieves 158
   Conclusion 160

7. Conclusion 165
   Survival of Lower-tier Elites 165
   Crisis and Means of Production 167
   Connected Offices 168
   Contentious Dynamics 170
   Conniving Narratives 171
   Politics of Liberalism 172

Select Bibliography 175
Index 193

Maps, Figures and Tables

Maps

1	Danube Province, from Sir R. Dalyell's 1869 report on the province	xii
2	Vidin County and environs (enlarged section from Map 1)	xiii

Figures

3.1	Some of the prominent members of the councils in Vidin	45
3.2	List of elected members in 1872	60
4.1	Vidin administrative council members' titles	85
4.2	Report of 4 August 1873	86
4.3	Report of 31 March 1874	89
4.4	The seal of Marin Novinov, upside down	98

Tables

3.1	Candidate lists for Vidin's administrative council	59
3.2	Candidate lists for Vidin's council of appeals and crimes	63
3.3	List of Vidin's administrative and judiciary council members in the yearbooks	64
3.4	Vidin's council members' appointment years	67
4.1	List of changes in titles and seal impressions in Vidin administrative council's copy register	91
4.2	Titles, names and seals of the administrative council members in Vidin in 1873	99
4.3	List of Vidin's commercial court members in the yearbooks	104
4.4	List of Vidin's municipal council members in the yearbooks	107
4.5	List of Vidin's commission of surveys members in the yearbooks	108

Abbreviations

BOA   Başbakanlık Osmanlı Arşivi [Prime Ministry Ottoman Archives], Istanbul
EI2   *Encyclopaedia of Islam, Second Edition*, edited by P. Bearman, Th. Bianquis, C. E. Bosworth, E. van Donzel and W. P. Heinrichs, Brill Online: Brill.
IA   *İslam ansiklopedisi*, Istanbul: Türkiye Diyanet Vakfı, 1988–2013.
IJMES   *International Journal of Middle Eastern Studies*
JOTSA   *Journal of the Ottoman and Turkish Studies Association*
NA   National Archives, Kew
NBKM   Sts. Cyril and Methodius National Library, Oriental Section, Sofia

I have used the following abbreviations for the *hijri* months for the dates in Ottoman documents:

Muharrem (Arabic Muharram):	(M)
Safer (Safar):	(S)
Rabiülevvel (Rabi' al-Awwal):	(Ra)
Rabiülahir (Rabi' al-Thani):	(R)
Cemaziyülevvel (Cumada al-Ula):	(Ca)
Cemaziyülahir (Cumada al-Thani):	(C)
Receb (Rajab):	(B)
Şaban (Sha'ban):	(Ş)
Ramazan (Ramadan):	(N)
Şevval (Shawwal):	(L)
Zilkade (Dhu al-Qi'da):	(Za)
Zilhicce (Dhu al-Hijja):	(Z)

Preface

Provincial governance was a very sensitive issue for the Ottomans, particularly during the tumultuous long nineteenth century, with its wars, uprisings and large demographic shifts. While conventional Weberian accounts of 'Ottoman Modernisation/Westernisation' continue to associate the provinces with resistance to centralisation or secessionist movements, this book subscribes to a critical view that warns against the urge to frame nineteenth-century Ottoman history in 'empire vs provinces' or 'state vs society' dichotomies. The tenuous provincial dynamics of the empire in this period were not only sensitive to imperial reforms but also influenced the design of such imperial policies. Many local agents successfully integrated into the post-1864 administrative structure, engaging in political negotiations to protect their interests. *Local Governance in Ottoman Bulgaria* provides a detailed picture of nineteenth-century provincial administration in the Ottoman Empire by focusing on a prototypical region and utilising untapped sources to reveal the dynamic interaction between imperial regulations and local politics.

Trying to reconstruct a decent understanding of how provincial administration operated in a beautiful but lesser-known corner of the Balkans during the nineteenth century proved to be a lengthy and arduous process. People discussed in this book are not among the known Bulgarian or Ottoman elite with an established estate or family records that might reveal some bits about their lives. Rather, they were relatively insignificant notables who strived to improve their lives through their involvement with organisations that produced generic reports, revealing very little about the concerns and negotiations of their members. Yet, whatever is left from their traces in these reports, reveal a complicated and lively political space with intriguing negotiations and networks.

The research for this dissertation was supported by the Ohio State University, the American Council of Learned Societies, Institute for Turkish Studies, Centre for Advanced Studies in Sofia, Nantes Institute for Advanced Studies and Bloomsburg University of Pennsylvania.

I am indebted to many friends and mentors in my struggle to understand the politics of local administration in nineteenth-century Ottoman Vidin.

I wish to thank my mentors at Ohio State University – Jane Hathaway, Kenneth Andrien and my adviser Carter V. Findley – for reading and critiquing my graduate work. I believe this project ended up being a bit different, if not more, than what I could argue within the bounds of my dissertation.

I am grateful to Charlotte Weber who read and helped me revise this text; the editors at EUP – Nicola Ramsey, Kirsty Woods, Eddie Clark and Lel Gillingwater – who assisted me throughout the complicated publication process; Kent Schull and the anonymous reviewers whose constructive feedback made me clarify my arguments; and Sue O'Donnell who assisted with the images in the book and designed the book cover.

I am also indebted to the staff members of the archives and libraries in Ankara, Istanbul, Sofia, Vidin, Kew and Maryland who patiently guided me through their catalogues. I owe special thanks to Margarita Dobreva, Zorka Ivanova, Stoyanka Kenderova, Rumen Kovachev, Evgeni Radushev, Genadi Vulchev and Aşkın Zorlu. Milena Methodieva and her wonderful grandmother 'Baba Radka' kindly helped me find my way around in Vidin. My discussions with Iris Agmon, Yiğit Akın, Virginia Aksan, Silvia Angelova, Febe Armanios, Sedat Bingöl, Musa Çadırcı, Boğaç Ergene, Adrian Gonzalez, Michael Hickey, William Hudon, Gerassimus Katsan, Meral Kaya, Atabey Kaygun, Christine Philliou, Avi Rubin, Kent Schull, Emre Sencer, Lisa Stallbaumer-Beishline and Zeynep Türkyılmaz helped me organise my thoughts into writing.

During the 2012/13 academic year, I had the opportunity to be a fellow at Nantes Institute for Advanced Study. The conversations that I had at the Institute with other fellows and staff, including Perry Anderson, Joseph Bergin, Emmanuel Droit, Parvis Ghassem-Fachandi, Roberto Fragale, Samuel Jube, Suleiman Mourad, Vidya Rao and Chaohua Wang, helped me significantly in revising earlier versions of this work and identifying new research questions that led me to my current project on the legal narratives and economic policies of the Ottoman Empire.

This project has its origins in my time at the Middle East Technical University and I still cherish the bonds that I established during those years. I became interested in how local administration produced statistical information while I was an economics student there. The politics around the gathering and representation of 'factual information' introduced me to the complexities of provincial governance. It has been a privilege to exchange ideas with Huricihan İslamoğlu even as the focus of my initial inquiry has expanded from my concerns back then. She has always been a stimulating intellectual mentor. In addition, I consider myself lucky to have discussed my work with Selçuk Dursun, Bogac Ergene and Alp Yücel Kaya. They have been inspiring friends and

Preface

supportive colleagues at METU and after, for over two decades. I also would like to thank Ayça Akarçaya, Bülent Anıl, Teoman Ekerbiçer, Gül Ertan, Nurhan Örün, Meltem Özmut and Ela Özver for their support and friendship.

My mother taught me to always ask why and to question everything. She pushed me to pursue my aspirations even if that meant being an ocean away. I cannot thank her enough for her support. In the process of research and writing, Heather and I welcomed Sofi Elif, Luke Emre and Marie Defne to our nomadic existence. As three beads of hope, they provided much needed entertainment and inspiration wherever we lived. They continue to brighten every single day of our lives, giving us something to look forward to tomorrow. My father-in-law Arnold Almer and my mother Nurcan Kaygusuz were invaluable to us as we often burdened them with our presence and requests. My sister Nihan Yolsal and her partner Ümit Yolsal gave continuous encouragement and support during the research and writing phase of this project.

Finally, I want to thank Heather, my love, for making my life meaningful. Her endless patience and insightful discussions gently guided me and the sacrifices she made allowed me to finish this work. She had faith in me when I did not; without her, this would not be.

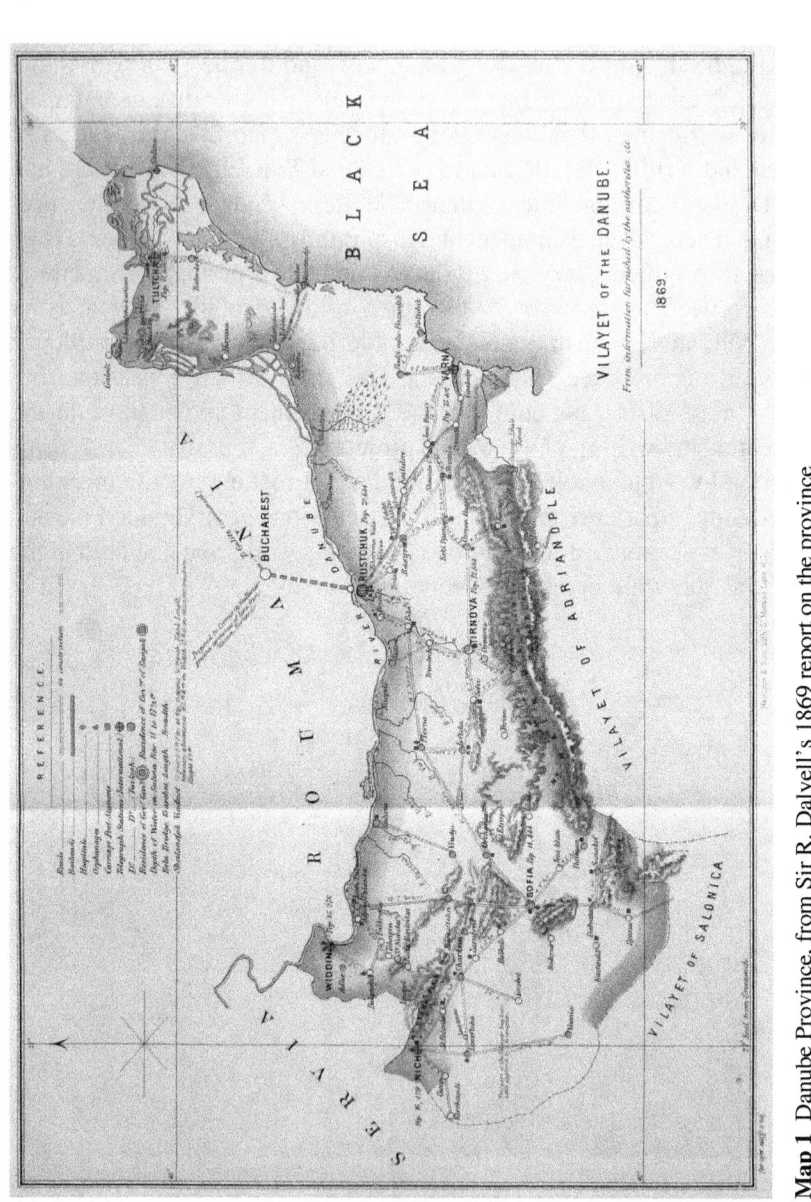

Map 1 Danube Province, from Sir R. Dalyell's 1869 report on the province
Source: PRO FO 881-2956, National Archives.

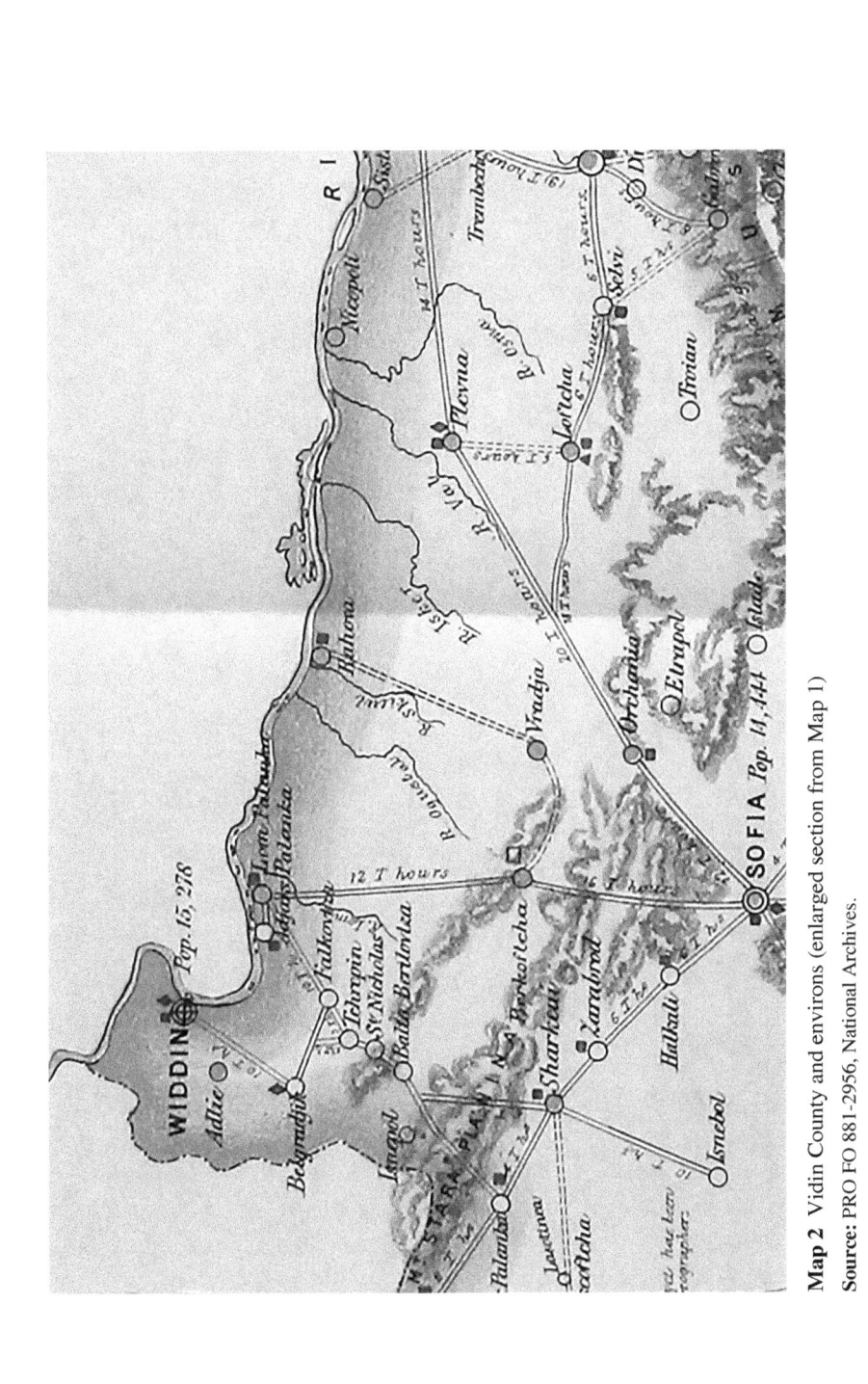

Map 2 Vidin County and environs (enlarged section from Map 1)
Source: PRO FO 881-2956, National Archives.

1

Introduction

This book examines the politics of judiciary and administrative practices in Vidin County during the 1860s and 1870s. Today Vidin County is in modern-day Bulgaria, but between 1396 and 1878 it was a county under Ottoman administration. It became a part of the Danube Province when the latter was founded in 1864 in conjunction with an imperial reform that redefined the administrative divisions of the empire; under the new system, Vidin County (*liva* or *sancak*) included the districts of Vidin (the administrative centre), 'Adliye (modern-day Kula), Belgradcık (Belogradchik), Berkofça (Bergovitsa), İvraca (Vratsa), Rahova (Rahovo) and Lom (Lom). The 1864 Ottoman Provincial Regulation also introduced a provincial bureaucratic framework that placed local judiciary and administrative councils at the centre of local governance. This book examines these councils to illuminate the contested politics of Ottoman provincial administration in the long nineteenth century.

Although the 1864 regulation marked a seminal moment in provincial administration, it was part of the larger Ottoman transformation to the 'liberal-capitalist social formation'.[1] Thus, the offices and procedures generated with this regulation provide a lens through which to view the broader imperial transformation from the provinces. It was the prominent Ottoman statesman, Midhat Paşa, who was responsible for this regulation and he first applied it in the Danube Province, where he served as the first governor of the first province established by the same regulation. Midhat Paşa's vision for the administrative divisions' structure and functions had its opponents but, at the end of the day, his perspective determined modern Ottoman provincial governance. Several of his contemporaries praised his personality and efforts, including John A. Longworth, British Consul General in Serbia, who visited the province in 1865 to observe the new order: 'A man [of] quick versatile powers ... [with a] love for order' who was 'peculiarly [qualified] for the task of organisation', which he executed with a level of 'intelligence and vigour ... [that] blinded [the Consul] to its shortcomings'.[2] Therefore, as part of Midhat Paşa's inaugural province, Vidin County serves as a good starting place to examine imperial change coming from the provinces. Through an examination of the Vidin administrative council's correspondence with the Danube Province and Istanbul, *Local Governance in Ottoman Bulgaria* explores the relationship between provincial politics and imperial transformation.

In Ottoman historiography, the imperial transformation of the late Ottoman Empire has been a lively field, shaped by modernisation–Westernisation debates in 1950s. With the rise of the New Left in the 1970s, revisionist scholars like İslamoğlu and Keyder (1977) rejected the modernisation narrative (Lockman 2004: 162–72). Despite the early start, the death of this narrative took a long time and particularly in the field of sociolegal studies it led to a false equivalence between unclearly defined notions of 'secularisation' and 'Westernisation' (Hathaway and Barbir 2008: 59–60; Rubin 2009: 121–5). Arguing for continuity between the eighteenth and nineteenth centuries, this book contributes to the expanding revisionist historiography and presents the nineteenth-century transformation of the empire as one driven predominantly by internal factors as opposed to a series of reforms that were designed by the imperial administration to impose 'modern Western' institutions on Ottoman society.[3]

State–society relations in the Ottoman provinces have been a topic of interest to scholars of the Ottoman Empire for decades.[4] Such works have shown clearly that provincial administration in the Ottoman Empire was a highly politicised arena, and that the boundaries of what constituted the state at the provincial level constantly changed, including and excluding certain members of the local community. However, the majority of these works focused on regions to the east of Istanbul, excluding Ottoman Bulgaria.[5] The Balkans constitute a significant but understudied region in both Ottoman and world history. As Frederick Anscombe (2012) noted, most Balkan histories focus exclusively on social unrest, emerging because of nationalism or class conflict. Anscombe invites us to examine how the Ottoman state operated in order to understand this transformation in the Balkans and how it fits within the rest of European history. In a similar vein, recent comparative histories of imperial rule underscore the role of imperial politics and institutional transformations (related to the rise of modern states) in the emergence of nationalist movements that destroyed several nineteenth-century empires (Bartov and Weitz 2013: 2; Burbank and Cooper 2010: 219; Leonhard and Hirschhausen 2011: 10). Focusing on the significance of imperial provincial administration in this understudied region that played a unique role in the nineteenth-century Ottoman imperial transformation, I argue that the Ottoman transformation is comparable to the histories of change and state formation in other world empires during this period.

Introduction

Delineating the 'internal social and political bases of the modern period', to use Dina Rizk Khoury's phrasing (Khoury 1997: 214), in their continuity over the last two centuries of the Ottoman Empire requires a different framing of Ottoman state–society relations following the direction suggested by Timothy Mitchell (1999: 77) to 'take seriously the elusiveness of the boundary between state and society . . . [and to] examine the parallel distinction constructed between state and economy'. Until recently, the literature on this topic in general has been dominated by two models: that of a strong state mitigating or co-opting oppositional groups or one of a weak state that existed separate from a relatively independent civil society (Khoury 1997: 213). The historiography on Ottoman administration in Bulgaria is no exception.[6] However, the relationship between state and society was not that simple. Following Albert Hourani's influential work on the 'politics of notables', particularly after the end of 1970s, an increasing number of scholars explored the connection between the local power elite and Ottoman imperial rule. As Khoury (2006: 137) has written,

> perhaps most critical for relations between the provinces and the central government, was the local social matrix within which the prerogatives of the government were played out. Although we have as yet relatively few and unevenly distributed studies of provincial Ottoman history, what is available points to the centrality of local familial and group networks in shaping the central state's relations with provincial societies.[7]

Local social matrixes constituted a grey zone where the boundaries between Ottoman state structures and provincial society became blurred. Elucidating the nature of this complex relationship and the procedures/structures that regulated it is essential to understand the nineteenth-century transformation in the larger context of the Ottoman legitimation crisis.

The Ottomans established these administrative councils at the provincial, county and district levels to handle essential local tasks, including tax collection, overseeing the planning and financing of provincial infrastructure, payment of state employees' salaries, and so on. Their tasks included reporting local incidents to the provincial capital and conveying orders from the provincial offices above to the units below their administrative supervision. The county administrative council's correspondence provides valuable information on Ottoman provincial governance in this period. However, the correspondence of this office at the imperial archives reveals a limited picture of such practices because several issues were resolved in the provincial capital before reaching the imperial centre, and those that actually made their way to Istanbul were quickly forwarded to various different offices of imperial bureaucracy. While such correspondence was recorded in the 'provincial incoming-outgoing ledgers' (Vilayet Gelen-Giden Defterleri) in the imperial capital, tracing it is a daunting task – if not entirely impossible – because the records of certain significant offices are still not available to researchers.[8]

One way to overcome these limitations is to analyse the copies of this correspondence kept at the local level. This book analyses the Vidin County administrative council's copy registers along with other documents available at Bulgarian and Turkish archives to get a better understanding of the institutional environment that produced them. The purpose of this analysis is to ascertain how local inhabitants in this particular county responded to the policies and reforms of the modern Ottoman state.

The Argument

My main argument is twofold: (1) the offices and practices of nineteenth-century Ottoman provincial governance served as a dynamic platform for the politics of local administration, and (2) the local inhabitants of Vidin effectively used this judiciary and administrative framework in this period of transformation to devise strategies for advancing their interests. *Local Governance in Ottoman Bulgaria* challenges an understanding of nineteenth-century local politics as polarised between a dominating local government trying to impose unprecedented reforms designed at the imperial centre on the one hand, and an oppressed but resistant people, rebelling against the insensitive policies of the state on the other. Without denying that a certain level of violence was prevalent, I argue, first, that the distinction between state and society was not as clear as presumed; second, that the local administrative branch of the state was not a monolithic body of state agents; and third, that society was not always oblivious to or rebellious against reform policies.

A perspective that presumes a state–society split at the local level easily lends itself to an unhealthy coalescence of theories on Ottoman decline and Bulgarian romantic nationalism (Anscombe 2012). Consider, for example, how Duncan Perry (1993: 3–4) characterises the nineteenth-century Ottoman experience in general as a 'downward spiral of ultimate dissolution, interrupted by one important era of progressiveness'. In Bulgaria, only Midhat Paşa's governorate, the Danube Province,

> prospered while he rooted out and quashed all revolutionary activity. But in general, reforms were not faithfully or fully implemented or sustained in the Balkans, and when Midhat [Paşa] was transferred [in 1868], his reforms

Introduction

eroded. However, for the increasing number of educated Bulgarians, even the imperfectly enacted reforms of this era provided a foretaste of liberty and fed their desire for still more.[9]

The 'decaying Ottoman administration' was functional only long enough (Perry does not note that Midhat Paşa's administration lasted only four years) to stimulate 'the increasing number of educated Bulgarians'. Michael Palairet (1997: 84) rejects Perry's assertion of political and economic collapse in the nineteenth-century Danube Province, arguing that 'although the most rapid phase of expansion was probably concluded in the late 1860s, the output of the Bulgarian lands . . . was at or near its peak at the time of the liberation [1878]'. As informative as Palairet's work is on the Balkan economies, he does not focus much on the political transformation of this period. His analysis, however, underscores the need to question claims regarding the impact of the 'decaying Ottoman administration' in Bulgaria.

I focus on the politics of local administration in the second half of the nineteenth century in an Ottoman county in modern-day Bulgaria with hopes of contributing to the still-emerging body of scholarship on the provincial history of the empire (Blumi 2012; Aymes 2014). Adding to that literature, I explore the nineteenth-century transformation of the empire's provincial judiciary–administrative structure by looking at a peculiar region, the Danube Province. The Ottomans established this province as a trial ground for an empire-wide reform under the governorship of Midhat Paşa who supervised the transformation of provincial administration in the whole empire (Todorova 1980; Abu-Manneh 1998; Göyünç 1982; Todorova 1993; Ceylan 2011; Petrov 2006).

While this is an attempt to understand the dimensions of the nineteenth-century transformation of the Ottoman Empire at the local level, its primary focus is on how the local notables and peasants utilised Ottoman local institutions to further their interests. An essential source for this investigation is the reports produced by the local administrative councils, which were copied in registers that were meant to be kept in the provinces. The correspondence of the administrative council – a product of various political processes – can reveal a lot about the breadth of political participation in the Ottoman administration during this period.

Vidin

Vidin is a town where the borders of Romania and Serbia meet along the Danube River. Under the Ottomans, it was a centre of a larger administrative unit bordered by the Iskar River to the east, the Stara Planina mountain range to the south and west, and the Danube River to the north. Fertile soil and a moderate climate made these lands suitable for agricultural production, mostly cereal and fodder crops, vegetables, fruit and grapes. An Ottoman survey published in 1873 indicated that 81 per cent of the population lived in rural areas (Petrov 2006: 63).

The county of Vidin spanned 4,092 square miles (10,600 square kilometres). It was, and remains, a predominantly non-Muslim region – with a Muslim population below 20 per cent in the 1860s and 1870s. This was the general character of the western counties of the Danube Province (Petrov 2006: 69–70). Ottoman statistics published in 1878 list a population of 37,185 Muslims and 154,992 non-Muslims in the county. The demographic composition was reversed in the town of Vidin, the fourth largest town in the Danube Province: a survey from 1866 reported 51.6 per cent of the population as Muslim, 34.1 per cent as Bulgarian, 6.2 per cent as Roma and 8.2 per cent as Jewish (Petrov 2006: 76).

In the nineteenth century, Vidin became an 'important economic centre, stimulated by navigation on the Danube' (Ivanova 'Widin').[10] The changes in the political arena reflected this change as well. One of the better-known *ayan*s[11] of the whole empire, Pasvanoğlu Osman Paşa of Vidin, died in 1807, bringing a sense of 'relief' to the Balkans.[12] His successor in Vidin, Molla Idris, did not cause much trouble for the imperial administration and was the last *ayan* to 'control' the region. From 1814 onward, the imperial centre directly appointed the region's administrator. 'When one looks at Vidin in the years following the death of Pasvanoğlu', notes Zens (2004: 193), 'there is very little evidence that the city was home to one of the most notorious *ayan*s in the Ottoman state, apart from buildings and other public works that bore his name.' Gradeva (2006: 149), on the other hand, notes that

> it was among the Janissaries and the rank-and-file Muslims that [Pasvanoğlu] earned his real and lasting fame. They created and circulated songs for him in which he emerges as a true hero. The age of nationalism had set in the Balkans.

These interpretations, however, do not provide a framework that could foresee the uprising that happened only a few decades later in 1849, when Vidin served as the centre of a tax rebellion that involved up to 10,000 people and dozens of villages from the region (Aytekin 2012: 197–8).

While there are some differences in the ways that scholars have explained the reasons behind the 1849 tax rebellion, overall they seem to agree that 'the land tenure regime and the highly exploitative relations between cultivators and landlords in the Vidin area' engendered a lot of discontent,

Introduction

particularly among non-Muslims.[13] At the centre of this problem were the large estates (*çiftlik*) owned by the 'landlords' (*gospodar* – Bulgarian for 'master'). Large estates did not emerge in the nineteenth century. As early as the seventeenth century such estates became common in the Balkans and western Anatolia (Zens 2004: 20; McGowan 1981: 73–9; İslamoğlu-İnan 1987: 101–59). In Vidin, political-military developments contributed to the formation of these large estates. As Svetlana Ivanova ('Widin') notes, the county remained on the militarised Ottoman frontier line against various enemies until the end of the eighteenth century when it became the centre for Pasvanoğlu Osman Paşa's highly charged secession movement.

For Vidiners, as inhabitants of a highly militarised zone, these two centuries meant gradual accumulation of usufruct in the hands of a military class, which, during the military reforms of Selim III, chose to ally with Pasvanoğlu Osman Paşa against the imperial administration (Dimitrov 1972: 13–28). Thus, the particular land regime that led to the uprisings had been established prior to the nineteenth century, worked – for the most part – to the benefit of the military class, and was further intensified during Pasvanoğlu's rule in Vidin when the Janissaries supported him in his resistance (Anscombe 2006: 120).

The complaints about this land regime centred around three districts in Vidin ('Adliye, Belgradcık and Lom).[14] According to the 1874 provincial yearbook, there were 161 villages in these districts; only three had mixed Muslim and non-Muslim populations and twenty-five had Muslim-only populations; the remaining villages had entirely non-Muslim populations.[15] The villages in these districts, not unlike the others, were highly segregated along religious lines. For the most part, the Muslim landlords did not live in the same villages as the actual cultivators.

In the eighteenth and early nineteenth centuries the land was becoming 'increasingly mobile, capable of being bought and sold' because of higher monetisation in the economy and centralisation in revenue-extraction mechanisms (Adanır 2006: 167). However, by the mid-nineteenth century, elevated costs and diminishing returns had made these estates less profitable (Findley 2010: 109; Palairet 1997: 43–6). This meant that, particularly after the Land Code of 1858, more of these estates were 'sold' to the cultivators, some of whom had been living on those lands. The Vidin uprising happened in the midst of this institutional transformation.

Following the uprisings, when this land regime (*gospodarlık*) was abolished, 'the usufruct of the lands was transferred to the state'.[16] After eliminating the peasants' basis for claims on these lands (the usufruct rights), the imperial administration sought to collect lump-sum payments from the peasants in return for a title deed which would make the peasant the legal owner of the property. A decree from the Supreme Council of Judicial Ordinances (Meclis-i Vala-yı Ahkam-ı Adliye) sent to Vidin on 13 May 1863 (NBKM, VD 96/38) indicates that even after fifteen years, cultivators refused to pay money to 'buy' the land they had been tilling. Unable to collect a lump sum, the Supreme Council decided that it would be easier to get the money from the cultivators by dividing it into small increments that would not exceed the amount of rent they used to pay to the *gospodar*s. As the old right-holders lost their claims on usufruct, the cultivators in the region became de facto owners of land.

The period of the nineteenth century prior to 1864 witnessed a significant transformation of the socio-economic structure in Vidin County. Pasvanoğlu and his supporters lost their political might during the first decades of the century while the imperial administration decided to abolish the *gospodarlık* regime in the immediate aftermath of the 1849 uprising. Vidin became a relatively more stable county with a different composition of the political elite, within which land ownership was still one of the more problematic issues. The settlement of Circassian and Tatar refugees in the region in the 1860s in the wake of the Crimean War further complicated the problematic nature of land ownership. In this highly charged environment, who took part in the politics of local administration and how they did so became a very important issue. This book focuses on this participation process.

Structure of the Book

The focus of Chapter 2 is the transformation of the Ottoman Empire into a liberal-capitalist social formation. This transformation was not limited to the nineteenth century and was definitely not a series of reforms imported from European countries. Rather, it was a consequence of inherent dynamics particularly associated with how people related to the means of production, and that began centuries earlier. By using Habermas's 'legitimation crisis' and the formation of liberal-capitalist societies as a framework, this chapter provides context for the rest of the book.

Chapters 3 and 4 describe the key organisational structure of the book: 'the judicio-administrative sphere' of provincial politics. One of the key arguments of this book is that there was a blurred line between the judiciary and administrative offices at the provincial level. Although the regulations that established these offices aimed to separate them, the particular nature of local notables' involvement with them meant that they could not function apart from each other. I refer to this combined space of governance as the judicio-administrative sphere. Chapter 3 explores the provincial

Introduction

administration as a key component of the nineteenth-century Ottoman reforms. Analysing the provincial regulations of 1864 and 1871, I describe the provincial administrative model designed primarily by Midhat Paşa in the course of his governorship of the region, focusing particularly on the administrative and judicial councils in the county of Vidin. This chapter underlines the importance of local notables in these councils and discusses the politics of election in the context of these councils.

The analysis of the provincial judicio-administrative sphere continues in Chapter 4, concentrating on these councils' functions. An examination of the attendance patterns of the council members reveals some irregularities in the way these councils operated. By looking at different organisations related to these councils, I elaborate on the complexity of the politics of administration in Vidin and its connection with the offices and practices of Ottoman governance.

Chapter 5 examines several case studies from the copy register of Vidin's county administrative council against other sources to reveal the political processes behind the council's reports. A close reading of some correspondence reveal interesting patterns in the political strategies of those involved in the writing process and how they chose to write these reports. My perspective is critical of the state–society divide, as the case studies reveal a more complex 'singular government of state and society'. The local administrative practices of the Ottoman modern state constitute an aspect of Ottoman 'governmentality' in which different agents (of this singular government) could and did participate to pursue their own goals.[17]

Chapter 6 explores the narrative function of the debates and correspondence associated with provincial governance. By looking at how the local agents problematised the refugee settlement process in provincial correspondence, I explore the parallels between provincial politics and the imperial transformation into a liberal-capitalist social formation, where a presumably autonomous market order determined the boundaries of governance. This perspective is essential in looking at the empire from the provincial level and challenges the presumed path of reforms as unidirectional from the imperial centre to the provinces.

This book explores the context of Ottoman local governance during the liberal-capitalist state reformation. The processes explored here focus mostly on the individuals' rights to the means of production; thus, many complaints and disputes coming from the provinces during the nineteenth century were concerned with property and taxation. These complaints, however, do not stem from a binary opposition between a state that coerces transformation and a society that opposes reforms. Such reductionism not only trivialises the complex nature of the local administration's politics but also presents nineteenth-century Ottoman subjects as reluctant partners to a transformation that the imperial centre initiated. Focusing on the offices and practices involved in composing such complaints reveals some of the complex patterns and politics behind the ink on these reports. Neither the notables nor the less wealthy inhabitants of Vidin were unaware of what to make of nineteenth-century reforms. Vidiners knew quite well how to utilise these reforms and their associated institutions to protect their own interests.

Notes

1. For a definition of the 'liberal-capitalist social formation', see Habermas 1975: 17).
2. 'Report by Mr Consul General Longworth on the Organisation of the Vilayet of the Danube' (National Archives [hereafter NA], FO 881-1393: 2, 12).
3. Consider Carter V. Findley's (2010: 34) comment on Selim III's reforms in the early nineteenth century: 'as the leading reformist statesmen's writings prove, the Enlightenment's "spirit of system" (*esprit de systeme*) intruded into Ottoman thinking in these very years. Selim's New Order started the Ottoman turn toward the rationalization that is of the essence of modernity.' As nuanced as his analysis may be, at the heart of Findley's empire-centric framework is the understanding that modernity is a European and predominantly nineteenth-century phenomena. Agents of change impose 'modernity' through top-down procedures ('most people experienced the impact of modernity largely through demands their governments made on them') and could be shared or borrowed from others. 'Consequently', Findley's 'study does not attempt to define a "Turkish modernity". It does talk about many modern Turkish phenomena, but their context is greater than national. They are all part of the Turkish experience of modernity, which is European in its origins but ever more global in its scope' (2010: 16–17). I subscribe to a different understanding of modernity, one that 'question[s] the close identification of modernity with state centralization and uniform administrative practice'. In this framework, suggested by İslamoğlu and Perdue (2001: 274, 281), modernity 'means the multiple institutional forms, or orderings of social reality, that since the sixteenth century responded to and enabled commercial expansion and competition among different political entities. In this sense, modernity does not merely indicate the institutional configurations of the nineteenth century but incorporates their early history in the sixteenth through eighteenth centuries.' Their analysis reminds us 'that the Weberian ideal-typical rational state cannot encompass the multiple contingent histories of modernities around the world'.

Introduction

4. While some historians focus on the seventeenth and eighteenth centuries – such as Jane Hathaway (1997) – others focus primarily on the nineteenth century, for example Jens Hanssen (2005), Eugene Rogan (1999) and Mahmoud Yazbak (1998). Yet, some others focused on local communities over longer periods, relating the nineteenth-century transformation to earlier centuries. Examples are Beshara Doumani (1995), Dina Rizk Khoury (1997) and Michael E. Meeker (2002).
5. Recent and welcome exceptions include an edited volume by Frederick F. Anscombe (2006), with only a few contributions focusing on Bulgaria in the pre-1850s, and Isa Blumi's work on Albania (2011).
6. Anscombe (2012; 2014) has been pointing out the particular weakness of the Balkan historiography on this front in his recent writings. For an example of those who argue for a strong Ottoman state, see Valentina P. Dimitrova-Grajzl (2007). As Fikret Adanır (2006: 157) notes, 'such research remain[s] more or less focused on the "classical" Ottoman regime, subscribing thereby rather uncritically to what the Weberian archetypal concept of "sultanism" implied – that is, a kind of patrimonialism that left little room for negotiated solutions on the basis of popular acceptance.' For the other model that argues for a weaker Ottoman state, see İnalcık (1992). The conviction that the contradiction between strong provincial magnates and the Ottoman state was evidence for Ottoman decline was more prevalent in the 1950s and 1960s among Turkish historians. Their works, with their notions of an Ottoman 'decline', served as secondary sources for historians of the Balkans who could not utilise Ottoman archival sources. R. J. Crampton (2005: 51), for example, notes that 'throughout the [nineteenth] century the quality of Ottoman administration was in decline . . . The most serious problem, particularly in the second half of the century, was the failure of the central government to control the *ayan*s. The *ayan*s were overmighty subjects.' For a more through discussion of this historiography, see Adanır and Faroqhi (2002).
7. Recent contributions by Isa Blumi (2011; 2012) or Marc Aymes (2010; 2014) serve as good examples of works that place the provincial political and economic relations at the centre of an analysis of the Ottoman Empire.
8. For example, the correspondence registers of the Refugee (*muhacirin*) Commission is available to researchers, yet the actual correspondence is not. The register includes only brief summaries of the correspondence and scholars like David C. Cuthell (2005) has utilised these summaries to write general accounts of the refugee problems. However, the unavailability of the detailed reports limit our ability to focus on a particular region. Similarly, the registers of Council of State (Şura-yı Devlet) are available for researchers but the registers of the Council of Judicial Ordinances (Divân-ı Ahkâm-ı 'Adliye) are not. So if a provincial case was reported to the imperial administration, a researcher can trace the office that the case was forwarded to (using the incoming–outgoing ledgers) yet still may not be able to access the

actual report if it was sent to the Refugee Commission or Council of Judicial Ordinances.
9. Mariia Nikolaeva Todorova (1996: 69–73) gives a summary analysis of similar dominant discourses on the Balkans.
10. This was closely related with increased stability in the region which eventually led to increased agricultural production (Palairet 1997: 49, 62).
11. A term that can be translated as 'notable' (Bowen 'A'yan').
12. Robert W. Zens (2004: 187), notes that Pasvanoğlu died, not at the hands of Ottoman officials, but because of gangrene he developed from an injury to his hand. Another recent work (Gradeva 2006) notes that he died 'probably of influenza'. The *Encyclopaedia of Islam* article (Bajraktarević 'Paswanoghlu'), on the other hand, notes only that 'his health was rather poor as a result of too great mental strain; ambition led him to aim at independence, as evidence of which we have the coins struck by him and known as Pazvančeta'. It is ironic that the cause of death of clearly the most prominent Vidiner and undoubtedly one of the most significant *ayan*s in Ottoman history seems so vague.
13. (Aytekin 2006: 36). Aytekin's dissertation is the most recent work on this topic. His discussion of the 1849 uprising relies heavily on Halil İnalcık (1992). While Aytekin analyses the uprising predominantly by focusing on issues involving land ownership, İnalcık (1992: 58–74) emphasises the influence of Serbian nationalists as well as the Russians and the British. Hüdai Şentürk (1992: 82–99, 101–424), takes İnalcık's emphasis on nationalist movements further and argues that these uprisings should be seen as the origins of the Bulgarian independence movement. Regardless of the differences they attribute to the role of nationalist movements and foreign powers, all three authors agree that the existing land regime in Vidin created significant discontent, particularly among the non-Muslim populations.
14. These three districts are noted in the Prime Ministry Ottoman Archives (hereafter, BOA) İ. DH. 13733, 13880, 15361, 15382, 16091, 17158, 19124. In a report that he submitted to the Supreme Council of Judicial Ordinances to explain the origins of the *gospodarlık* system, the governor of Vidin, Zarifi Paşa, limited the places in which this system was prevalent to a few villages in these districts: BOA, İ. DH. 15687, dated 26 June 1852 (8 N 1268). In fact, in one document the Supreme Council of Judicial Ordinances notes that this regime was limited to these three districts only (Sts. Cyril and Methodius National Library, Oriental Section (hereafter NBKM) VD 96/38, dated 13 May 1863 (24 ZA 1279)). For more, see Aytekin (2006: 39–59).
15. (*Salname Tuna*: 7:176–83, 86–9, 92–7). Cf. Teplov (1877: 175–88).
16. '*Hukuk-ı tasarrufiyeleri canib-i miriye alınarak*' (NBKM, VD 96/38).
17. Foucault (1991: 102–3) gives three interrelated meanings for 'governmentality'. Here, I refer to Foucault's first definition of the term as 'the ensemble formed by the institutions, procedures, analyses and reflections,

Introduction

the calculations and tactics that allow the exercise of this very specific albeit complex form of power, which has as its target population, as its principal form of knowledge political economy, and as its essential technical means apparatuses of security'. While I use governmentality in reference to this larger ensemble, the closely related term 'governance' refers to the institutions and procedures, that is, rules and practices, associated with governmentality.

2

Contextualising the Nineteenth Century

> Turkey was not a corpse, but a body paralyzed: it revived as soon as the enlightenment of the present generation recalled it to life, and the rare and interesting spectacle is presented of a country having totally altered its political condition in the short space of sixteen years, through the spirited and patriotic exertions of a few individuals, while that salutary change promises to be permanent, because the system will be continued by the pupils and imitators of those few eminent Statesmen, each of whom is surrounded by a chosen band of disciples brought up in their principles. (Porter and Larpent 1854: 10)

Such were the optimistic words of Sir George Larpent, who extended and published the memoir of his grandfather, Sir James Porter, in 1854, fifteen years after the beginning of the Tanzimat (the Reforms) period. Sir George Larpent recounts vividly the event that marks 'the beginning' of this era, the reading of the Gülhane imperial decree on 3 November 1839, soon after sixteen-year-old Sultan Abdülmecid came to power (1 July 1839). These words reflect what appears to be a prevalent way of interpreting these reforms:[1] as an enlightened recall to life, a sudden reawakening of a seemingly paralysed body through the efforts of a few 'spirited' individuals. Such unsubstantial interpretations of the Tanzimat era as 'Western-inspired reforms imposed from above' in a declining empire prevent us from seeing a long process of transformation that began before the 'long nineteenth century' (1789–1922).[2]

This chapter focuses on the long nineteenth century to understand the imperial framework of transformation behind the central topic of this book: the politics of local administration. The nineteenth-century Ottoman experience was not merely a series of Western-inspired reforms that unexpectedly transformed a stagnant empire. Instead, this was a period of socio-economic crisis that coincided with the culmination of a long-term transformation that began in the seventeenth century.[3] Focusing on how people's access to the means of production transformed in the period leading up to and during the nineteenth century, and tracing the impact of this change on the fiscal and bureaucratic practices of Ottoman governance provides a better framework for examining the emergence of the liberal-capitalist social formation in the Ottoman Empire. Rather than a detailed account of this era and its reforms, I present here a broad overview of a long-term transformation in order to contextualise the emergence of the provincial administrative structure analysed in the rest of the book.

While the Ottomans established the administrative councils that I examine with the 1864 provincial regulation, initial attempts to create such bodies date back to the formation of tax collection councils (*muhassıllık meclisi*) in 1840. Councils and other provincial offices that flourished in the nineteenth century extended the administrative capacity of professionally trained staff and provided a platform for the local populace to engage with Ottoman governance. These offices served as complementary elements of a complex state–society relationship focusing on effective administration and participatory politics. On the one hand, they enabled the systematic administration of Ottoman provinces and continuous monitoring of their subjects' wealth and security; on the other hand, the councils in particular served as platforms for the politics of local administration. As such, local councils and other offices served as a means of communication between the imperial centre and provinces and connected the formation of an Ottoman civil officialdom, with the transformation of the tax structure and the establishment of the infrastructure for modern Ottoman governance. I develop these themes further in the remainder of this chapter, where I examine the long nineteenth century as a period of crisis and transformation.

The Tanzimat Era: Marking a Crisis and a Transition

Contextualising the Ottoman social formation is necessary to analyse the nature of the transformation of the Ottoman statecraft and its technologies in the long nineteenth century.[4] This period, including but not limited to the Tanzimat era, was part of a larger transformation that began with the crisis of the 'traditional social formation' (starting, arguably, in the seventeenth century) and culminated in a capitalist social formation.[5] The principle of organisation, that is, the defining economic and social feature, in the traditional social formation is 'class domination in political form' (for example aristocracy); in the liberal-capitalist social formation, on the other hand, it is the relationship of wage labour and capital, which is anchored in the system of bourgeois civil law (Habermas 1975: 15). Following Rifa'at Abou-El-Haj (1991: 62–4), I argue that the transformation in the long nineteenth century was part of a transition from one social formation to another, indicating a change in the principles of organisation in response to a legitimation crisis.[6]

Nineteenth-century Local Governance in Ottoman Bulgaria

A system's survival depends on forces of production and a set of 'discursively redeemable and fundamentally criticisable claims' that justify the rule of dominant classes and legitimise the existing social order (Habermas 1975: 9). Legitimation, in this sense, integrates a system centred around the means of production. Crises are indicative of a paralysis of social integration: a discordance in the institutional harmony of a system caused by a disintegration of the principles by which individuals or actors relate to one another in a society. This is where the legitimacy of a certain hegemonic order becomes crucial: so long as the hegemonic domination of a certain class remains unchallenged in the system, institutional problems can remain under control. Otherwise, crises lead to the transformation of social orders.

The crisis of the traditional social formation, therefore, follows the collapse of the legitimation of a political-administrative system that regulates 'the privilege of disposition of the means of production and the strategic exercise of power' through a legal order. In other words, the structures that regulate ownership of the means of production, primarily land, need to be legitimised through different ideologies, 'by falling back on traditional world-views and a conventional civic ethic' (Habermas 1975: 19). Up until the mid- to late sixteenth century the Ottoman ruling elite reserved the major benefits from the system for themselves by setting up 'institutional structures . . . to facilitate regulated and legitimized exploitation of material and human resources' (Abou-El-Haj 1991: 59). This structure began changing by the end of the sixteenth century and intensified as the empire faced the crisis of the seventeenth century. In his definitive work on this global crisis, Geoffrey Parker (2013: 185) notes that the Eastern Mediterranean suffered more than 'almost any other part of the northern hemisphere'. Focusing on the Ottoman experience in particular, Sam White (2011: 39–51), concurs with Parker's claim and adds that the crisis led to particular tensions between the nomads and settled communities. Abnormal climatic conditions (drought years, heavy rains and floods, El Niño) during the Little Ice Age, various political and economic problems (disenfranchised clerics, military and peasants; episodes of extensive mutiny/political unrest; and regicide), wars with Russia, Poland, Austria and Venice, and episodes of plague, contributed to a disastrous century for the Ottomans (White 2011: 123–226; Parker 2013: 185–210). This crisis led to a transformation of landholding patterns and an eventual shift of political and economic resources to the countryside (Abou-El-Haj 1991: 12, 48–54; Hathaway and Barbir 2008: 62–9).

Prior to the eighteenth century, Ottomans experienced a gradual transformation to 'commercialized, and often export-oriented agriculture' (White

2011: 293). Despite the shift of fortunes associated with this transformation, the eighteenth-century Ottoman political-administrative system was led by a socially mobile, new ruling elite that included the provincial dynasties, like that of Pasvanoğlu Osman Paşa of Vidin, whose hegemony was legitimised by 'the religious law . . . tailored to meet the needs of the ruling class whenever its interests demanded such an adjustment' (Abou-El-Haj 1991: 60).[7] Yaycioglu (2016: 14) argues that by the late eighteenth century Ottoman polity was shaped by the conflation of (1) a top-down reformist agenda, (2) a partnership of imperial and provincial elites on fiscal and political matters and (3) bottom-up pressure from communities for increased participation. The merging of these three movements around discourses of reform marked the beginning of the nineteenth century. A significant turning point in this transformation was the abolishment of the Janissary forces in 1826, after which Mahmud II's reforms gradually eliminated the power of the provincial dynasties and increased local communities' participation in provincial governance (Yaycioglu 2016: 229).

Thus, the nineteenth-century transformation of the Ottoman Empire was a prolonged response to this crisis. The numerous imperial decrees issued and the codification movement associated with the century provides an opportunity to examine this response. The language of the Gülhane imperial decree (1839) and the reaction of some contemporaries can help explain the significance of 'justification of authority' in this context. The paragraphs below are from the beginning and the end of this decree, as translated and recounted by Sir George Larpent, whose grandfather, Sir James Porter, actually witnessed the reading of the decree in Istanbul:

> It is well known that during the early ages of the Ottoman monarchy the glorious precepts of the Koran and the laws of the empire were ever held in honour. In consequence of this the empire increased in strength and greatness and all the population, without exception, acquired a high degree of welfare and prosperity. For 150 years, a succession of incidents and various causes have checked this obedience to the sacred code of the law, and to the regulations, which emanate from it, and the previous internal strength and prosperity have been converted into weakness and poverty; for in truth an empire loses all its stability when it ceases to observe its laws.

> The enactments thus made, being a complete renovation and alteration in ancient usages, this Imperial rescript will be published at Constantinople and in all the towns of our empire, and will be officially communicated to all the Ambassadors of friendly Powers residing in Constantinople, in order that they be witnesses of the concession of these institutions, which, with the favor of the Almighty, will endure [forever].[8]

Porter claims that the imperial decree is somewhat puzzling, as it

> starts by imputing the decline of the state principally to the transgression of the old laws, and then proceeds to adopt new regulations in the state, and then ends by praising the restoration of old manners and customs, as the sole means of salvation.

'[S]till', he explains, 'there were numerous parties to be pleased in Constantinople, and ... it was necessary to satisfy the demands of the Reformers, without outraging the feelings of the old Turkish party' (1854: 17, 24). Other contemporary observers of the reform movement echo Porter's amusement at the seemingly contradictory message of the decree – advocating civic reform and seeking to restore traditional worldviews – and his explanation of this swing with reference to the demands of opposing parties (Baker 1877: 169–70; Engelhardt 1999: 43–5; Michelsen 1854: 27–31; Spencer 1851: 261–2; Ubicini 1856: 27–30). The 'confusing' decree wherein the Ottoman authorities not only introduced reforms but also fell back on 'traditional worldviews' was symptomatic of the crisis of the traditional Ottoman social formation that led to the Tanzimat era, a crisis which was not a rupture but, rather, extended over the transformative decades of the nineteenth century.

Means of Production and Ottoman Social Formation

The pre-Tanzimat Ottoman legal order regulated 'the privilege of disposition of the means of production and the strategic exercise of power' (Habermas 1975: 19) through a complex set of laws. Land was the most significant means of production and a dominant element in the distribution of wealth and income well into the mid-nineteenth century (Hershlag 1995: 121). In the legal framework of the sixteenth century, the land was '*de jure* the property and de facto under the control of the sultan ... [who] distributed it as fiefs' (Imber 1997: 121). The Land Code of 1858 transformed this legal framework by restructuring different rights on land; it signalled the culmination of a change that led to increased mobilisation of land and other means of production during the previous two centuries (Adanır 2006: 167).

Before the Land Code of 1858, a different set of rules regulated the privilege of disposition of land wherein agricultural lands, woods and open steppe were considered the 'property' of the Ottoman state (Faroqhi 2006d: 381). The preference for state ownership of property in Ottoman law (as opposed to private ownership in freehold form) did not mean lack of legal protection of use rights on state land, nor of ownership in freehold over other means of production (buildings, trees, gardens). The state distributed use rights and tax rights of land as part of its particularistic negotiations with different groups at the imperial and local levels (İnalcık and Quataert 1994: 141–2), and a complex 'institutional framework' (North 2005: 49) of tax, usufruct and possession rights regulated various claims of different groups on land, providing them access and protection.[9] Although this complex system prevailed throughout the seventeenth and eighteenth centuries, 'the application of officially promulgated rules in [these] centuries was less clear-cut than had – mostly – been true in the 1500s' (Faroqhi 2006d: 381). Increased mobilisation of land in these centuries within the framework of these alternative forms of rights posed a challenge to social integration and prepared the institutional background for the Land Code (Abou-El-Haj 1991: 47–52). The 1858 code established a singular claim of ownership by the title-holder and promulgated individuals' right to alienate their property. This was a response to the crisis of the traditional Ottoman social formation stemming from the mobilisation that Abou-El-Haj and others discussed. Ottoman legislators in drafting the Land Code fell back on 'traditional worldviews' and 'shunned all talk of a revolutionary change in property rights but were adamant in pointing to the fact that their task had been simply one of compiling and codifying old regulations and not introducing any new ones' (İslamoğlu 2000: 34).

The pre-1858 legal order was an established property regime regulating the complex rights and claims on land. As such, it was consequential to particularistic negotiations between the government and its allegiants such as usufruct holders or tax collectors.[10] 'Free alienability' is not a precondition for ownership (Giddens 1985: 68–71; Arıcanlı 1998); different rules and regulations protected the usufruct of those who worked on state (*miri*) lands in the Ottoman Empire even when they did not have the right to dispose of land.[11] Peasants could inherit and transfer the usufruct of the *miri* lands. Another category of land in the Ottoman Empire was 'privately owned' *mülk* lands. The owners of these lands could transform their holdings into pious endowments (*waqf*) (Cin 1987; Gerber 1987: 9–17; Meriwether 1999), which constituted another 'flexible tool at the disposal of individuals who wished to customize . . . their property transmission strategy' (Doumani 1998: 7).[12] As İslamoğlu (2000: 17) argues, the pre-1858 property relations were 'inseparable from the differentiated and particularistic claims over revenues of different groups, on the one hand, and from the claims of subsistence producers to land use, on the other'. The sovereign's authority over the title of the land (*raqaba*) translated to the prerogative of the central government over the distribution of the rights to revenues from land among negotiating parties.

Various 'irregularities' further complicated the complex set of property relations. In Nablus, for example, peasants did dispose of state lands to which they held usufruct (Doumani 1995: 157–65).[13] Ownership of buildings and trees (including the right to alienate them) were separate from the land they stood on, and limits on the disposition of land did not necessarily apply to them. In addition to such variations, Boğaç Ergene (2003: 170–88) raises important questions regarding the courts' institutional authority on land disputes; peasants did not necessarily go to court for all disputes. The rigidity of Islamic rules regarding property transmission does not change the fact that 'the application of these rules, in reality, was often the last resort for families and individuals; that is, property transmission was often a conscious and strategic social act, not an automatic, passive or formulaic process' (Doumani 1998: 7).

Centralised regulation and standardisation of the claims on landed property were a priority for nineteenth-century Ottoman governance (İslamoğlu 2000). This is partially visible in the frequency of regulations issued regarding land ownership in the nineteenth century. In *Külliyât-ı Kavânîn* (Karakoç 2006), one of the most comprehensive compilations of Ottoman laws and regulations, there are eight decrees regarding landed property prior to 1800. There is a visible increase in this number in the next century: Ottomans issued twenty imperial decrees pertaining to landed property between 1800 and 1858. The Land Code did not seem to reduce the government's attention to land disposition. In the four years between the Land Code and the imperial decree of 21 February 1862 (which ordered a survey of all the land in the Ottoman Empire), there were seven regulations pertaining to property rights. While a mere quantitative analysis of legislation does not say much about the nature of these decrees or a change in the processes that produced these decrees, the relative abundance of regulations indicates that the topic of land tenure occupied the legislative offices in Istanbul for a significant amount of time in this period.

There were similar reform attempts in the nineteenth century concerning other means of production, such as buildings and trees. An individual could buy, sell, rent a whole building, or just hold shares of it. A similarly complex system operated for trees (Imber 1982); Hyde Clark, the vice president of the Imperial Land Commission in Asia Minor in the 1860s, had the chance to observe the 'ancient institution of property in trees' in detail and suggested that this may 'be conceived to precede property in land' (Clark 1890: 201). The fatwas of sixteenth-century jurists reveal, for example, that not all trees had undisputed freehold status, but only 'wild trees onto which a cultivator had grafted new stock' (Imber 1982: 767).

Such separation of the ownership of land from the structures and trees on it was not a practice unique to the Ottomans. Sabrina Joseph (2007: 35) notes that a similar system existed in eighteenth-century Lower Brittany.

A series of decrees issued during the nineteenth century regulated the transfer of such means of production in an increasingly dynamic economic environment. An 1838 regulation announced a 90 per cent reduction in the commission taken by brokers or public criers (*dellal*) for the sale of inns and real property belonging to orphans and to the insane, mentally incompetent or missing persons.[14] The third section of the new penal code (issued after the Gülhane imperial decree in 1839), opens with a statement banning confiscation of the 'properties and possessions' of anyone in the empire (*Mecmu'a-yı kavanin*: 153), even as means for collecting debts. An 1848 regulation required all sale contracts to be drafted by local administrators and to be written on official paper (*Mecmu'a-yı kavanin*: 42–5). Imperial income and property (*temettuat*) surveys of 1840 and 1845 recorded shops, inns, workshops, mills and barns as revenue-generating assets that people could buy and sell easily. Similar surveys from 1875 include not only these revenue-producing assets but also estimated values of the houses in which people were living.[15] In nineteenth-century Palestine, freehold over olive trees was very much a part of peasants' capital accumulation process. Elizabeth Anne Finn, wife of the British consul of Jerusalem, relates the story of a mid-nineteenth-century Palestinian peasant whose father-in-law 'pledged his olive trees for 500 piasters and wrote a bond upon himself to pay fifteen jars of oil' to a local merchant.[16]

The nineteenth-century Ottoman transformation, manifesting itself through these regulations on land and other means of production, helped reorganise provincial judiciary and administrative practices, ensuring their compatibility with the principle of organisation of the liberal-capitalist social formation: the relationship of wage labour and capital anchored in a system of bourgeois civil law. This period, therefore, marked a crisis of the traditional social formation, out of which a liberal-capitalist social formation eventually emerged. The crisis of the traditional social formation, according to Habermas (1975: 21), is a consequence of the contradiction that exists 'between validity claims of systems of norms and justifications that cannot explicitly permit exploitation, and a class structure in which privileged appropriation of socially produced wealth is the rule'. The imperial decree of 1839 announced a 'system of norms and justifications that cannot explicitly permit exploitation' by extending guarantees of 'life, honour and property' to all Ottomans. This was not the launching of 'a trackless domain to pursue the paradoxical goal of legal Westernisation (and therefore secularisation) in an explicitly Islamic state' as argued by

Carter Findley (1989: 31). The decree and the following reforms challenged the empire's legal authority and the existing political order that privileged certain groups over others. While the decree's introduction, quoted above, praised 'the early ages of the Ottoman monarchy', when 'the glorious precepts of the Koran and the laws of the empire were ever held in honour', its conclusion acknowledged that 'the enactments thus made, [were] a complete renovation and alteration in ancient usages' (Porter and Larpent 1854: 17, 21). Changes to the taxation practices exemplify the impact of this 'renovation and alteration' on the means of production.

From Tax Farmers to Tax Collectors

In 1838, Sultan Mahmud II established a financial affairs ministry and turned the 'chief treasurer' into a 'minister' while reconfiguring the imperial administration into the 'Sublime Porte' (Cezar 1986: 264; Findley 1980: 140; Şener 1990: 25–7; Çakır 2001: 35). This restructuring at the imperial centre coincided with a more drastic change in tax categories and collection methods partially due to the fact that the cash-strapped empire was not able to secure loans from foreign governments until 1854 (Birdal 2010: 18). These changes had a ripple effect in the Ottoman provinces. Prior to 1839, tax farmers (*mültezim*) administered the assessment and collection of a vague bundle of customary (*'örfi*) and *shar'i* taxes.[17] This order was abolished when the former group of taxes was consolidated under the title 'collectively assessed tax' (*'an cema'atin virgü*), a new category that was based on regular surveys, conducted by appointed tax collectors (*muhassıl*).[18] This reconfiguration, imposing a collective tax burden for a village, or a neighbourhood in a town, led to resistance in various parts of the empire.

The position of *muhassıl* was temporary; the imperial centre abolished it two years after its introduction. The conventional argument on *muhassıls* explains the 'failure' of this experiment as due to a limited imperial capacity to make the shift from fiscal decentralisation to fiscal centralisation (Findley 'Muhassıl'). Local administrative practices, however, did not revert to their status prior to the introduction of these agents. For the purposes of this analysis, it is important to understand the introduction of *muhassıls* and even their presumed 'failure' as part of a transition that relegated the task of supervising economic activity to provincial councils operating in a larger complex framework of authority, security and information (Saraçoğlu 2015).

The term *muhassıl* comes from the Arabic verb حصل (to cause something to happen) and refers to 'one who makes [something] happen'

(Sayın 1999: 141; Devellioğlu 1997). This definition seems appropriate when one considers the full responsibility of the *muhassıls*. Together with the officials working underneath them and the local tax-collection councils, the tax collectors were key provincial agents of the Ottoman state (Cezar 1986: 282). The assessment, apportionment and collection of the taxes were left to the tax-collection councils (*muhassıllık meclisleri*) that employed indirectly elected local notables and other appointed members in addition to the tax collectors. In addition to supervising the tax collection, *muhassıls*' duties, in the context of the nineteenth-century fiscal/administrative transformation, included surveying the income and properties of the local populace, supervising the postal services, contracting infrastructural projects (such as maintaining the bridges and irrigation canals) and keeping an account of the annuities sold by the Ottoman treasury (*esham*). The assessment of the tax base obligated the tax collectors to survey the countryside with their aides. Once completed, the imperial fiscal office would use these surveys to determine the amount of annual tax each village should pay (Kaynar 1985: 254–64; Efe 2002: 30, 72–8). In addition, they were required to recruit a local police force that would guarantee the safety and property of the inhabitants (Efe 2002: 25–48). A regulation governing the tax-collection councils' members described their responsibilities as handling all of the significant financial, policing and infrastructural issues in the provinces (*Mecmu'a-yı kavanin*: 33–5).

The 1845 surveys of some districts in Anatolia reveal how the tax-collection councils apportioned taxes: a single household's share in the communally assessed tax for the village was roughly equal to its share in the total revenue of the village (Saraçoğlu 1998: 48–54). Thus, within each village (or neighbourhood), the households would be required to contribute to the communally assessed tax burden in relation to their share in the total wealth of their community.[19] The peasants could – and did – dispute the total amount of tax assessed for their villages and demand reassessment. If external factors (such as drought, leading to a bad harvest) required a reassessment of a particular village's communal tax burden, the tax collectors and the tax-collection councils would conduct the necessary surveys on the tax base and report to the Supreme Council of Judicial Ordinances which, then, would issue an imperial decree (Şener 1990: 86) reflecting their decision. Among the particular collection of imperial decrees issued by this council, there are more than forty decrees just for the year 1841[20] that concern readjusting the communal tax burden in various parts of the empire.[21] The new tax, which the ministry qualified as 'collected among neighbours' (*komşuca alınan vergiler*), then, was negotiated on two levels: the communal (on the basis of the surveys) and the individual (in a collaborative manner); and the local councils were essential in both processes (Çakır 2001: 49; Şener 1990: 95–6).

Eventually, in 1859, a fixed-rate property and income tax replaced the collectively assessed tax (Nuri 1992: 289; Engelhardt 1999: 58). Although by that time the office of the tax collector had been defunct for seventeen years, the collectors' fate was not shared by the councils (and other judicio-administrative offices) employing civil officials at the provincial level and serving as the backbone of local governance.[22] Among other factors, the disappearance of the *muhassıls* seems to be related to common complaints about the application of the tax reforms, which were indicative of a crisis of the traditional Ottoman social formation and related to the means of production. As İslamoğlu (2000: 17–18) emphasises, claims on tax revenues were an essential component in the bundle of rights over land. Indicative of this significance perhaps, the taxation system's transformation in the early 1840s was at the centre of the reconfiguration of property relations, particularly for the post-1858 political administration of the new property rights (Mundy 2000: 64).

Introduction of tax-collection councils under the temporary directorship of *muhassıls* was part of an attempt to curb the power potential of advantaged tax farmers and administrators in establishing claims over the revenues from the primary means of production (Nuri 1992: 283–8). The tax reforms' socio-economic impacts, therefore, were consequential for the provincial societal order. The tax collectors, as representatives of a new Ottoman state, were responsible for overseeing the application of imperial reforms; their success, some argue, became identical with that of the imperial administration (Cezar 1986: 282; Efe 2002: 8). Such high expectations translated into serious responsibilities for tax apportionment and collection and created significant power potential for the *muhassıls* and the local councils, making them intermediaries in the negotiations between the imperial government and the provincial populace regarding tax claims.

Despite their powerful position, the tax collectors had to share their authority. Field marshals (sing. *müşir*) and divisional generals (sing. *ferik*) who were supposed to serve as chairs of the tax-collection councils between 1836 and 1839 administered the provinces and the counties.[23] These councils included the *muhassıl* and his two clerks (*katib*), one for financial matters and the other for population/property surveys (Ortaylı 2000: 34); the judge (*hakim*); the mufti; a military officer (*'asker zabiti*); and four local notables who were 'shrewd and honest in their manners' (*Mecmu'a-yı kavanin*: 33–5). If there were Christians in the region, these councils would include the metropolitan and two people from among their chief elders, bringing the total number to thirteen (Çadırcı

1997: 121; Ortaylı 2000: 34; Efe 2002: 72; Kaynar 1985: 238). As organisations that involved different powerful agents (from religious leaders to the judge, from local notables to the tax collector), these councils constituted a suitable arena for the politics of local administration.[24]

The tax reforms designated the tax collectors as key figures in provincial administration, but the councils often challenged their powers. Despite – or perhaps because of – this there were several complaints about the tax collectors (Çadırcı 1994; Çakır 2001: 101–40; İnalcık 1993; Kaynar 1985: 283–94; Uzun 2002). Tax farms' replacement with the *muhassıl* councils changed the provincial socio-economic structure; different groups competed to carve out positions of power for themselves. The old tax farmers were no exception to this hegemonic process: the return of tax farming practices in two years allowed some of them to remain as powerful actors in local politics (Çakır 2001: 47–8). Nevertheless, they had to share their power with a bourgeoning cadre of other local figures in the context of the provincial judicio-administrative structures. In that sense, this particular transformation reflected a larger one associated with the crisis of the old order and its organising principle.

Taxation was a 'steering mechanism' with which the central authority related the political administrative system to the economic system. Problems with the 'steering mechanisms' of political-administrative systems turn into a full-fledged systems crisis 'if (and only if) they cannot be resolved within the range of possibility that is circumscribed by the organisational principle of the society' (Habermas 1975: 5–7). The tax reforms of the Tanzimat era were not an isolated issue, but an essential component of the crisis of the Ottoman traditional social formation. Tax farmers were significant actors in the traditional Ottoman social formation, with a legal order that regulated 'the privilege of disposition of the means of production and the strategic exercise of power' (Habermas 1975: 19). Politically defined class relations (an integral part of these institutions) constantly reproduced and maintained the system until 1839, when the egalitarian declarations of the empire shattered the legitimacy of such politically privileged classes. This legitimation crisis related closely to the primary means of production, the land and claims over it. The bourgeoning regional/local elite replaced the tax farmers as significant agents, using the provincial judicio-administrative councils with imperially decreed reform narratives securing their rights over their property.

The transformative period of the crisis in the traditional Ottoman social formation and the emergence of a liberal-capitalist formation expanded beyond the Tanzimat era (1839–71). This study does not aim to establish a specific date for the beginning or the end of the crisis. Disintegration of the old political classes in the Ottoman Empire did not begin with, nor was it limited to, the abolition of the tax farming. Nevertheless, tax farming was a relatively early stage in the process, and the new offices that emerged because of the tax reforms, tax-collection councils, established the basis for the judicial and administrative bodies on which this work focuses. The crisis and formation provide a context for the documents that I examine here; they explain why problems pertaining to the means of production – issues of land, tax, forests and the like – appear so frequently in local correspondence. Understanding this temporal and imperial background is essential to avoid an anachronistic perspective on the councils (Abou-El-Haj 1991: 8 and *passim*) and in understanding the 'transitoriness' of the historical phenomenon (Abou-El-Haj 1994: 173).

The Liberal-capitalist Ottoman Social Formation

A concise analysis of the transformation into the liberal-capitalist Ottoman social formation reveals what other changes accompanied the evolution of the tax structures. Liberal-capitalist social formation is organised around 'the relationship of wage labour and capital anchored in the system of bourgeois civil law' (Habermas 1975: 20–1). The rise of this relationship requires the disintegration of the political class structures that characterised the traditional social formation. Within this new system, a presumed 'natural order' of market-centred relationships (rather than titles and privileges) ensures class domination while the practices of the modern state complement the spontaneous order of market commerce with civil law. In this particular framework, where economic exchange is the dominant steering medium, the exercise of the state's power within a legitimate institutional framework (modern governance) focused on

> (a) to the protection of bourgeois commerce in accord with civil law (police and administration of justice), (b) to the shielding of the market mechanism from self-destructive side effects (for example legislation for the protection of labour), (c) to the satisfaction of the prerequisites of production in the economy as a whole (public school education, transportation and communication) and (d) to the adaptation of the system of civil law to needs that arise from the process of accumulation (tax, banking and business law). By fulfilling these four classes of tasks, the state secures the structural prerequisites of the reproduction process as capitalistic. (Habermas 1975: 21)

In the long nineteenth century, the Ottomans took up these tasks as a presumed spontaneous order of a market economy became more dominant in Ottoman governance.

The protection of bourgeois commerce in accord with civil law: Count Léon Hrabia Ostrorog, former judicial advisor to the Ottoman government and a lecturer in Islamic law at the University of London, remarked that in the wake of the Ottoman Empire's collapse, 'the [*'ulama*] considered [commercial quarrels] as being, rather than theirs, the business of tradesmen, between themselves, or of their guilds, to settle' (1979: 50). Islamic law is indeed compatible with bourgeois commerce; however, the codification attempts in this century focused on establishing a standardised institutional framework for the regulation of commercial activity in the Ottoman Empire. After the turn of the nineteenth century, some commercial disputes were resolved in commercial tribunals that included Ottoman and foreign merchants and operated under the authority of the Comptroller of the Customs House (Ekinci 2000: 768). A decade after the formation of the Council of Trade and Agriculture in the wake of the Anglo-Ottoman Commercial Treaty of 1838, the commercial tribunal in Istanbul was restructured to include ten Muslim and ten non-Muslim Ottoman subjects in agreement with the European powers holding capitulary privileges (Bingöl 2004: 113–31).[25] A new commercial code, based on the French code of 1807, was issued in 1850 (*Düstur* 1:375–466) and after 1861, commercial courts, which were established in the provinces on the basis of need until that period, became a systematic component of the provincial judicio-administrative structure (*Düstur* 1:445–65). The British jurist Sir Travers Twiss (1880: 11–17) noted how

> these commercial tribunals [had] one great advantage over the ordinary civil tribunals, inasmuch as they [executed] their own [judgements], whereas the ordinary civil tribunals have to report their decisions to the Governor-General of the Province, who . . . directs the Minister of Police to give effect to them.

The new tribunals and code seem to have coincided with Ottoman intentions to protect commerce via institutional transformation.

Legislation for protection of labour: this is relatively less self-evident because the modernisation paradigm's Eurocentric focus on equating the protection of labour to organised labour movements meant almost exclusive focus on urban factory workers and the Ottoman Strike Law of 1909 (Quataert 2001: 96–7; Atabaki and Brockett 2009: 6). This law, based on a bill issued a year earlier (Ökçün 1996: 111–14) was triggered by a powerful wave of strikes among different groups of workers (Karakışla 1995; Yildirim 2015; Nacar 2014) and established procedures to resolve labour disputes through bilateral negotiations with company representatives under the supervision of the Ministry of Trade and Public Works.[26] While protests led to legislation to protect labour by the turn of the century, the industrial work force, as Quataert pointed out (2001: 100), 'formed a tiny fraction of the non-agricultural work force. The "real story" ... involve[d] unorganized workers in small-scale work sites'. Works on Palestine and the Balkans point at how policies of local *ayans* and the Ottoman state helped boost small-scale industrial production at the local level.[27]

Quataert's reference to 'unorganized workers' includes those who were associated with artisanal guilds. Recent work on guilds, by Suraiya Faroqhi and others, explain how these organisational units were not under the exclusive control of the Ottoman state. Guilds provided a dynamic structure for their members (the most significant organised workforce in the empire) that they were able to utilise protecting their interests in response to changing global economic conditions in the late eighteenth and early nineteenth centuries (Akarlı 2004; Deguilhem 2005; Faroqhi 2006a, 2009; Ghazaleh 2005; Yildirim 2001). In addition to the labour laws and guild policies aimed at regulating working conditions to maintain capitalist production, prevention of corvée labour became a priority for the Ottoman government earlier in the nineteenth century (Ortaylı 2000: 87). The empire, however, was not able to enforce the decree, and this became an issue of provincial discontent (İnalcik 1992: 37). The regulations focused on attempts to prevent the overburdening of the peasants by the governors in the provinces (Ortaylı 2000: 87). Corvée was always a part of the provincial political economy in the Ottoman Empire, yet there was an unprecedented increase in the nineteenth century. In the case of Ottoman Egypt – and probably elsewhere in the empire, as some of the cases I explore in the rest of this book indicate – this was a 'result of a transition in the energy regime ... from animal to human labour' (Mikhail 2013: 346). Ottoman governance actively focused on encouraging industrial production and limiting labour exploitation.

Banking and business law: the formation of the Agricultural Credit Fund (Menafi'-i 'Umumiye Sandığı), first in 1863 at the Danube Province, under the administration of Midhat Paşa (Midhat 2004: 97; Midhat 1903: 38; 1997: 49–50) and then in the rest of the empire, complemented measures regulating the sphere of production and commerce.[28] The rationale behind the introduction of this fund was to extend credit to farmers in need. At the end of 1867, the total accumulation of the Agricultural Credit Fund in the Danube Province was twenty million *guruş* (Güran 1998: 150), the equivalent of £178,571.40.²⁹ This was approximately 10 per cent of the total tax revenue from the province in the fiscal (Rumi) year of 1283 (13 March 1867–13 March 1868) and roughly a quarter of the tithe from agricultural produce in that year (1869). The Agricultural Credit Funds, which eventually led to the Agricultural Bank (Ziraat Bankası) established in 1888, were 'not only a first attempt to organize agricultural credit in the Ottoman Empire but also one of the first such attempts in Europe' (Todorova 1993: 117). Another innovation that addressed provincial capital needs was the Orphans' Funds. The Hanafi tradition holds that an orphan 'who has not yet reached puberty but who is clearly of rational judgment, may, if his guardian so authorizes him, enter into commercial transactions' (Shaham 'Yatim'), giving significant leverage to the guardians and limiting the availability of the inheritance to other potential debtors. The Orphans' Funds (together with the Agricultural Credit Funds) were standard components of the provincial administrative structure starting with the first yearbook of the Danube Province (1869). They were under the authority of the Authority for the Supervision of Orphans' Properties (Emval-ı Eytam Nezareti) and acted as banks holding and managing the inheritance monies of orphans 'and other physically and mentally challenged persons' until the orphans became legal inheritors. They lent money to the general public at interest rates set forth in the procedures governing the funds (Agmon 2006).

Availability of funds through banks had a positive impact at the provincial level. According to the provincial yearbooks, the sum accumulated in the Orphans' Funds at Vidin increased from 1,406,358 *guruş* (£12,557) in 1868 to 2,298,400 *guruş* (£20,521) in 1876 – and only 35 per cent of this amount was physically present; the rest was loaned out to individuals. In a report dated 22 January 1873, the British consul Humphrey T. Sandwith noted how the Cretans continually failed to 'secure a prolific crop since its prosperity received the terrible blow inflicted by the last prolonged insurrection [1866–9]'. This, he added, 'left the islanders plunged in debt', rendering them 'insolvent' and 'paralyzed'.³⁰ Facing the possibility of losing the property they had mortgaged for their loans, the peasants requested help from the local administrative council. Eventually the Council of State debated the issue . In their report to the Grand Vizierate, the Council informed the former that the Orphans' Fund of Crete had twenty million *guruş*, and the Agricultural Credit Fund six million *guruş*. The Council suggested lending these funds to the villagers to pay back their debt; however, it found the 12 per cent interest rate too high and deemed it more appropriate to halve the rate to 6 per cent.³¹ As it was trying to encourage borrowing from these early creditor organisations, the Ottoman state was also trying to block the way of other unofficial institutions, such as the *selem* money-lending contracts, by referring to them as 'illegal'.

Public school education, transportation and communication: Henry C. Barkley, a British civil engineer who lived in the Danube Province during the 1860s while working for the Ruse–Varna railway construction, noted this about road conditions:

> I have said there were no macadamized roads in Turkey, but perhaps I ought to have said in the parts of Turkey I have visited, for lately I have seen it mentioned in a letter from a special correspondent, that there is an excellent macadamized road leading out of [Vidin], made by Midhat [Paşa] when he was governor of the [Province].
>
> Midhat Paşa arrived at [Ruse] soon after we commenced the railway, and at once set about making a chaussée from that town to Varna . . . [He] also made a fairly good macadamized street through the Bulgar quarter, which he continued for one mile out of the town in the direction of [Silistra], and I believe scratched a little at a road towards [Vidin]. (Barkley 1877: 94, 97)

Midhat Paşa's son, Ali Haydar Midhat Beğ, echoed Barkley's cautious remarks (1903: 36): 'Roads were now being laid out in every direction, and bridges constructed over the Morava and other rivers, so as to meet the requirements of an agricultural population, and facilitate the outlet for their produce.' Roughly 1,864 miles (3,000 kilometres) of road were built during Midhat Paşa's four-year tenure as the governor (Midhat 1903: 38). In addition, he established a coach company for mail and travellers, and a steamer service on the Danube (Midhat 2004: 99–100; Todorova 1993: 116). Midhat Paşa's efforts were representative of the increased systematic attention on the part of the Ottoman state to the prerequisites of capitalist economic production.

Educational reforms coincided with infrastructural investments (Fortna 2002: 1–43; Somel 2001: 1–13, 271–7). The first modern military schools were founded in the 1770s and were followed by the first civil secular schools in the 1830s (Findley 1989: 132). Earlier schools focused on professional formation. In 1842, a girls-only, multi-confessional school for midwives was founded (Somel 2000: 224–5). In 1845, a plan for a generalised system of schools was instated (Findley 1989: 134). The three-tiered system consisted of Qur'anic elementary schools, upper elementary schools known as *rüşdiye*, and universities. In 1857, the Ministry of Public Education was established to coordinate the increasing number of government schools (Somel 2001: 8). The first university suggested in the 1845 plan was opened in Istanbul in 1900, and by 1918 there were eleven *lycées*

(Findley 1989: 134). The Education Act of 1869, which did not come into force until 1880s, introduced a compulsory, centralised school system (Evered 2012). The Ottoman state was clearly concerned with establishing a modern education system in the nineteenth century.

Roads, railways, steamer and coach lines; a modern education system that emphasised secular as well as religious values; and improvements in the postal services and communication techniques including the electric telegraph (Mardin 1961: 262; Davison 1993: 53–7) are among what Habermas refers to as the 'structural prerequisites of production'. Ottoman governance focused on such prerequisites intensively during the nineteenth century as the modern state directed its activities toward complementing the functioning of self-regulative market commerce. The transformation from the traditional social formation to a liberal-capitalist social formation was not a rupture but rather a protracted transformation. As the means of production played a key role in the crisis of the traditional social formation, problems pertaining to their control dominated the general disputes related to the transformation.

Governance, Official Print and Information Flow

Although useful in understanding the imperial context behind the focus of this study, Habermas's taxonomy of social formations cannot address the details of the local dynamics behind this transformation. Through a variety of different tools, the Ottoman state maintained its legitimacy and control at the local level during the crisis of the old order and the transition to the liberal-capitalist one. The Ottoman bureaucracy, with its procedures and the information flow it regulated between the centre and the provinces, was essential to this legitimising process. Kemal Karpat (1972: 257) argues that the Ottoman bureaucrats were essential partners in a 'socio-economic order based on private property and free trade'. Ideologically they considered themselves as the foundation of the state; yet they also fulfilled a functional role that necessitated professionalisation.

The particular relationship between printing and politics in the nineteenth-century Ottoman Empire reveals the functional role of the imperial and provincial bureaucracy.[32] Anthony Giddens (1985: 179) relates the nineteenth-century rise in the amount of cheaply available printed materials directly to the 'enlargement of the sphere of the political'. Textually mediated organisation of the modern state played a key role in the development of an environment in which debates and discussions gained an 'intertextual' nature owing to the readily available public texts on governance. The common presence of such printed material did not preclude censorship. The discursive arena of governance in this new form of state could function under the watchful eye of policing organisations; what 'marks the decisive shift... towards a new form of state' is the referential nature of publications.

During the nineteenth century there was a significant increase in official publications. On 17 February 1851, the imperial printing house (Takvimhane-i 'Amire), established eight years before the Gülhane imperial decree, published a 142-page volume of codes and regulations, which appears to be one of the earliest attempts by the imperial government to collect its codes and regulations in printed, bound volumes during the Tanzimat period.[33] Almost a decade later, in 1863, a 586-page corpus came out under the title *Düstur* (*Düstur-ı atik* 1st ed.).[34] Immediately following the table of contents, a cover page explains that the title means 'a collection that comprises laws and regulations' (*Kavanin ve nizamatın münderic olduğu mecmu'aya zamm-i dal ile Düstur denilir*) and notes that the particular volume is an extended version of the previous volume from 1851 (*Mecmu'a-yı kavanin*). The second edition took only three years when an extended 904-page *Düstur* came out on 17 April 1866 (*Düstur-ı atik* 2nd ed.).[35] Seven years later, *Düstur* became a regularly published series of volumes of Ottoman law. The modern Turkish Republic adopted the title and is still publishing the *Düstur* series as officially published legal volumes today.

Giddens (1985: 179) argues that

> [p]rinted codes of law, within an increasingly literate culture, made for the increasing integration of 'interpreted' law within the practice of state administration and for a much more consistent and direct application of standardized juridicial procedures to the activities of the mass population.

Consistency and intertextuality in judiciary and governance in this framework relate closely to the referable nature of printed laws. As Ottoman official corpora, *Düstur* volumes had a character of referability, as compilations of new laws and regulations issued after the Gülhane imperial decree (1839) – which was the first decree included in all the earlier editions (*Mecmu'a-yı kavanin; Düstur-ı atik* 1st ed.; and *Düstur-ı atik* 2nd ed.), and the first volume of the 1872 series. The cover page of the 1863 volume emphasises how the empire would maintain the referable character of the compilation by adding the future laws and regulations to the new editions of this volume. The Ottoman state not only printed these volumes but also distributed them to different parts of the empire and ordered their translation into the languages of its minority populations.[36]

Also in the middle decades of the century, the Ottoman state ordered the publication of imperial yearbooks. Higher-level bureaucrats who were involved closely with the Tanzimat reforms published the first yearbook (*salname*) in 1847, a few years prior to the 1851 *Düstur* (*Mecmu'a-yı kavanin*).[37] In the preface, they noted the purpose and the structure of the yearbooks as follows:

> In order to aid all those working in clerical and other related work, individual lists have been compiled, these lists quoting the names and ranks of the ministers of our state, the [viziers] and officials in the provinces, and the foreign ambassadors within our nation. In order to provide information about the world abroad, the rulers and ministers of state in Europe have been presented along with a brief summary of the legal statuses of the respective nations. A calendar has also been added, and the holy days of the various religions listed. In addition to this a register of the fiscal incomes and expenditures of the European states has been added, together with the exchange rates of their currencies compared with the Ottoman currency, as well as the rules and regulations concerning the state minting house have been listed. The land postal service operating within our state, and the steamboat routes, both [international and domestic], as well as their running times have also been recorded. This [yearbook] will be printed and published every year. Although its quality may not be perfect this year, it is certain that in the future it will find itself a much sought after work. (Duman 2000: 22)

The yearbooks not only helped their readers to locate the Ottoman Empire in a comparative legal and financial framework with other states, but also provided a wealth of detail regarding the imperial administration, from the names of the people employed to the timetables of important ferry lines. 'A time table', as Giddens (1985: 174) points out, 'is a time–space ordering device, which is at the heart of modern organisations. All organisations . . . operate by means of time tables, through which the sequencing of activities in time–space is choreographed.' People did not necessarily rely on the yearbooks to check the times of the steamboats but the fact that such information was included, together with an explanatory preface, implies that the empire was operating at a 'time–space convergence' and that it was supplying its bureaucrats and other citizens with certain tools to operate at that level as well.

The price of the yearbooks were six *guruş* initially; eventually this came down to five *guruş*. Hasan Duman (2000: 22) claims that this was an 'extremely high price for that time'. However, the annual subscription to the official weekly of the empire, *Takvim-i Vekayi*, cost 120 *guruş* when it began publication on 1 November 1831. *Tuna-Dunav*, the official weekly of the Danube Province, offered an annual subscription for forty *guruş* in its first issue (14 March 1865).[38] With one *guruş* in the Istanbul wholesale market of 1851, one could buy approximately four pounds of wheat for making bread (Findley 1989: 364–7). The yearbook, with the wealth of information included in it, was relatively inexpensive for those who wanted to have a reference copy.[39]

In 1866, almost two decades after the first imperial yearbook, the first provincial yearbook (for the Bosnia Province) came out. Two years later Danube Province followed suit with a yearbook published in its capital, Ruse. In its preface, the editors emphasise the significance of publishing statistics and apologise for possible errors in a work that the local government strived to do perfectly. An eleven-page list (almost 10 per cent of the entire yearbook) of the 'significant days' of the year and the exact prayer times on these days follows this preface. The editors warn the readers that they took the exact latitude of Ruse (43° 5' north) as the basis for calculating the prayer times, adding that the prayer times in Ruse would vary across seasons and be different than other places at a different longitude or latitude (*Salname Tuna*, 1:3). Following the list is a universal chronology – with special emphasis on the Ottoman Empire – beginning with Adam's 'birth' (6,216 years before the Hijra) and ending in 1846 (the founding of the *rüşdiye* schools). These two tables are exemplary of Ottoman efforts to create a 'homogenous, empty time' that Benedict Anderson (1983: 36) emphasised as crucial in imagining communities. The provincial government in Ruse published ten provincial yearbooks (*Salname Tuna* 1868–77). The earlier volumes that I consulted did not have a price tag, but the 1871 volume did: eight *guruş* – arguably not very expensive.

Düstur and the yearbooks were essential components of the increasingly public 'discursive arena' of nineteenth-century state administration, to use Giddens's phrase. The 'textually mediated organisation' of Ottoman governance was essential for the liberal-capitalist social formation. The comparative perspective presented through such judicio-administrative texts as the *Düstur* and the yearbooks contributed to the 'legitimation' of the Ottoman state. Habermas (1975: 22) argues that the dominant 'bourgeois ideologies' of liberal-capitalist social formations 'can assume a universalistic structure and appeal to generalizable interests because the property order had shed its political form and been converted into a relation of production that, it seems, can legitimate itself'. Within the 'public sphere' of Ottoman governance that was inseparable from 'textually mediated organisation', the modern Ottoman state appeared in universal, generalised categories, comparable to 'European' states.

As the preface to the first imperial yearbook indicates, such texts were to serve as functional tools for the professionalisation of the new Ottoman bureaucracy that 'maintained the view that it was the foundation of the state' (Karpat 1972: 257). They were manuals for provincial administrators, explaining the modern state structure. Furthermore, they constructed a universal textual description of the empire with the facts and procedures that the local administrators provided. If such 'textually mediated organisation' explained Ottoman governance for its people, then the collection of provincial data and application of standardised provincial procedures required people to perceive the empire in the categories that the empire provided.

Conclusion

In one of his lectures at the University of Vermont in 1982, Michel Foucault (2000: 404) identified a new field of investigation for himself. He described it as 'the way by which, through some political technology of individuals, we have been led to recognize ourselves as a society, as a part of a social entity, as a part of a nation or of a state'. The lecture was a part of Foucault's broader, emerging focus on the political exercise of sovereignty by the state over its population. In investigating what he referred to as the 'reason of state', Foucault focused on the relation between politics as a practice and as knowledge, and argued for the possibility of a specific 'political knowledge'. 'Government is possible', he noted,

> only when the strength of the state is known: it is by this knowledge that it can be sustained. . . . [The] art of governing characteristic of the reason of state is intimately bound up with the development of what was called, at this moment, political 'arithmetic'.

He added (2000: 407–10) that this 'political arithmetic' was nothing but

> a statistics related not at all to probability but to the knowledge of state, the knowledge of different states' respective forces . . . Here we meet the problem I would like to analyse in some future work . . . What kind of political techniques, what technology of government, has been put to work and used and developed in the general framework of the reason of state in order to make the individual a significant element for the state?

The significance of local administration is obvious. The new Ottoman bureaucracy geared towards functionalism and professionalisation was involved heavily in the creation of this 'political knowledge' that made the government possible.[40] As the official yearbooks, newspapers and corpora published the numbers, structure and procedures of Ottoman governance, the 'reason of state' became obvious to bureaucrats and subjects alike.

This was a phase of the dissolution of the Ottoman traditional social formation and the formation of the liberal-capitalist one. A process that began a century prior, the Gülhane imperial decree did not mark the beginning of this process but rather its intensification during the Tanzimat era. Those involved with the politics of local administration created this 'political knowledge', but not by themselves. They had to rely on their informants, the people they counted and whose wealth they measured.

Of course, there were those who did not want to participate fully in the creation of political knowledge. On 1 December 1838 *Takvim-i Vekayi* reported the sad story of a Mehmed 'Ali, who attempted to conceal one of his dwellings from a surveyor who came to the village. 'With the divine wisdom of God', the house of Mehmed 'Ali was burned down while he and his household had to run out 'stark naked to save their lives'. 'As there had not been a precedent of fire in the district' until then, the event should serve, the piece in the official paper added, as a 'warning' to others. Despite such 'divine warnings', however, some subjects of the empire refused to comply with the demands of an inquisitive state at all times.

Concealing information and armed resistance were among the many different ways people chose to respond to the transformation of the Ottoman social formation. Others' reactions were more compliant; after all, the local populace and bureaucrats were a part of this transformation too, and adapting to the transformation of the Ottoman state's technologies proved beneficial at times. The knowledge that these groups provided constituted the Ottoman 'political arithmetic'. As I discuss in Chapter 5, different agents benefited from this transformation by incorporating the 'reason of state' into their daily lives and their strategies.

This chapter began by outlining the crisis of the traditional Ottoman social formation and the emergence of a liberal-capitalist one over the course of the Tanzimat era. Local notables and other subjects of the empire were fully involved in this transformation. The clear boundaries of the state–society duality, a salient feature that dominates conventional empire-centric works on this period (Stanford Shaw, Carter Findley, İlber Ortaylı and others) were part of the Ottoman imperial discourse and its 'textually mediated organisation'. The legal corpora supported the idea of a uniform legal structure to govern the whole empire; the yearbooks categorised the personnel, resources and the subject population of this structure; and the official newspapers told stories of 'divine justice' supporting the new practices of the state. It would be misleading to adopt the state–society split suggested by the imperial perspective. As the next chapter reveals, the local notables became a very strong component of the new provincial judicio-administrative sphere.

Contextualising the Nineteenth Century

To explain the transformation of the Ottoman social formation, I focus on the provincial judicio-administrative sphere in the following chapters. The modern Ottoman state of the emerging liberal-capitalist social formation utilised 'textually mediated organisation' to establish its 'legitimation' and to explain a 'reason of the state'. Essential for the dissemination of this 'reason of state' was the information flow. This flow of information not only constituted the state's 'political arithmetic', but also gave the local agents the means to protect their interests by incorporating themselves within the information flow through petitions and requests.[41] Because the crisis of the traditional Ottoman social formation was about the rights over means of production, a majority of the disputes that in the confines of the textually mediated organisation of this new state focused on means of production. Understanding the structure and the transformation of the local administrative framework is crucial to an analysis of the politics behind the correspondence between the provinces and the centre. The following two chapters explain some of the organisations that produced and conveyed this particular kind of information to the state and thereby introduce us to the politics of local administration.

Notes

1. At least among contemporary foreign observers and Ottoman historians who examined that period in the second half of the twentieth century. Ironically, the recently published, four-volume *Cambridge History of Turkey* has 1839 as the cut-off date between the last two volumes: (Faroqhi 2006c) and (Kasaba 2008).
2. Carter Findley, summarises the Tanzimat era (1839–76) as 'a continuation and intensification of [modernising] reform' that began earlier in response to 'emerging global modernity in both its Janus-like faces, the threatening aspect (separatist nationalism in the Balkans, imperialism in Asia and Africa) and the attractive aspect (the hope of overcoming Ottoman backwardness by emulating European progress)' (Findley 2008: 11–14). My discussion in this chapter diverges from Findley's analysis that represents the current commonly accepted general perspective on the nineteenth cenruty. We share some common foci: the imperial centre, political rule and bureaucratic transformation. Yet the analysis in this book distances itself from such modernisation-centred analyses that explain organisational reform as a top-down response to secessionalist/imperialist threats or to the appeal of Westernisation. Instead, this books emphasises the relationship between these reforms and the means of production to explore the connection between these reforms and the development of a liberal-capitalist social structuration.

3. Here, the 'crisis' refers to what Jürgen Habermas (1975) defines as the 'legitimation crisis' (discussed below). The Ottoman Empire suffered concurrent environmental, military and political crises throughout the nineteenth century. However, this chapter does not focus on these crises in detail.
4. 'Social formation' refers specifically to the complex set of relations – economic, political and ideological – that determines the mode of production and all other aspects of social life. My use of the term is consistent with Habermas's analysis (1975: 9–10), which defines sociocultural reproduction as a function of 'outer nature' (the resources of the non-human environment) and 'inner nature' (the organic substratum of members of the society). The survival of social systems depends on their hegemonic classes' successful adaptation of the outer and inner nature to the needs of the social formation through system integration and social integration, respectively.
5. Habermas's taxonomy of social formations allows us to focus on the institutional reconfiguration of the long nineteenth century as a process instigated not by exogenous factors in a brief period but as a transformative course motivated primarily by internal factors. For more on these categories, see Habermas (1975: 17–31). Since the 1990s, Ottoman historiography has increasingly focused on the transformative potential of the provinces. (Some examples include: Abou-El-Haj 1991; Blumi 2012; Doumani 1995; Hathaway and Barbir 2008; İslamoğlu 2004b; Khoury 1997; Meeker 2002.)
6. Habermas borrows the term 'crisis' from General Systems Theory: 'Crises arise when the structure of a social system allows fewer possibilities for problem solving than are necessary to the continued existence of the system . . . when the consensual foundations of normative structures are so much impaired that the society becomes anomic. Crisis states assume the form of a disintegration of social institutions' (Habermas 1975: 2–3).
7. Cf. Tezcan (2012: 227–43). Casale's interesting analysis (2010) suggests that this transformation might also relate to the increasing political power and autonomy of the merchants particularly associated with Indian Ocean long-distance trade.
8. (Porter and Larpent 1854: 17, 21). Roderick Davison (1963: 55) refers to this apparent conflict as 'split personality' in comparing the reform edict with its successor, the reform decree of 1856.
9. Imber argues that Turks inherited the basic principles of the pre-1858 land tenure system from the late Byzantine Empire and its successor principalities in the Balkan Peninsula and western Anatolia. First the Seljuk Sultanate and then the Ottomans retained this system with certain modifications. The annexation of Hungary in 1541 gave the necessary impetus to systematise Ottoman land tenure. This was done by Ebu's-su'ud Efendi – then the military judge of Rumelia, a member of the Imperial Council, and one of the most powerful Ottoman legal scholars of his time (Imber 1997: 136; İnalcık 1998).
10. Usufruct rights, tax claims and the right to dispose of land are different 'resources' that may be owned by different individuals (Waldron 1988: 38–9).

Contextualising the Nineteenth Century

In theory, the Land Code of 1858 aimed to combine the first and last of these resources in the hands of the 'title-holder'. Consolidation of these rights obviously involved negotiations at various levels – a process that is explained in detail by Huricihan İslamoğlu (2000; 2004a) – and was paralleled by the consolidation of tax claims.

11. An imperial decree dated 23 April 1847, for example, guaranteed the inheritance rights of daughters on their parents' land – that is, *miri* lands that were cultivated by their fathers or their mothers (*Mecmu'a-yı Kavanin*: 40–2; Berki 1938: 10–12). Barkan (1999: 360) notes that this code was revolutionary for the female inheritors. Prior to this law, in theory, the widows and the daughters of deceased males could inherit the usufruct only in the absence of a son. Meriwether's (1999: 153–77) account of inheritance in Ottoman Aleppo reveals the discordance between theory and practice.

12. In theory, God owned the *waqf* lands, and people could use their revenues to fund the activities of the endowment. Yet in practice, the status and the boundaries of such foundation lands changed frequently, as *waqfs* provided a legal framework for land transfers (Singer 2000). The patterns of property transmission in such endowments were by no means uniform; they responded to the differences in their political economies and cultural environments (Doumani 1998) yet they were common and regular enough, as noted by some of the contemporaries visiting the empire (De Kay 1833: 421–2).

13. Cuno (1992: 77–84) notes that some Muslim jurists were supporting peasants' claims to private ownership of land. The 'sale' of *miri* lands was not a problem limited to the late eighteenth and early nineteenth centuries; İnalcık (1998) notes similar practices in the previous centuries due to 'loopholes and legal devices by which the law . . . could be circumvented'. See also (Faroqhi 2006d, 381–3).

14. *Takvim-i Vekayi*, 1 December 1838 (14 N 1254). The rate came down from 2 per cent of the sale to 0.2 per cent. This does not explain other relevant issues such as how one establishes ownership over the property of a missing person. Yavuz Aykan (forthcoming) explores an interesting case study of the complicated strategies of litigants in establishing property rights.

15. This establishes a value of 'the home' of an individual. The survey, therefore, assesses the wealth of an individual, which is different from a calculation of the revenue from rented property. The shift reflects an increase in the awareness of one's own house as capital that she/he can liquidate. I do not wish to make a general statement for the whole empire. Such awareness might be because Istanbul ordered the building of houses for the large number of immigrants who settled in the region, as I discuss later.

16. This case, as Doumani (1995: 131–81) elaborately argues, has wider implications. The *salam* money-lending contracts, as exemplified here, facilitated accumulation of capital in the hands of particular classes in olive-based villages.

17. Tax farming, as a mode of collection, intensified in the first half of the seventeenth century as a solution to the liquidity crisis of the central state (Genç 2000; Parry 1970; Sahillioğlu 1970). The unit of taxation was the *mukata'a*, which was a single or combination of tax base(s) representing a certain amount of tax revenue usually known or estimable to the finance office. The procedure adopted was one of public auction to prospective tax farmers (*mültezims*). The imperial administration would grant a certificate to the highest bidder entitling him to the title of tax farmer of a particular *mukata'a* up to three years. The tax farmer could request to extend his privileges up to twelve years through reappointment via the same bidding procedure. This practice did not emerge as a life-term contract, although it eventually turned into that. The *mültezim*, after paying the amount specified in the contract, could save the remaining part of the tax, which he collected as his profit in accordance with the laws (Salzmann 1993: 398–401). When lending bankers pressured the tax farmers, the latter tended to exploit the peasants, leading to social upheavals in the seventeenth century.
18. (Kaynar 1985: 226–54; Çakır 2001: 41–8). The imperial administration determined the tax liability of each village or neighbourhood through surveys (Sûdi 1888 (1306): 78–84; Güran 1989: 12–13; Şener 1990: 94–102; Çakır 2001: 48–55).
19. These results are valid only for the surveys of 1845 and may not reflect the reality. Nevertheless, they are useful in understanding the logic of tax apportionment and what the administrators considered as a 'just' tax load.
20. The powers of the Supreme Council over administrative and financial issues increased when the council moved from the palace to a new building in the Ottoman administrative complex, the 'Sublime Porte', in 1840 (Seyitdanlıoğlu 1999: 44–6).
21. BOA, İ. MVL. 14/220, 14/224, 14/225, 15/230, 15/235, 15/238, 16/241, 16/243, 16/245, 16/255, 16/256, 16/259, 17/267, 17/270, 17/271, 19/291, 20/316, 20/320, 21/322, 22/322, 23/356, 24/378, 25/388, 25/390, 25/391, 25/397, 26/410, 26/414, 26/418, 26/419, 26/421, 27/426, 27/427, 27/428, 27/439, 27/443, 27/444, 27/452, 27/459, 28/469, 29/488, 29/489, 30/499, 30/506, 31/525, 31/526, 31/538. These decrees responded to the petitions from the villagers or the tax collectors' reports; as such, they represent the negotiational character of the communal tax assessment process.
22. See Akiba (2009). Although we know that the method of collection reverted to auctioning to tax farmers, there is not much research on the power of tax farmers in the second half of the nineteenth century. There is no reason for us to assume that tax farmers were able to maintain their previous powers, especially after the 1864 provincial regulation. Procedures of communally assessed tax gave these councils advantage in challenging the authority of the tax farmers. Çakır (2001: 121–6) argues that this leverage was essential in opposing the *muhassıls* prior to their abrogation.

23. (Kaynar 1985: 238–9). Musa Çadırcı (1997: 14–23, 63) notes that these military titles appeared as part of the 1836 military reforms: field marshals and divisional generals took over the duties of the governors (*vali*) and sub-governors (*mutasarrıf*) until 1839. The military restructuring following the destruction of the Janissary corps (in 1826) served as a basis for the new provincial division of the nineteenth century.
24. Akiba (2009) explains these councils in a larger context. While the earlier, foundational works by scholars like İnalcık (1992), Çadırcı (1997) or Ortaylı (2000) on the political role of the nineteenth-century provincial elite emphasise the 'resistance' to the imperial transformation, revisionist historians – for example, (Zens 2004; Philliou 2011; Blumi 2012; Meeker 2002; Aymes 2014; Doumani 1995; Blumi 2011; Aymes 2010) – provide a more nuanced picture. Nevertheless, they all seem to agree that these councils provided a platform for local politics.
25. Mübahat S. Kütükoğlu (1974) emphasises the British role in this transformation. Maria Todorova (1980: 72–172), on the other hand, points out that the British were more concerned with their anti-Russian policies than with interfering with the Ottoman Empire until the Crimean War of 1853. It would be wrong to presume that the legal–commercial transformation within the Ottoman Empire occurred for the most part due to the pressure of foreign powers and that the Ottomans became a part of the world economy in a passive manner. Ottoman merchants' involvement in this transformation remains a relatively understudied topic. Beshara Doumani (1995: 236–45) proves that Ottoman merchants were not as vulnerable and passive as supporters of the conventional 'integration into the world economy' theory would argue. Scholars like Isa Blumi (2012), Giancarlo Casale (2010), Baki Tezcan (2012) or Ali Yaycioglu (2016) also emphasised the political power of the emergent Ottoman merchant class.
26. 'Public service providers' could not strike (Ökçün 1996: 112). The strike wave of 1908, however, marked the culmination of a larger worker discontent. Prior to these strikes, coal miners in Zonguldak staged a walkout in 1863, and the telegram workers in the Beyoğlu post office in Istanbul went on strike in 1872. Note also that the empire's early industrial establishments in the late 1830s exclusively served the Ottoman army, and used soldiers in place of paid workers (Karakışla 1995: 19).
27. Habermas's framework does not explain the provincial reality well. Doumani (1995) and Palairet (1997: 63–84), point to the significance of small scale manufacturers' accumulation.
28. The largest of these funds belonged to the Edirne and Danube Provinces (Güran 1998: 151).
29. 112 *guruş* for £1 sterling exchange rate (Public Record Office [PRO], 'Report by Mr Vice-Consul Blunt on the Manufacture in the Vilayet of Adrianople in the Year 1867', 20 February 1868, Accounts and Papers, Commercial Reports, Session LXVIII (19 November 1867 – 31 July 1868): 169–74).

30. PRO, 'Report by Consul Sandwith on the Trade of Crete for the Year 1872', 22 January 1873, Accounts and Papers, Commercial Reports, Session LXIV (6 February – 5 August 1873): 628–9.
31. BOA, A. MKT. ŞD. 18/69, dated 1 January 1874 (12 Za 1290). Following the suggestions of the Council of State, the Grand Vizierate issued orders to the Crete Province BOA, A. MKT. ŞD. 19/25, dated 7 February 1874 (19 Z 1290), and issued a regulation on how the Orphan Funds of Crete should operate to resolve the issue. See BOA, A. MKT. ŞD. 20/10, dated 17 April 1874 (29 S 1291).
32. My discussion here does not focus on Ottoman literature and the advent of 'print capitalism'.
33. *Mecmu'a-yı kavanin (Düstur)*. Many thanks to Musa Çadırcı for lending his personal copy of this volume and for directing me to other prototypes of the *Düstur* series mentioned here. This early volume does not have a title page or an introduction, nor is there a name printed on the leather binding of the copy. The later volumes of *Düstur* in 1863 (*Düstur-ı Atik* 1st ed.) and 1866 (*Düstur-ı Atik* 2nd ed.), however, give reference to a similar volume published at this date and mention that the later volumes are extended reprints of this earlier volume. Furthermore, in his *Külliyât-ı Kavânîn*, Sarkiz Karakoç refers numerous times to this earliest volume as *Mecmu'a-yı kavanin* (A Collection of Laws), and to the latter two volumes as *Düstur-ı atik, sene 1279* and *Düstur-ı atik, sene 1282* (The Old *Düstur*, editions 1863 and 1866, respectively).
34. The decree for this edition's printing: BOA, İ. MVL. 462/20854, dated 20 February 1862 (20 Ş 1278).
35. The decree for this edition's printing: BOA, İ. MVL. 529/23729, dated 11 April 1865 (15 Za 1281).
36. On 20 February 1880 the imperial administration sent thirty copies of the whole set of existing volumes to different counties and districts of the Yemen province: BOA, DH. MKT. 1330/26, dated 20 February 1880 (9 Ra 1297). On 3 May 1871 the editor of the newspaper *Konstantinopolis*, D. Nikolaidis, received honours for translating *Düstur* into Modern Greek. BOA, İ. HR. 249/14805, dated 3 May 1871 (12 S 1288).
37. Ahmed Cevdet Paşa and Ahmed Vefik Paşa (1823–91) were among those involved with the first volume (Duman 2000: 22). At the time of the yearbook's publication, Ahmed Cevdet Paşa was serving as the judicial advisor to the grand vizier Mustafa Reşid Paşa, mastermind of the Gülhane imperial decree and a leading figure of the Tanzimat era. Cevdet Paşa served as the official court chronicler (*vak'anüvis*); the governor of different Ottoman provinces; a member of a commission to reform the official newspaper, *Takvim-i Vekayi*; and the president of the Council of Judicial Ordinances. In this last position, he supervised and was a driving force behind the official codification and consolidation of the Hanafi private law for the empire known as the Mecelle (Bowen 'Ahmad Djevdet Pasha'). This was a significant

codification movement but it was not strictly Hanafi – the final work did not limit itself to the majority opinions within the Hanafi school of law (Ayoub 2015) – and it was not the first codification attempt within the Ottoman Empire (Rubin 2016). Ahmed Vefik Paşa came from a family of interpreters and began serving at the translation office in 1837. He became the chief translator in 1847, the same year that the imperial yearbook came out. Aside from serving as the Ottoman ambassador to Persia and France, he was the imperial commissioner in the Danubian principalities, and presided over the First Ottoman Parliament in 1876–8. In 1879, he became the governor of Bursa, where he sponsored important reforms in sanitation, education and agriculture and established the first Ottoman theatre (Deny 'Ahmad Wafik Pasha').

38. Beyazit Library, Ali Emiri Mecmua Collection no. 311 and Gazete Collection no. 267 respectively.
39. The price cut and the continuous publication of these yearbooks are indicative of the Ottoman state's intention to publicise such information. This study, however, does not intend to make any claims about demand for the yearbooks. For that we would need to know the actual number of copies sold.
40. The Ottoman state emphasised the significance of statistics as a modern technology. See, for example, BOA, DUİT 37-2/18 (1), dated 2 January 1879 (8 M 1296).
41. Petition writing was an integral component of Ottoman bureaucracy that helped maintain imperial legitimacy at the provincial level (Ben-Bassat 2013: 2–6; Lafi 2011: 73–4).

3

Sitting Together: Local Councils and the Politics of Election in the County of Vidin

Conventional historians of the Bulgarian national 'revival' (*vŭzrazhdane*, lit. 'rebirth') commonly consider the local notables who worked 'for' the Ottoman government as an 'enemy of the people' (Daskalov 2004: 116). This is not surprising considering that socialist Bulgarian scholarship viewed the Ottoman period as 'an era of cultural stagnation' (Buchanan 2007: 45), and until recently, Bulgarian historians rarely treated the Ottoman administration in a dispassionate manner. Instead, they have been dismissive of the nineteenth-century Ottoman modernisation process (Petrov 2006: 39–49). However, this perspective cannot explain the role that some 'Turkish Muslims' who were associated with Ottoman provincial administration, such as Ma'ruf Ağazade Ahmed Beğ of Vidin, played in the autonomous Bulgarian administration after the Ottomans lost control of the region in 1878. From as early as 1864 until the end of Ottoman rule in Vidin, Ahmed Beğ (Figure 3.1) was a council member in the provincial judiciary and administrative structure, the focus of this chapter. Interestingly, in 1879, after the collapse of Ottoman rule, he became a member of the new Bulgarian Constituent Assembly, and in 1883 he was still a municipal council member in Vidin. The provincial judicio-administrative sphere's structure provided a space for Ahmed Beğ and other local notables, including all those listed in Figure 3.1, to remain influential despite their religious differences or the change of rule in Vidin. This coincides with what Toledano (1997: 148; 2007: 26–8, 108) describes as the 'localisation and Ottomanisation' of rule in the provinces in the eighteenth century. In fact, even after the elimination of large households, the less-prominent notables retained a significant position in the politics of provincial administration as part of Ottoman governance.

This chapter focuses on the nineteenth-century Ottoman administrative unit *liva* (or *sancak*), which is equivalent to a county. I examine the politics of administering such a unit, starting with a general analysis of its structure and moving on to a specific analysis of the local offices within Vidin County. Local agents and appointed officials interact with others

Local Councils and the Politics of Election in Vidin

Figure 3.1 Some of the Prominent Members of the Councils in Vidin
Source: Photos courtesy of Genadi Vulchev.

by using certain practices in accordance with a set of bureaucratic roles. These political interactions constitute local administration.[1] Imperial rules and regulations determine the idealised forms of such interactions. A close reading of the official regulations against an analysis of local agents' and appointed officials' interactions within the framework of the provincial administrative and judicial offices reveals that provincial reality did not match these idealised forms. The imperial administration was aware of this, but was seemingly unconcerned about it.

In the period under study, the Ottoman government issued two comprehensive regulations on provincial organisation (in 1864 and 1871) that made counties essential units of organisation and their administrative and judicial councils central to the larger provincial judicio-administrative complex.[2] These regulations outlined a particular election system that privileged the influence of local notables on these councils. In fact, some of these local inhabitants were prominent political figures prior to the 1864 regulation and retained equally significant positions even after Ottoman rule in Vidin County de facto ended in 1878.

The first two sections of this chapter provide an outline of the county structure based on the provincial regulations of 1864 and 1871. The third section explains the structure of two particularly central organisations: the county administrative council (*liva idare meclisi*) and the council of appeals and crime (*meclis-i temyiz-i hukuk ve cinayet*). Following this introduction, the fourth section traces the politics of these councils as expressed in their reports to the higher administrative centre in Ruse. In the fifth section, I examine the election process for these councils and the environment in which the councils drafted the local correspondence on the county's judicial and administrative issues. This analysis provides a basis for the following chapters, which provide a close reading of the texts these councils produced.

The Many Parts of the Imperial Dominions: the County as an Administrative Unit

The 1864 provincial regulation (*Düstur* 1:608–24), defines the 'county' (*liva*) as the basic unit in the new administrative geography:

> The many parts of the imperial dominions are divided into various circumscriptions according to the relationships among [their constituent] counties and each circumscription shall be known as a province (*vilayet*).
> Article 1: The general administration of each circumscription is entrusted to the administrative organisation that is specified in the following articles, and this administration is established at a single centre.
> Article 2: Each circumscription being divided into counties (*livalar*) including the county (*sancak*) that is the administrative centre, in every county there will be an administration of a subgovernor (*mutasarrıf*); and the principal city will be the seat of authority.[3]

Arguably, the most important aspect of the 1864 regulation was the hierarchical administrative order it introduced: counties constituted provinces, districts (*kaza*) combined to form counties, and villages (*karye*) made up districts. In the cities and towns, every fifty houses formed a neighbourhood (*mahalla*), a unit that was identical to a village in this administrative hierarchy. Although traditionally the individual *shar'i* courts' jurisdictions matched district boundaries, the imperial administration often changed the boundaries of districts or transferred villages from one district to another during the nineteenth century (Petrov 2006: 84). Such redistricting often aimed at maintaining a relative demographic and financial equality among counties, which served as the primary tax unit for imperial administration after the fiscal reorganisation of 1840 (Shaw and Shaw 1978: 84). The county maintained its significance as an administrative unit in the 1864 regulation and the following administrative transformations of the nineteenth century.

The Danube Province stood out from the others. It encompassed more counties and its formation predated the rest. There were twenty-seven provinces and 123 counties in the Ottoman Empire (Çadırcı 1997: 63). In the European part of the empire, each province contained an average of 4.4 counties (for the empire as a whole, the average was 4.5). The Danube Province exceeded this average, with seven counties: Ruse (the administrative centre), Vidin, Varna, Tulcha, Sofia, Tarnovo and Nish (Teplov 1877: 3). This new composition significantly expanded the former boundaries of the province, which was established in 1846 to include only three of these counties: Nish, Vidin and Silistra (which, in 1864, became a district of the newly established Ruse County). The provincial regulation of 1864 was almost a verbatim copy of the unique regulation drafted for this province only a month earlier.[4]

Most of the districts that constituted the Vidin County were in existence prior to the 1864 regulation. In fact, Vidin was the seat of a subgovernor (*mutasarrıf*) for a larger county extending further east along the Danube (Çakır 2001: 246). By 1864 Vidin had become the administrative centre of the districts of 'Adliye (modern-day Kula), Belgradcık (Belogradchik), Berkofça (Bergovitsa), İvraca (Vratsa), Rahova (Rahovo) and Lom (Lom), with a total of 461 villages within these districts.[5]

Midhat Paşa played the leading role in the establishment of the Danube Province, which served as a prototype for the larger administrative reorganisation (Şentürk 1992: 170; Todorova 1993: 115). His influence over the provincial reform was mostly due to his successful governorship of the troubled province of Nish (1861–3). His success entitled him to an imperial decoration (his second) and engendered further recognition in imperial administration. The administrative model he devised in the course of his service in Nish set the blueprint for the provincial regulation of 1864 as he secured the post of the governor of the newly founded Danube Province.[6]

Midhat Paşa's model emphasised a separation of administrative, judicial and commercial aspects of governance. Different councils made up of local representatives and appointed clerks were to handle these issues relatively independently of each other. This model defined the general framework of the emergent modern Ottoman provincial administration, keeping the power potential of the local notables and *shar'i* judges under check by bureaucrats, regulations and a codified legal system.[7] In little more than six years, the 1871 regulation further crystallised the institutional framework that the 1864 regulation aimed to introduce. The 1864 regulation introduced a structural division of the administrative units that constituted the basis for a new regulation further qualifying the administrative and judicial council's bureaucratic functions. The new provincial regulation, issued on 22 January 1871, 'annulled' the regulation of 1864 without necessarily altering it altogether. It specified each administrative division's power potential and responsibilities (*Düstur* 1:625–51).

The 1871 Regulation: the County as a Reflection of the Province

The 1871 regulation is more organised and structured than its 1864 counterpart. It is mostly a revision, clarifying the titles and responsibilities of the employees of each provincial unit, from the province to the village in the administrative sphere of the existing system.[8] It emphasises the separation of the judicial offices from the administrative ones at its opening:

> Special regulations for the state courts (*mehakim-i nizamiye*) having been put in place, these regulations do not discuss the administration of the courts but rather define the duties of the administrative officials, the administrative and municipal councils and the district administrations. (*Düstur* 1:625)

Similar to its 1864 predecessor, the new regulation made the subgovernors accountable to the governors (*vali*) who were appointed from the imperial centre. The structure of the 1871 regulation echoes this subordination: the first sixty of the 130 articles define the official positions at different levels and the remaining articles discuss the councils.[9] In both parts, the lion's share of articles pertains to the highest level of local representation in the Ottoman state: the province. The first thirty-four articles deal with the duties of the provincial-level personnel. The following eight articles focus on county-level administration. Article 35 of the 1871 regulation lists the administration of the civil, financial and constabulary affairs, and enforcement of criminal and civil laws as among the duties of the subgovernors. In consultation with the governor, they were to determine the meeting schedule of the district councils and oversee the actions of the district heads and the councils to ensure their concordance with the general regulations and the practices/decisions of the county administrative council. Article 36 made the subgovernors responsible for supervising other officials in the county as well. In addition, they were to report to the governor their regular inspections of public works and occasional investigations of administrative irregularities (*Düstur* 1:634).

These two articles reveal the limits on the power potential of subgovernors at the county level and, to a certain degree, the logic behind the organisation of the first part of the 1871 regulation. The county, as a provincial unit, did not have a unique administrative style that allowed for civil, executive or legislative independence. All such affairs at the county level made sense as part of a more powerful unit, the province. The governor and the county administrative council members limited the authority of the subgovernor. Recent works (Rubin 2011: 28) point at the significance of this hierarchical order in creating a homogenised sphere of administrative practices across the imperial domains. The separation of administrative and judiciary powers was at the heart of these codes. However, this separation was not observed at the local level.[10] The subgovernors were supposed to ensure that the general principles of administration defined for the province were effective at the county level, at least on paper. They 'shared the responsibility of the governor' at the county level and 'reported back to him' if there was anything wrong. Only the regular tasks required to achieve those predetermined goals could be performed at the discretion of the subgovernor, and that had to happen 'with the required decision of the county administrative council'.[11] In theory, councils and local administrators were to provide checks and balances for the modern Ottoman bureaucratic order.

Councils: Inevitable Dynamism?

One of the biggest novelties the provincial regulations of 1864 and 1871 introduced was the system of administrative and judiciary councils. These were not the first provincial councils Ottomans introduced in the nineteenth century: tax collection councils (*muhassıllık meclisi*) established in 1840 and the provincial councils formed following an 1849 regulation preceded them (Petrov 2006: 97–9; Akiba 2009). Yet administrative councils and councils of appeals and crime were part of a more sophisticated organisation that commanded most of the provincial judicio-administrative sphere, while their predecessors had limited power over the judicial sphere. These councils were essential components of Ottoman governmentality in the provinces. They incorporated local notables into the judicio-administrative sphere and imposed limits on the powers of high-ranking administrators – governors, subgovernors, district head officials – and the *shar'i* judge. In addition, they mediated between the districts and the provinces.

The 1864 regulation required both county councils to have appointed and 'elected' members. Subgovernors chaired the administrative councils, which had four appointed members: the judge of the *shar'i* court (*hakim el-şer'*), the religious leader(s) of the region (*müfti-i belde* for Muslims and *re'is-i ruhani* for non-Muslims), the accountant (*muhasebeci*) and the director of correspondence (*müdür-i tahrirat*). The administrative councils were to have an equal number of elected members (*a'za*). For counties with mixed religious composition these were required to be a mix of Muslims and non-Muslims. The judicial councils had a simpler composition: The *shar'i* judge served as the chair of the council of appeals and crime, which had six 'elected' members.

The ratio of appointed to 'elected' members in the administrative councils changed in favour of the former group as the regulation of the Danube

Province (issued on 13 October 1864) became the general Provincial Regulation a month later. While the number of appointed members in the county administrative councils did not change, there was a reduction (from six to four) in the number of members 'elected' from among the local notables. The local leaders of major religious communities sat on the council *ex officio*.[12] The regulation of 1864 eliminated this advantage by establishing the ratio at 4:4.[13] Typically, the majority ruled in these councils; therefore, this flux in numbers significantly challenged the power potential of the elected members (should they choose to unite and act against the appointed members of the council). The number of elected members in the council of appeals and crime, on the other hand, remained at six until 1873, when it was reduced to four.

In clarifying the duties of the councils, Part Two of the 1864 regulation focuses on the administration of the affairs of the county and has two subsections: 'Civil Affairs (*umur-ı mülkiye*)' and 'Legal Affairs (*idare-i livanın umur-ı hukukiyesi*)'. Article 34, in the first subsection, notes the administrative council's responsibilities:

> The administrative council will be in charge of implementing matters pertaining to civil and financial affairs, police, revenue-collection, public works, property transfer and agriculture, and will not interfere with legal affairs.

Article 37, in the second subsection, defines the judge (*hakim*) as the judicial authority on the *nizami* and *shar'i* courts and article 40 explains (*Düstur* 1:615) the duty of the council of appeals as distinctly separate from the *shar'i* courts:

> This council of appeals is charged with the investigation, hearing and supervising of suits that can be separated and identified as legal (*kanuni*) and regulatory (*nizami*) cases apart from [the following]: first, the particular cases that pertain to Muslims and thus need to be heard in *shar'i* courts and likewise cases that pertain to non-Muslims and are heard in their spiritual administrations; and second, issues that relate only to commercial affairs and are heard at the council of commerce.

The regulation of 1864 marked a significant point in the judicial sphere's compartmentalisation in provincial administration (Rubin 2011: 27–8). The title for the county judge in this regulation, *hakim*, differs from that in the Danube Provincial Regulation, *kadı* – the traditional term for a *shar'i* judge. This terminology shift overlapped with a restructuring of the Ottoman judiciary.[14] Article 40 limits the judicial authority of the religious courts to 'the spiritual needs of the community' curbing the power of religious authorities over some judicial practices. Yet, it falls short of specifying what constitutes 'the particular cases that pertain to Muslims and thus need to be heard in *shar'i* courts and ... cases that pertain to non-Muslims and are heard by their spiritual administrations'.[15] Numerous cases of conversion to Islam in Vidin's administrative council registers indicate that even such religious cases were debated by these new councils.[16] The 1864 regulation also distinguishes commercial suits from civil and criminal ones. The commercial code served as a blueprint for the reorganisation of the legal system along secular lines prior to the 1864 regulation.[17] True to this legacy, the 1864 regulation confirms that commercial affairs lie outside the authority of the *hakim*.

In addition to handling some local administrative tasks, the administrative council and council of appeals and crime served as mediators in transferring a local issue or a dispute to the imperial centre. Land disputes, issues pertaining to taxation and administration, and criminal cases fell within the jurisdiction of these two councils. Through a chain of such councils at different administrative levels, the regulation separated civil cases from criminal ones: the administrative councils in the provinces, counties and districts focused on civil cases, and the councils of appeals and crime dealt with criminal cases. A similar two-council structure operated at the district level. District administrative councils (*idare meclisi*) and councils of litigation (*de'avi meclisi*) would report on and transfer 'cases of significance' and appeals to the relevant councils at the county level. Likewise, the councils at the county level would transfer the cases to the provincial centre and from there to Istanbul.[18] From 1864 to 1868, cases coming from these local councils to Istanbul were sent to different departments of the Supreme Council of Judicial Ordinances (Meclis-i Vala-yı Ahkam-ı 'Adliye).[19]

Local representatives came to serve in these councils through a complicated election process that created a necessary space for the local politics of administration. I should qualify using the term 'elected' for council members. This was a two-stage process, wherein candidacy depended on nomination by a special committee. The 1864 regulation outlines the procedure for electing local notables to the county administrative council. While the four members of the inaugural council would be newly elected in the first election, the subsequent elections would replace only half of the four members. The appointed members of the council – the judge of the *shar'i* court, the religious leader(s), the accountant and the director of correspondence – would form a 'nominating committee' (*meclis-i tefrik*) for the elected members of the council. In Vidin County, the members of this committee were mostly from the region. In their correspondence about hiring for positions such as the director of correspondence, the county administrative council emphasised the significance of local knowledge and experience in fulfilling the tasks of this position.[20]

For the first year, the nominating committee would identify three times the number of needed candidates for election (for the county administrative council this would be a total of twelve candidates). Maintaining an equal ratio of Muslims to non-Muslims was important in these nominations.[21] The names of these twelve candidates would be distributed to all the district councils in the county, whereupon the members would vote for two-thirds (eight) of the twelve candidates and report their names back to the nominating committee at the county level. Following this, the nominating committee would determine the four candidates who received the most votes and send their names to the subgovernor, who would pick two names and send a final list to the provincial governor for approval.[22]

The subgovernor's selection concluded the initial election determining the four members who would serve in the first year the councils were established. Every year thereafter, through the same complicated process, half of the members were replaced. (The regulation does not clarify which two members had to resign after serving only one year.) In these subsequent elections, the initial list sent to the districts included only six names, from which the district administrative councils would select four. The county administrative council determined the top four candidates, and the subgovernor chose two of the four to submit to the province for approval. Re-election of those who had completed their terms was permitted, which made it possible for some members to continue serving.

A member's re-election was not a simple process. He would have to be relisted by the county nominating committee, selected by the district administrative councils and favoured by the subgovernor, who then selected the final two council members. Finally, he would have to receive the governor's approval. In a county like Vidin, with six districts, even when an ex-member's name appeared on the initial list, the chances of him being chosen as one of the top four at the county level were fairly low. In theory, this complex mechanism made the re-election of council members difficult and threatened the stability of any two-party alliance between the subgovernor and elected members. It limited the power potential of members and subgovernor alike, since the subgovernor could not guarantee that a member he considered an 'ally' would be selected by the district administrative councils. Theoretically, one might expect a high level of turnover in the membership of these councils due to the low likelihood of re-election.

Another factor that contributed to change over time in the composition of these councils was the rotation of their appointed members. The 1871 register of the Vidin County administrative council is replete with reports of clerks in the region being reassigned from one post to another. The frequent replacement of appointed Ottoman officials was partially due to resignations over low pay, bad working conditions and work overload.[23] Whenever possible, someone with experience in a similar post would replace an appointed member, which could lead to vacation of another office.

Two examples from the register of the administrative council in Vidin help to clarify how these appointments were determined. Osman Efendi, the registrar of title deeds (*tapu katibi*) in the district of Lom, was fired from his position after an investigation into claims that he had been unlawfully soliciting money from deed holders (NBKM, VD 107/16). The council considered Osman Efendi's continuation in his post 'impermissible', and replaced him by Mahmud Efendi, the land registrar (*arazi katibi*) of the district of Vratsa, who had 'sufficient ability to fill the post'. Subsequently, the county administrative council decided to hire a certain Mustafa Efendi from Vratsa to replace Mahmud Efendi. In all these appointments, the clerks had to provide a guarantor who would vouch for them.

It is curious that the administrative council hired Mustafa Efendi from Vratsa although he had not served as a registrar before. A month later, the same council refused to allow Hacı İlyas Ağazade Mehmed Beğ to replace Yeter Beğ, the resigning land registry clerk (*tahrir-i emlak katibi*) of Vratsa District, because the former did not have previous experience. The council was concerned that 'someone who had not been employed in land registry might throw the survey procedures into disorder'. In their report to the Danube Province, the council referred to a decree of the governor requesting that someone with knowledge and experience should replace the resigning land registry clerk.[24] The district administrative council in Vratsa reported that no one was available in the district to replace Yeter Beğ and asked the county to dispatch a replacement.

Regardless of the seemingly inconsistent attitude of the administrative council on the appointment of Mustafa Efendi and Mehmed Beğ, these two cases provide insight into the status of clerks in Vidin by the early 1870s. The shifting pattern of employment created a constantly changing pool of clerks within Vidin County. In 1871 alone there were more than fifty cases of shifting appointments due to resignations or expulsions. Most of the resignations refer to insufficient pay, decrease in salary or excessive workload. Cases of bribery and resignation suggest a general dissatisfaction with demanding working conditions and insufficient pay.

A suspicious administration that required guarantors to hire clerks and insisted that these guarantors be checked and verified as alive and still qualified twice every year accompanied this dissatisfaction (Record 151 in NBKM, VD 107/16). This high turnover rate, contributed to the accumulation of power in the hands of select local notables. Shifting their position in the local administrative ranks, certain notables remained embedded in the politics of local administration.

Councils: Conveying or Constituting Reality?

The administrative councils' reports provide evidence for the significance of local notables' participation in administration. As the two cases I discuss in this section indicate, the relationship between these councils' reports and the events they discuss were less than straightforward, thanks to the politics of provincial administration. The report concerning the first case refer to a certain Şakir Efendi, who claimed that he was representing the Christians from the Rahovo District in Vidin, and complained about high taxes. 'Upon investigation', it turned out that not only was there no excessive taxation, but people did not appoint Şakir Efendi as community representative. Apparently, Şakir Efendi, used his authority as a former state clerk and 'coerced' the region's inhabitants into signing a petition. The council dealt with another case concerning Rahovo in the same month. When they received the news that 200 people had taken a certain Mustafa from the district prison by force, the council appointed someone 'to investigate' the issue. Again, 'upon investigation', the case proved to be false. Apparently, a chief clerk, in dispute with the district's governor, fabricated the story to get Mustafa out of prison (Records 154 and 205 in NBKM, VD 107/16). Such cases demonstrate the difficulties associated with information gathering at the local level.

I would like to focus on the source of our information rather than the results of these investigations. A certain Marin Ağa 'investigated' both cases and played an instrumental role in constituting the 'reality' in these reports. Vidin's administrative council, which was an essential source of local information for the Danube Province and Istanbul, had to rely on the reports of its investigators. Marin Ağa, an elected member of the council serving as an informant, and the reports of the administrative council were at the centre of this imperfect information system. Despite the system's deficiencies, the province and Istanbul often had to rely on his information. Writing, as Jack Goody argues, is a 'technology' that 'has a particular kind of internal influence, since it changes not only the way we communicate but the nature of what we communicate, whether to others or to ourselves'.[25] It is with this understanding of writing as a technology that I would like to approach the register of 1871.

Local Councils and the Politics of Election in Vidin

The communication from the county administrative council to the provincial administrative centre is a technology of Ottoman governmentality; it is a procedure aimed at establishing the authority of the Ottoman state over its population.[26] These reports, petitions and letters also provided the local populace an opportunity to participate in the official depiction of social reality. They offered the inhabitants a means (however limited) to challenge the Ottoman governance from within. This practice of report writing was a platform for what Anthony Giddens refers as the 'dialectic of control'. According to Giddens (1985: 10–11), regardless of the scope or degree of power the 'superordinate' groups have, their authority relies on the compliance of the 'subordinate' ones in this dialectic. The subordinate agents can use certain strategies to protect their interests. Analysis of the copy register in which these reports were recorded can therefore help us understand how the dialectic of control functioned within Vidin.

The reports themselves offer insight into three different aspects of this dialectic. First, they illustrate how the councils represented Vidin County affairs to the empire.[27] The register included information on the number of people and the taxes for which they were liable. It labelled certain practices 'unacceptable' or 'unlawful', certain people as 'exempt from taxes', and certain people as 'old' rather than 'new' inhabitants. In short, the register constituted a lens that rendered the countryside 'visible' to the gaze of the imperial administration.[28] By establishing categories to be used in these reports – such as 'title deeds' – the modern Ottoman state was asking the council to describe the social reality of Vidin from a particular angle. People's 'traditional' rights on certain previously designated communal lands, for example, became 'illegal claims' since ownership was now defined in terms of possessing the title deed to a piece of land. Despite the authority of the 'superordinate', the modern Ottoman state, to impose a vocabulary that defined what was legitimate, the 'subordinate' organisations, the councils, were able to use their authority to determine what and how to report using the particular vocabulary of by the Ottoman state. This dialectic becomes more apparent in the election process discussed below.

Second, the reports of the administrative and judiciary councils reveal something of the negotiated settlements among the members of the council. Council members did not work in harmony on issues that related to the distribution of land to immigrants or to the auctioning of the contracts to provision the armed forces. In fact, there is enough evidence to suggest that this was not the case; there were serious discussions that took place in these organisations. The difficulty in analysing this particular dialectic of control, however, is identifying the 'subordinate' and 'superordinate' parties. I do not have access to the council minutes, which would provide insight into the shifting power balances within these bodies.[29] Michael Meeker (2002) has pointed out that local notables who held government posts were also likely to belong to big families or certain interest groups. The power configuration within the county would have an impact on the functioning of these councils, with alliances and oppositions forming among the members. The discussion of the election results below covers only a single aspect of these shifting power balances, namely, the struggle between the appointed and elected members.

Third, these councils' reports demonstrate how the local populace employed the language of the modern Ottoman state in order to achieve their goals. For ordinary townsmen, these councils represented an authority whose subjects were 'men as a population in relation to the state'. As an organisation, the council served as an apparatus for what Foucault (2000: 409) refers to as 'marginalistic integration of individuals in the state's utility'.[30] By submitting their complaints to the councils, the inhabitants of Vidin County were agreeing to identify themselves as 'individuals', that is, as part of a social entity defined in relation to the modern Ottoman state. The presence of the council as an office that organised and classified people and their possessions according to their potential benefit or harm to the state also forced the people to use similar terms in defining themselves and others in their communications with the councils.

Nonetheless, considering the council and its reports only as technologies of government does not do justice to the situation in Vidin County in the second half of the nineteenth century. They also need to be viewed as a means of resistance to and negotiation of regional political and economic power. My argument on this second conceptualisation is based on works by Huricihan İslamoğlu (2004a; 2004b) and Michael Meeker (2002) who argue that the modern state did not have absolute power over its population. İslamoğlu proposes a 'constitutivist perspective' within which administrative orderings – and law – are conceptualised as hegemonic processes that are dynamic and reflective of the struggles of different groups. She calls for a more detailed analysis of the processes that generate the modern state. The state, in İslamoğlu's (2004a: 278) argument, is a 'hegemonic environment'.[31] In this environment, in order to maintain authority the dominant groups must continually reconstitute the environment through negotiations that order social reality (such as laws that regulate access and allocation of resources). This dynamic and negotiational conceptualisation of the state as a hegemonic environment allows room for other actors to interfere with and challenge the Ottoman governmentality at different levels. This conceptualisation invites us to analyse the dynamic politics of what Foucault (1991: 102–3) referred to as a 'very specific albeit complex form of power'.

Michael Meeker's elaborate analysis of the town of Of on the eastern Black Sea coast focuses on this negotiational coexistence of state and society at the local level. In defining how 'a single government of state officials and local elites' (2002: 185) in this Black Sea town began to take shape in the course of eighteenth century, Meeker emphasises how lower-rank military officers formed interpersonal associations with the local notability, giving the latter the ability to mobilise armed followings. In the course of the nineteenth-century transformation of the state apparatus, as these notables remained relevant for the functioning of the essential governmental tasks in Of, they kept the provincial governors in the dark by systematically filtering out information. According to Meeker (2002: 260) the combination of centralised bureaucratic structure with interpersonal association circles rendered such filtering more consistent.

As the local social structures adapted to Ottoman governmentality and devised new strategies to protect their interests within it, the dynamism inherent in the hegemonic Ottoman state was matched by different groups' and alliances' negotiations at the local level, where the boundaries of the modern state were not very clear. At times, local agents were very much a part of this hegemonic environment; at other times, they were conspicuously absent from the imperial view. Resistance to Ottoman governmentality did not always fit into the categories defined by the institutions of local administration.

The adoption of a modern state language by the 'subordinates' implies utilisation of a new code in the 'dialectic of control' by both the superordinate and the subordinate groups as an essential governing practice.[32] The discrepancy between local realities and official categories in this dialectic creates a necessary space for politics of administration at the local level. To understand the relationship between the coding of information a modern state utilises and its administrative power, one needs to examine the negotiations within the hegemonic environment in which this coded language is constructed. The administrative power, according to Giddens (1985: 47) is conditional on the utilisation of this particular coding in direct supervision (and ordering) of social reality. As İslamoğlu and Meeker suggest, however, this ordering is a hegemonic process – constitutive of the hegemonic environment that is the state itself – where one can observe the single government of state officials and local elites interact with the local populace.

Thus, the language of reports, a language that speaks of 'title deeds' and 'income surveys', orders the social reality to fit into the yearbooks and detaches it from local community life. This, however, does not imply that the subordinates were altogether pacified. Even in the context of this detachment, those who were not a part of the Ottoman administration had the potential to act as agents with 'transformative capacity' over structures in the dialectic of control taking place at the local level. The local notables and the populace at large were able to integrate themselves into the council to filter information and constitute a social reality readily visible to the eyes of the provincial administration. It is through these means that the institutions of local administration of the modern Ottoman state were continually challenged and reconstituted. I give some examples of this dialectic in Chapter 5.

Vidin in the nineteenth century did not have a monoblock 'state' operating in opposition to a dominated 'society'. The administrative council's election results suggest that local notables were able to integrate themselves into the local mechanisms of administration as they did in the previous centuries. The council did serve Ottoman governmentality. Through its repeated procedures, it contributed to the 'discursive dispersion' of the narrative of a powerful state (Foucault 1982: 31–9). Yet the local notables and other agents knew how to manipulate these procedures and the reports of the administrative council to filter out information and paint a particular image for the provincial administration. The negotiations on what these reports should say constituted a significant component of modern Ottoman governance.

Of Permanency and Change: the Politics of Election

The provincial regulations of 1864 and 1871 describe the framework of a highly dynamic system and reports from Vidin's administrative council confirm a high turnover rate among most of the appointed and some elected members. The appointed members had to change posts due to the above-mentioned replacement policies. On the other hand, half of the elected members were replaced every year. Understanding who the elected members were, their terms of service and interactions with other council members is essential for analysing the local politics of administration. This section focuses on the election – and re-election – of the members of these councils. The provincial administrative structure gave significant powers to the council members in local politics, making membership elections important, politically charged events. Getting elected and re-elected to these councils was a difficult, complex, but essential, political process.

Being an elected member in the local councils meant having a certain level of authority in the provincial judicio-administrative sphere. Through

Table 3.1 Candidate lists for Vidin's administrative council (from the copy register)

Year	Candidate 1	Candidate 2	Candidate 3	Candidate 4	Candidate 5
1871	Ma'rufzade eminent Ahmed Beğ, administrative council member	İvraniyelizade İsma'il Efendi	Eminent Sevastaki Ağa, former member of the court of appeals	Merchant Hacı Todor Ağa	
1872	Eminent 'Ali Beğ, *from the Vidin dynasty*[a]	Hacı Ömer Beğ, from the Vidin dynasty[b]	Duhani Derviş Ahmed Efendi[c]	Candle maker Kristo Ağa	Dye-maker Marin Ağa
1873	Hacı Ömer Beğ, *from the notables of Vidin*[d]	Osman Beğ, from the notables of Vidin,	Safer Ağa, member of the court of appeals	Eminent Canko Ağa of Vidin	
1874	Ma'ruf Ağazade eminent Ahmed Beğ	Hacı Tahir Ağa, former member of the court of appeals	Marin Ağa, former member of the administrative council	Merchant Zayko Ağa	

Source: NBKM, VD 96/41 and VD 107/16.

[a] Emphasis mine, the original text: *Vidin hanedanından.* A note above the name of the candidate indicates that "'Ali Beğ resigned although he won the majority'.
[b] A note above the name of the candidate indicates that 'Hacı Ömer Beğ resigned as well'.
[c] A note above the name of the candidate indicates that 'Although Ahmed Efendi got two votes less than 'Ali and Ömer Beğs, due to their resignation, employment of this member is contingent on [the governor's] exalted opinion'.
[d] Emphasis mine, the original text: *Vidin eşrafından.* A note above the name of the candidate indicates that 'Hacı Ömer Beğ resigned mentioning excess personal affairs'.

Nineteenth-century Local Governance in Ottoman Bulgaria

re-election, notables could stretch this authority over a longer period. This chance, however, was rather low – in theory. Several factors determined whether someone's name would be on the initial list of candidates distributed to the districts including their local reputation and relationship with the council's appointed members who served as a nominating committee determining the initial list. When a candidate's name appeared on the initial list sent to the districts, the mathematical likelihood of the same name appearing among the top four of all the names the subgovernor received was only 22 per cent. Even if the subgovernor, who chose two out of the four, were to prefer a lucky candidate over the others, the governor could veto the subgovernor's choice.

The elections took place in Muharram, the first month of the *hijri* year. Table 3.1 presents the candidate lists that Vidin's subgovernor received for the years 1871 to 1874. The entries in the table are from two separate registers of the council's reports to Ruse, which span the period from March 1871 to February 1874 (NBKM, VD 107/16 and VD 96/41). The subgovernor was to forward two names (a Muslim and a non-Muslim) out of the four on the list to the governor. Yet, Vidin's subgovernor reported all of the names on the list to the governor, explicitly stating that the choice belonged entirely to the governor. These lists' composition and the appended remarks (explained in the notes at the bottom of the table) provide insight into the politics of the nomination process.[33]

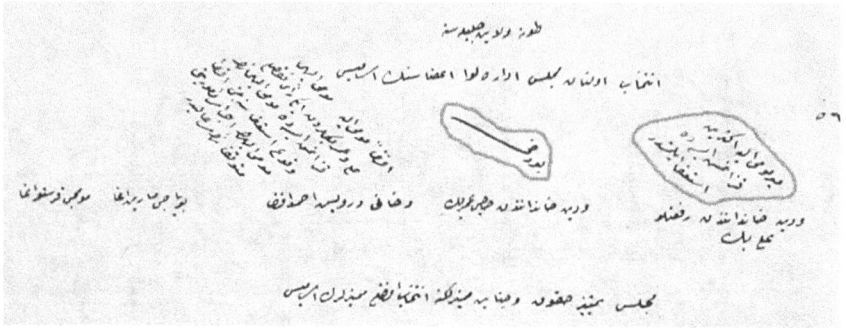

Figure 3.2 List of Elected Members in 1872

Source: NBKM, VD 107/16. The circled areas explain why the candidate resigned.

There are four names in the final list for all the years except 1872, when the resignation of the top two candidates left a third candidate as the only (Muslim) candidate. 'Ali Beğ and Hacı Ömer Beğ, both among the notables in Vidin, resigned for unknown reasons, and Duhani Derviş Ahmed Efendi was elected as the new Muslim member of the council.

Something similar happened the following year, when Hacı Ömer Beğ appeared as a candidate again but resigned, 'mentioning the excess of his personal affairs'.

Resignation notes in these entries are right above the individual's name (the circled areas in Figure 3.2 and notes in Table 3.1). There are no explanations for 'Ali Beğ and Hacı Ömer Beğ's resignations in 1872. In 1873 a note explains the latter's resignation with 'the excess of his personal affairs'. Regardless of his reasons, Hacı Ömer Beğ's decision led to the automatic election of another Muslim candidate in both years without giving the governor the chance to pick a candidate from two names. The report of 1873 explicitly states that the governor needs to appoint 'a Muslim and a non-Muslim' from among the four candidates.

Hacı Ömer Beğ's resignation in two consecutive years may be a reflection of the local politics. We do not know how the nominating committee compiled the initial candidate lists to distribute to the districts and it is unclear if Hacı Ömer Beğ, or any of the candidates on the initial list, wanted to be listed. If the committee composed the list without the candidates' consent, then an elected candidate's only choice to not serve would be to resign. But if Hacı Ömer Beğ opted to be on the list, then his resignation would reflect to his own calculations, or perhaps, the pressure of others.[34] There are no further details regarding the resignations, nor is there evidence of a deal among notables. Any guess with this much information would be speculative due to lack of direct evidence. One thing that is certain, however, is that the administrative council in Vidin did choose to report a single candidate. It presented the results of a local decision-making process at the county level to the provincial government at Danube as the only possible legitimate outcome and the governor did not appear to have challenged this.

The administrative council's reaction to the elected candidates' resignation seem to have been designed to secure the election of particular members. When the top two Muslim candidates who got the most votes from the districts resigned in 1872, the council did not hesitate to add the notable who ranked third, Duhani Derviş Ahmed Efendi, but they did not add a fourth candidate. In order to give the right to select a candidate to the governor – as the council seem to have done in the past – the two candidates' resignation should necessitate two additional names on the list, not just one. Furthermore, in 1873, when Hacı Ömer Beğ resigned for the second year in a row and left another local notable, Osman Beğ, as the only candidate, the council could have named a third candidate, just as it had a year previously, but it chose not to. These choices left a particular candidate's name as the only viable option in both cases. The council used the report, an official document, to legitimise the settled outcome of local power negotiations. There are other intricacies of the 'election process' besides these irregularities.

A brief look at the lists reveals that certain names occur more than once in this short interval. Ma'rufzade Ahmed Beğ, for example, was a candidate in 1871 and, with a slightly different title, Ma'ruf Ağazade Ahmed Beğ, in 1874.[35] As mentioned in the report of 1871, Ahmed Beğ had served on the administrative council prior to that date as well. In addition to Hacı Ömer Beğ – who resigned twice – Marin Ağa, dye-maker and 'former member of the administrative council', appears in 1872 and 1874. Furthermore, these people were candidates not only for the administrative council but for the judiciary council.

Every year, along with choosing two members for the administrative council, the governor also made the final decision on candidates to replace half of the examining clerks (*mümeyyiz*) on the council of appeals and crime. This council, focusing mostly on judicial affairs within the county, was another way for notables to become a part of the local judicio-administrative sphere. The list of candidates for the examining clerkships was reported together with the candidates for the administrative council, but the number of candidates for each varied. In 1871 there were eight candidates for the examining clerkships, in 1872 only six, and from 1873 onward, only four.

There were a total of thirty-nine candidate positions for the two main administrative and judicial offices of local government in Vidin County.[36] The reports contain a total of thirty different names; twenty-two of these appear only once and eight appear multiple times. Moreover, some of the members appear to be from the same family groups.[37] Table 3.2 lists the candidates for the council of appeals and crime on the candidate lists submitted to the province. As in Table 3.1, certain names appear more often than others, indicating the importance of certain people in Vidin's judicio-administrative sphere. This point becomes clearer when one considers those on the lists who were actually selected to serve. Because these lists do not tell us the governor's final choices, we need to consult another source for this information.

Table 3.3 presents the names of elected members from the yearbooks (*salname*) of the Danube Province from 1868 (AH 1285) to 1877 (AH 1294). The lists were composed in the first month of the lunar calendar year (Muharram) and provided the names of potential members for the coming year. The yearbooks, however, give the names of local administrators of the previous year.[38] Combined with the candidate list in the local register, the information included in the provincial yearbooks, which were

Table 3.2 Candidate lists For Vidin's council of appeals and crimes (from the copy register)

Year	Candidate 1	Candidate 2	Candidate 3	Candidate 4	Candidate 5	Candidate 6	Candidate 7	Candidate 8
1871	Şerif 'alemdarzade Matyaş Ağa	Former district head official of Mecidiye, eminent Mansur Beğ	Ahmed Beyzade Mahmud Beğ	From the Belgrad immigrants Kerim Beğ	Tailor Çako Ağa	Hacı İlyazade Taso Ağa	Arslan oğlu Salamon Efendi	Yusuf Vagitora (?) Efendi
1872	From the Vidin dynasty Ramiz Beğ	Hacı 'Ali Şah Efendizade Cafer Efendi	Hacı Todor Ağa	Rukail Bazirgan	Tailor Sado Ağa	İlyaco's son-in-law Yako Efendi		
1873	Member of the court of appeals eminent Mansur Beğ	From the Belgrad immigrants eminent Şakir Efendi	Şaul Efendi from Vidin	Salamon Efendi from Vidin				
1874	Hacı Ömer Efendizade Remzi Beğ	Şerif 'alemdarzade Matyaş Ağa	Former member of the court of appeals Hacı Todor Ağa	Hacı İlya oğlu Taso Ağa				

Source: *NBKM, VD 96/41 and VD 107/16.*

Table 3.3 List of Vidin's administrative and judiciary council members in the yearbooks

Publication year	Elected members of Vidin's administrative council according to the *Salnames*			
1868	Zayko Ağa	Ömer Beğ	Hacı Tahir Ağa	Angel Ağa	
1869	Zayko Ağa	Ömer Beğ	Hacı Tahir Ağa	Angel Ağa	
1870	Zayko Ağa	Ömer Beğ	Hacı Tahir Ağa	Angel Ağa	
1871	Zayko Ağa	Ahmed Beğ	Mehmed Ağa	Zelko Ağa	
1872	Sevastaki Ağa	Ahmed Beğ	Mehmed Ağa	Zelko Ağa	
1873	Sevastaki Ağa	Ahmed Beğ	Ahmed Ağa	Kristo Ağa	
1874	Osman Beğ	Seko Ağa	Ahmed Ağa	Marin Ağa	
1875	Ahmed Beğ	Seko Ağa	Hacı Tahir Ağa	Zayko Ağa	
1876	Ahmed Beğ	Seko Ağa	Hacı Tahir Ağa	Zayko Ağa	
1877	Ahmed Beğ	Ahmed Ağa	Hacı Petko Ağa	Aleksandire Efendi	Mehmed Efendi	İshak Efendi

Publication year	Elected members of Vidin's council of appeals and crime according to the *Salnames*				
1868	Sevastaki Ağa	Mahmud Efendi	Hacı İliya Efendi	Ahmed Beğ	Ahmed Şükrü Efendi	Mişon Kalaf Efendi
1869	Sevastaki Ağa	Mahmud Efendi	Hacı İliya Efendi	Ahmed Beğ	Ahmed Şükrü Efendi	Mişon Kalaf Efendi
1870	Sevastaki Ağa	Mahmud Efendi	Hacı İliya Efendi	Ahmed Beğ	Ahmed Şükrü Efendi	Mişon Kalaf Efendi
1871	Sevastaki Ağa	Mahmud Efendi	Nako Efendi	Şakir Efendi	Ahmed Şükrü Efendi	Persiyado Efendi
1872	Mansur Beğ	Matyaş Ağa	Nako Efendi	Şakir Efendi	Salomon Efendi	Çako Ağa
1873	Mansur Beğ	Matyaş Ağa	Hacı Tahir Ağa	Hacı Todor	Salomon Efendi	Çako Ağa
1874	Mansur Beğ	Hacı Tahir Ağa	Hacı Todor	Şaul Efendi		
1875	Remzi Beğ	Matyaş Ağa	Hacı Todor	Şaul Efendi		
1876	Remzi Beğ	Matyaş Ağa	Hacı Todor	Şaul Efendi		
1877	Remzi Beğ	Matyaş Ağa	Hacı Todor	Petra Ağa		

Source: *Salname Tuna* 1868–77.

compiled to inform the centre, allows for a more critical approach to the politics of election.

In analysing Tables 3.2 and 3.3, the first thing to notice is the systematic reduction in the number of listed candidates for the council of appeals and crime: from eight in 1871 to six in 1872 to four the following year. The governor apparently selected four, three and two members in those years respectively. The first decrease in the judicial council's candidates does not conform to the results given in the provincial yearbooks. The yearbook of 1874 indicates that in 1873 the membership of the council declined from six to four (see Table 3.3). However, no explanation can be found in the yearbooks as to why there were eight names on the candidate list of 1871. In the report accompanying this particular candidate list (NBKM, VD 107/16), the administrative council explains that the regular procedure has been followed to replace half of the examining clerks:

> Inasmuch as annual election of half the members, with provision for re-election of outgoing members, is among the requirements of the special article of the provincial regulation, eighteen persons were found appropriate in the nominating council (*cem'iyyet-i tefrik*) for [1871] to replace half the members and the examining clerks of the administrative and appeals councils. Of the eighteen men who were nominated for election, as listed at the head of this report, four got the most votes, with unanimity of opinion, for membership in the administrative council and eight for the examining clerkship of the appeals council.

The council concludes its report with a request that the governor of the Danube Province 'elects' half of these candidates for the councils without necessarily indicating why, in that year (1871), the number of the candidates was eight instead of six. Two years later, in 1873, the report accompanying the candidate list (NBKM, VD 96/41), sent by the council to the province, refers to an 'imperial decree' (dated March 1873) that reduced of the number of the examining clerks in the council of appeals from six to four. The council sent the candidate list in the same month with this order: 10 March 1873. This explains why there were only four examining clerks listed in the yearbook of 1874.[39] Yet it does not clarify the presence of an extra name in that particular year's candidate list; nor does it explain the mismatch between the local registers and yearbooks.[40]

The eight names on the candidate list for the council of appeals and crime in 1871 imply a council with eight members (four of the names would replace *half* of the council members). The results in the yearbook, however, tell a different story. The candidate list of 1871 corresponds to the line for 1872 in Table 3.3, and there are six elected examining clerks on the council of appeals and crime. Four of them – Mansur Beğ, Matyaş

Ağa, Salamon Efendi and Çako Ağa – are different from the previous year's members and are included on the candidate list of 1871. It appears that Persiyado Efendi began serving on the council a year before he had to leave his post, and a fourth elected member replaced him.[41]

A similar irregularity in the tenure of the elected members appears in the first three lines of Table 3.3. All the names are the same for three consecutive years. The structure and content of the yearbooks suggest that a typographical error is an unlikely explanation for this irregularity. For the first three years, the names of the elected members are the same in both councils while the names of other clerks change. Clearly, the compilers did not use the same information regarding members of these councils for the first three years. Tables of errors at each volume's end say nothing that relates to this irregularity. And it is also unlikely that the information sent from the county was wrong for three consecutive years.

The presence of these names in the yearbooks does not mean that these people were actually serving. As I discuss in the next chapter, the information in the yearbooks is not always reliable. However, the provincial government published and distributed the yearbooks and they serve as public statements attesting to members' positions in local government. If the recurrence of the names for three consecutive years was not due to a typographical error, or an inaccuracy in the information sent, other factors must explain it. I discuss this in more detail in the next chapter.

The number of elected members for the administrative council in Table 3.3 increases to six for the year 1877. This appears to be the case for Vidin County alone. None of the other counties had administrative councils with six elected members. That this was not the general application in all counties might imply a certain change in the power configuration of Vidin County. Such details support the thesis that there were irregularities (or peculiarities) in the election process and the composition of these councils. It was possible to have a different number of elected members in similar administrative units in different counties, such as the councils mentioned above. It was also possible for a member to resign even after he was elected, or in the middle of his two-year term. As they were outcomes of the politics of local administration, such seeming irregularities reflect the particularities of the local power balance. Perhaps more important, the provincial government was aware of these irregularities. It did not hesitate to publish such irregularities in the yearbooks that were sent to different counties in the region as well as to Istanbul.

Table 3.4 lists the names of the elected council members, together with when and where they served, in order to give a better sense of their total duration of service. The last column of the table indicates how many times

Local Councils and the Politics of Election in Vidin

Table 3.4 Vidin's council members' appointment years

Name	'68[a]	'69	'70	'71	'72	'73	'74	'75	'76	'77	FR[d]
Ahmed Beğ	MT[b]	MT	MT	IM[c]	IM	IM		IM	IM	IM	9
Sevastaki Ağa	MT	MT	MT	MT	IM	IM					6
Hacı Tahir Ağa	IM	IM	IM			MT	MT	IM	IM		7
Zayko Ağa	IM	IM	IM	IM				IM	IM		6
Ahmed Şükrü Efendi	MT	MT	MT	MT							4
Mahmud Efendi	MT	MT	MT	MT							4
Matyaş Ağa					MT	MT		MT	MT	MT	5
Hacı Todor						MT	MT	MT	MT	MT	5
Şaul Efendi								MT	MT	MT	3
Seko Ağa							IM	IM	IM	IM	4
Angel Ağa	IM	IM	IM								3
Hacı İliya Efendi	MT	MT	MT								3
Mişon Kalaf Efendi	MT	MT	MT								3
Ömer Beğ	IM	IM	IM								3
Mansur Beğ					MT	MT	MT				3
Nako Efendi				MT	MT						2
Şakir Efendi				MT	MT						2
Ahmed Ağa						IM	IM				2
Çako Ağa					MT	MT					2
Marin Ağa						IM	IM				2
Mehmed Ağa				IM	IM						2
Zelko Ağa				IM	IM						2
Remzi Beğ								MT	MT	MT	3
Salamon Efendi					MT	MT					2
Osman Beğ								IM			1
Persiyado Efendi				MT							1

Source: *Salname Tuna* 1868–77.

[a] The last two digits of the yearbook's publication ('68 = 1868)
[b] MT = council of appeals and crime (*meclis-i temyiz-i hukuk ve cinayet*)
[c] IM = administrative council (*idare meclisi*)
[d] FR = total amount of years that a member served in either of the councils

a candidate served on one of the councils. The table shows how certain local notables switched from one council to another, thus remaining an integral part of the provincial judicio-administrative sphere. Despite possible inaccuracies in the yearbooks, the details of Table 3.4 are too striking to be ignored.

Table 3.4 makes it possible to reach some conclusions regarding the re-election process for these councils. On the one hand, through limiting the number of elected members from the local population and imposing a complicated election system that made re-election relatively unlikely, the imperial centre tried to keep the power potential of the local notables under control. On the other hand, through local politics and resignations, local notables were able to maintain their membership of these councils. This becomes more obvious from the provincial yearbooks. Tables 3.3 and 3.4 indicate not only that certain figures such as Ahmed Beğ, Sevastaki Ağa, Hacı Tahir Ağa or Zayko Ağa served continuously for several years, but also that (despite the two-year terms) several members served for an odd number of years.

The regulations required each member to serve for a two-year period. To achieve an odd number of service years, one would resign (or be dismissed) in the middle of a two-year term. It was not possible for the provincial administration at Ruse to be unaware of such political events. Yet at the same time, it was not necessary (or even not possible) to prevent these irregularities. The language of the provincial regulation provided a framework that members of the judicio-administrative sphere negotiated and interpreted in light of local politics. Instead of preventing Ahmed Beğ from serving for nine years (which would have been in line with the intentions of the regulation that imposed two-year terms), the governors at Ruse kept him as a member of these judiciary and administrative councils. While Ahmed Beğ was a member of local government in Vidin for nine years, from 1868 to 1877, the governor of Ruse changed ten times during this period.[42] Through re-election, local notables maintained their presence within the Ottoman judiciary and administration. To the best of our knowledge these members were not being paid a salary for their service in the councils, yet their position allowed them to have significant influence in local politics.[43]

The provincial regulations of 1864 and 1871 define the nominating committees as composed of the appointed members of the administrative council of the county. The local registers confirm that indeed this was the case for Vidin. A rough draft of a report, sent to the provincial administration on 2 April 1876, sheds light on problems with the election process.[44] The report takes note of a dispute between two camps that were supposed to elect eight candidates out of the twelve that the nominating committee decided upon for each council. The nominating committee did not send the list to the district councils. Instead three to four members from the administrative and judicial councils (*idare meclisi* and *meclis-i de'avi*) of each district came to Vidin to elect two-thirds of these twelve candidates. These electors (*intihabcı*) met the electors from the head district, Vidin.[45] However, the lists of names offered by the district council members did not match those offered by the electors from Vidin. The report does not refer to the gathering in the head district as an unusual incident, it may have been their usual practice. However, since they could not agree on a common list, it was necessary to draft the report.

The report's details present a clearer picture of the dispute. The number of electors in each group appears to be rather uneven. On the one hand, twenty-one electors from the districts, all of them members of the district councils, represented a larger body of electors in the districts. On the other, eight electors from the central district, Vidin, which served as the centre of the whole county, represented sixty-one electors from the villages and towns around Vidin. There is no detailed explanation in the report of who these sixty-one electors are, only that they are from the neighbourhoods and villages of Vidin District.[46]

It is likely that the sixty-one electors were notables from villages within the district of Vidin and that they agreed upon eight representatives in order to elect eight council members for that year. It is not possible to know the details of local politics in this election; nevertheless, it is clear that the eight representatives from Vidin had a significant influence on the process. Even the majority from the districts could not exert authority over the Vidin representatives. They were able to insist on a list different from the one supported by the other twenty-one electors, and this disagreement led to the report.

Based on their names, at least five out of these eight representatives were non-Muslims. Three of the five had the names of their villages clearly identified: Yovan (Ioan) Ağa of Slanatruna, Karin Dimitri Ağa of Helvacı, and Yovan (Ioan) Orta (?) of Bregova. All three villages – Slanatruna, Helvacı, and Bregova – occupy a narrow strip to the north of Vidin. That some representatives used their village names together with their own names implies either that the other representatives were from the town of Vidin, or that they were familiar to the members of the administrative council to whom the report was addressed. Of the remaining five, Süleyman Efendi identified himself as the former Muslim religious leader of the region (*müfti-i sabık*). Another, Anastas Hacı İliya, was a member of the council of appeals and crime for three consecutive years, from 1868 to 1871.[47] A third representative not affiliated with a village, Aleksandri Nikolço Ağa (another report suggests that he was from Vidin), also appears on the list made by the twenty-one council members from the districts.

These details give some clues about the electors from the villages and neighbourhoods of Vidin. The electors were not evenly (geographically) distributed across the county and a candidate's prior involvement with the local administration did not prevent him from serving as an elector. Knowing the general pattern of the results of the 'election process' for the councils, however, it would not be unreasonable to expect that these representatives would have been on good terms with some of the county councils' frequently elected members. It comes as no surprise, then, that the lists compiled by both groups have a number of names in common, including Ma'ruf Ağazade Ahmed Beğ, who served on the councils for nine years beginning in 1868, and Zayko Ağa, who served for seven years during the same period. It should also be noted that the representatives' list features one candidate from the village of Slanatruna and one from Helvacı. It appears that notables from these northern villages of Vidin District were prominent enough to make it onto the candidate lists.[48]

Getting elected and serving on the county councils were significant achievements in the politics of local administration. Council membership meant power for the local notables who were elected and were able to maintain their positions. The report on the above-mentioned dispute regarding the drafting of the candidate lists indicates that there was a relatively stable domination by certain notables at the county level. The central district of the county and the other districts were expected to agree on certain names to represent local interests in local administration. Yet, as this dispute and the analysis of the election process indicates, getting re-elected to these councils was rather difficult.

Given the mathematically low likelihood of getting re-elected and the intricacies of local politics, it is difficult to understand how people like Ma'ruf Ağazade Ahmed Beğ served for such long periods. In fact, a core group of local notables played key roles in regional politics well before the first provincial yearbook was compiled in 1868. The 19 July 1865 issue of the newspaper *Dunav* reports the establishment of an orphanage (*ıslahhane*) for orphans and poor children in Ruse. The donors from the region include not only Ahmed Beğ but also Zayko Ağa. An interrogation report (NBKM, VD 123/17), dated 23 June 1865, bears the seal of Sevastaki Ağa as an examining clerk on the council of appeals and crime, with clearly identifiable letters, С İ Г, representing his full name, Sevastaki Ivanov Gunzovyanov (Севастаки Иванов Гънзовянов). Even prior to the decree of 1864, the seals of Ahmed Beğ and Zayko Ağa are prominent on a report (NBKM, VD 91/14) regarding the bakers of the town, and indicate their position as members of the tax collection council that preceded the administrative council.

The discussion here has been limited mostly to the last ten years during which the two councils were active. However, there were other opportunities besides the councils for local notables to participate in the activities of the Ottoman state. In addition to many other civilian and military members of local government, all volumes of the yearbooks except the first one list the members of a commission of surveys (*tahrir komisyonu*). The dye-maker Marin Ağa, who served as an interrogator in many cases, including the two above, and who was a council member for two years, was also listed as one of this commission's four members in all the yearbooks (*Salname Tuna* 1868–77). In fact, it is possible to find many names that reappear over the years in different bodies, indicating a provincial judicio-administrative sphere serving as a means for local groups to wield influence through the Ottoman governance.

Sources other than the yearbooks further attest to the complicated relationship between these local notables and the modern Ottoman state. With a language that is typical of the pro-independence newspapers that were published outside the Ottoman Empire, the author of an anonymous article from the nationalist Bucharest-based weekly *Svoboda* asks who should be blamed for 500 years of Ottoman brutality: 'Whom should we accuse? Who is to blame?'[49] The 'Turcophilic' Sevastaki Ağa provides the author with a convenient representative of those 'who wish to feed themselves alone, just like the Turks, and are ready to live comfortably'. 'Sevastaki', our reporter continues, 'has big mansions naturally full of wealth: silk curtains, velvet cushions and pillows, sultans' portraits, etc.' *Svoboda* was one of several newspapers whose reporters associated regime change with the elimination of the local notability, the *chorbadzhia*, who worked with the Ottoman government.[50] The regime change, however, did not eliminate the names that I have been discussing so far.

Genadi Vulchev's recent works explicate the family lineages among some of the prominent local notability prior to and after Bulgarian independence. For example, Sevastaki Ağa (Sevastaki I. Gunzovyanov, 1825–98) was married to Efimia Shishmanova, the younger sister of Ekaterina Shishmanova, Hacı İliya Efendi's (Ilia T. Tsanov, 1835–1901) mother (Vulchev 2001: 32, 158). Hacı İliya's brother, Nako Ağa (Naicho Tomov Tsanov), was later elected as a member of the judicial council. Their father, Tomaki Tsanov, worked for the Ottoman administration and died in exile in 'Asia Minor' (Vulchev 2001: 390). Some of these people retained their prominence after the regime change, and were able to integrate themselves into the new regime. While Sevastaki Ağa, coming from a notable family of Vlach descent from the village of Gumzovo (approximately nine miles north-east of Vidin), appears to have lost his prominence after Ottoman rule in Vidin County de facto ended in 1878 (Vulchev 2006: 148, 156–7), Zayko Ağa (Tseko Vanchov) represented Vidin in the Second General National Assembly (Obiknoveno Narodno Subranie) of the newly established Bulgaria in 1881 (Vulchev 2003: 624). Both he and Ahmed Beğ – with the semi-Slavicised name of Akhmed Beg Marufov – were members of the municipal council and among the thirty-eight people who donated 8,131 leva to the municipality in 1883.[51]

Although he was affiliated with the Ottoman administration and a 'Turkish Muslim', Akhmed Beğ was appointed by the Russian imperial commissar Kniaz Dondukov-Korsakov to the Constituent Assembly in Veliko Tarnovo in 1879 (Vulchev 2001: 73). Together with Sevastaki Ağa's nephew by marriage, Ilia T. Tsanov (Hacı İliya Efendi, a council member for several years), they were among the 229 intellectuals who drafted the Tarnovo Constitution that served Bulgaria from 1879 to 1947 (Vulchev 2001: 32, 158, 622).

Perhaps what is more interesting is that Ma'ruf Ağazade Ahmed Beğ's and Sevastaki Ivanov Gunzovyanov's fathers appear to have been members of the former local council established in 1849. A 1851 correspondence conveying the local *gospodars*' letter of appreciation to the imperial administration for the inheritable treasury certificates the *gospodars* received in exchange for the land that was formerly under their control bears the seals of the fathers (Ma'ruf Ağa and Ivan Ganzov) as elected council members.[52] The influence of some families appears to have continued over generations, as the 'end' of the *gospodarlık* regime evidently did not prevent these two families from using the new administrative structure to perpetuate their influence. Sevastaki Ağa must have ceased claiming a space for himself for more complex reasons; after all, other members of the Ottoman administration continued into Bulgarian administration.[53]

Conclusion

The regulations of 1864 and 1871 were attempts by the modern Ottoman state to establish a dynamic administrative structure that functioned in communication with but separately from the judicial structure at the local level. Although local councils were not a novelty for the empire, it was only after the provincial regulation of 1864 that we see the establishment of a separate judicial organisation, council of appeals and crime, in every county. These were state courts (*mehakim-i nizamiye*) that allowed the participation of local notables.[54] The provincial regulations of 1864 and 1871 focused mostly on the local administrative councils and put special emphasis on separating the structure and duties of these state courts. This attempt by the empire to separate the administrative sphere from the judicial one, however, appears to have failed in Vidin County. By moving from one council to another, the local notables, such as Zayko Ağa, Sevastaki Ağa, Ahmed Beğ and Hacı İliya Efendi, established a link between these councils.

In addition to emphasising relatively independent administrative and

Local Councils and the Politics of Election in Vidin

judicial councils, the regulations of 1864 and 1871 established a deliberate procedure of election that aimed to prevent the local notables from serving for long periods on these councils. Lists of members in the yearbooks indicate that this attempt did not succeed either. Several notables managed to get re-elected continuously for extended periods. That these yearbooks were published by the province indicates that the imperial administration was aware of this situation. The details of the election process described above also prove that the provincial centre at Ruse did not do much to prevent the re-election of certain candidates. Perhaps it did not have any reason to try to push notables away.

The design, duties and functioning of these councils enabled local notables to participate in the local judicio-administrative sphere. The nature of this participation made getting elected – and re-elected – a very important aspect of the politics of local administration. The information available about some of these council members indicates that they retained their prominence even after the collapse of the Ottoman administrative structure. In that sense, the local notables outlived the empire in the region as agents of the new Bulgarian governmentality. Surviving the crisis of the Ottoman traditional social structure, these agents were able to integrate themselves into the emerging modern social structure and be a part of Ottoman/Bulgarian governance despite the political turmoil in the region. Regime change, coming with the collapse of the Ottoman administrative structure in the region, did not lead to a dramatic rupture in the local socio-economic institutional structure.

So far I have focused mostly on how the agents of this structure came to power and retained their agency. This, however, does not mean that these councils functioned in unanimity, without any conflict. The next chapter extends this chapter's focus on the politics of election by discussing how the members of the council might have interacted with each other.

Notes

1. İslamoğlu (2004a: 277) discusses the political nature of administration at the imperial level.
2. Petrov (2006: 99) notes that the councils established by the 1864 regulation aimed to provide 'an institutional avenue for easier implementation of governing principles and policies conceived . . . in Istanbul rather than as a means for soliciting the political participation of people's representatives'. In that sense, this regulation was a part of the series of reforms targeting a more effective centralisation of Ottoman governance. He also argues that 'the 1871 revision of the system made the [administrative councils] even less

representative by generally lowering the quotas of elected members in them'; the results in this study prove otherwise. The provincial councils allowed for increased participation in Ottoman local governance.

3. In these articles, the Arabic term *liva* and its Turkish counterpart, *sancak*, (both meaning 'banner') are used interchangeably when referring to the administrative unit, the county.
4. The changes, except one (regarding the number of elected council members), are stylistic, such as changing 'this province' to 'all provinces' (Şentürk 1992: 253–71). I discuss the issue regarding the number of elected members below.
5. NBKM, VD 93/36, VD 96/44.
6. The most comprehensive work on his governorship is Petrov (2006).
7. (Agmon 2006: 69–73). Within the *shar'i* judiciary, nineteenth-century reforms led to the introduction of new posts such as lawyers (Agmon 2006: 168–95) or transformation of existing ones, such as 'naibships' (Akiba 2005)
8. The 1864 regulation divided the county administration in two sections titled 'civil affairs (*umur-ı mülkiye*)' and 'legal affairs (*umur-ı hukukiye*)'. This division-by-tasks changed into separation-by-personnel in the 1871 regulation. The latter refined the responsibilities of existing posts. Accordingly, section titles changed to 'the subgovernor's (*mutasarrıf*) duties', 'the county accountant's (*muhasebeci*) duties', 'the chief surveyor's duties (*tahrirat müdürü*)', and so on.
9. (*Düstur* 1:625–51). The sixty/seventy division into two types of articles is paralleled by a similar division in pages. Starting at page 625, the first part ends at page 639; the second part, beginning at the same page, concludes at page 651. The articles of the second part are relatively shorter in general, but it would not be misleading to say that the two parts of the regulation of 1871, one focusing on appointed members and the other on partially elected bodies of provincial administration, are comparable in length.
10. Rubin (2012: 999–1000) suggests that 'the intention of the legislature to separate the judicial from the administrative had been stated since the mid-1860s, but it was really applied with rigor in 1879 as part of the overall reform of the court system'. However, he cautions that the consuls had practical reasons to exaggerate the separation of powers: 'This idyllic description of the governors, contrasted with the general incompetence that the ambassador repeatedly attributed to the judicial officials in many consular reports during the early 1880s, should not be taken at face value . . . Hence, there appeared to be a sort of ad hoc collaboration between some governors and the consuls in an effort to work against or around the independence of the courts.' My argument does not contradict this observation. *De jure* there was an attempt to separate the powers. However, when we consider how and where the local elite was serving and the political nature of the way in which 'the separation of powers' were debated at the local level we are left with a general impression that such a separation was problematic and not uniform.

Local Councils and the Politics of Election in Vidin

11. (*Düstur* 1:634–5). The assignment to perform only the less significant tasks and the obligation to report anything of importance was not unique to the subgovernors. The governors had to perform within such ambiguous parameters as well. Given these vague terms, the regulation does not establish a clear relationship between higher- and lower-ranking administrators in the provinces. A risk-averse lower-ranking administrator might report more than a risk-taking one; or a stricter higher-ranking administrator might ask for more say in lower-level provincial affairs.
12. It is difficult to include the local religious leaders in either of these groups. Their composition and patterns of tenure varied from one county to another, reflecting local religious composition. There were complaints that not all religious groups were equally represented in these councils (Ortaylı 2000: 75). Even when they were all included, we have very limited information on how influential they were in the decision-making process. In Vidin, for example, the metropolitan did not participate in all the meetings (see Chapter 4).
13. The same thing happened in the provincial administrative councils as well. For the county administrative councils, compare articles 32 of the provincial regulation of the Danube Province with article 30 of the empire-wide regulation of 1864: (Şentürk 1992: 259).
14. Akiba refers to this transformation as 'formation of a new secular court system' (Akiba 2005: 43). Akiba's significant contribution notwithstanding, this is not a nuanced description. As Rubin (2009: 123) notes, the formations of secular has not been a subject of serious discussion in Ottoman sociolegal studies. Following Talal Asad's (2003: 5–12) work on the subject, this work considers secularism as a Euro-American doctrine that is closely connected with the rise of the capitalist world system of nation states and its associated political medium of citizenship.
15. (*Düstur* 1:615). Whatever the intentions of the separation were, as argued by Agmon, the *shar'i* courts remained very involved 'in the reproduction of the legal notions gender, social justice, and family' (Agmon 2006: 139).
16. These cases are discussed in Chapter 5.
17. See the report of the commission engaged in drawing up the Ottoman civil code (Mecelle) to the grand vizier on 10 March 1869, in Grigsby (1895: i–x). Cf. Demirel (2003: 22 and *passim*) and Bingöl (2004: 110–44).
18. What constituted 'cases of significance' here seems ambiguous. In an unpublished manuscript, Cevdet Paşa ([1869?]) explains that provincial councils of commerce were not allowed to reach a final decision on cases involving sums greater than 5,000 *guruş*. Bingöl (2002: 15) notes that district litigation councils could reach a final decision on cases that involved prison sentences of up to a month, and the councils of appeals and crime in the counties could finalise prison sentences of up to a year. Longer sentences would have to be referred to the appropriate councils in the provincial centres or in Istanbul (Baker 1877: 446–8).
19. For more information on the structure of the Supreme Council see

(Seyitdanlıoğlu 1999). In 1868 the Supreme Council was divided into two: the Council of State (Şura-yı Devlet) and the Council of Judicial Ordinances (Divân-ı Ahkâm-ı 'Adliye), chaired by Midhat Paşa and Cevdet Paşa respectively. Correspondence from the provinces was recorded in the Provincial Correspondence Registries (Vilayet Gelen-Giden Defterleri), then delivered to the Supreme Council of Judicial Ordinances or, after 1868, to the Council of State or the Council of Judicial Ordinances. These imperial offices would hear the cases and issue detailed reports on them. These reports would then be delivered either to the office of the grand vizier (*sadaret*) or to the sultan. Only these two offices had the right to issue orders to the provinces. Correspondence between these offices and the office of the grand vizier can be found at the Prime Ministry Ottoman Archives. Because the Council of Judicial Ordinances debated and reached a decision on criminal disputes coming from the provinces, and because the documents of this council are not available to researchers yet, the possibility of tracing the course of the criminal disputes referred from the provinces to Istanbul is fairly limited.
20. 'Local' here refers not strictly to Vidin County but to the Danube Province as a whole. All the appointed clerks who appear in the register of Vidin County in 1871, including those who were appointed at the district level, were from the Danube Province (NBKM, VD 107/16).
21. This ratio depended on the actual composition of the population. In places where there were few or no members of either population, it was not observed.
22. At the provincial level the final list would have to be approved by Istanbul. Such an elaborate 'election' system guaranteed that those who were not desired by Istanbul were not elected to the provincial councils. Yet, at the county level, the imperial government did not have a direct say. Istanbul could influence the 'election' process only through the leverage of its governors.
23. Such problems, especially the low salaries, were not unique to the provincial administration (Findley 1989: 292–333).
24. (Record 160 in NBKM, VD 107/16). These reports were mostly directed to the provincial administration. Occasionally they were directed to the imperial treasury or different military offices, but both reports mentioned in this case were directed to the province.
25. Goody (2000: 132) uses the National Academy of Sciences definition of 'technology': 'codified ways of deliberately manipulating the environment to achieve some material objective'. I would like to thank Boğaç Ergene for bringing Jack Goody's work to my attention.
26. It is crucial to note the difference between the 'Ottoman government' and 'Ottoman governmentality'. While the former is limited to the offices of the modern Ottoman state and the local notability affiliated with those organisations, the latter involves all members of the society who, through their choices of action, agree to be a part of this complex power network. A Circassian refugee, for example, might not be a participant in the Ottoman government;

nevertheless, he would contribute to Ottoman governmentality by agreeing to be 'registered' by the local council to receive a weekly allowance from the government. In that way that particular immigrant (and his family) would become part of the measured 'population' which is the target of Ottoman governance.

27. These reports were not the only ways in which the imperial centre was able to gather information regarding the provinces and the councils. Yet the authority given to these councils in handling and reporting local administrative and judicial cases rendered them the main source of information for the imperial centre.
28. I am using 'visible' in the sense that James C. Scott (1998) does. However, as İslamoğlu (2004a: 277) points out, Scott's analysis 'positions statecraft or administration too readily in opposition to society which comprises a domain of politics involving negotiations among multiple and diverse actors'. I do not consider administrative practices as a separate domain from local politics.
29. In Chapter 4, however, I reveal the patterns of participation through a structural analysis of the administrative council registers for the county of Vidin.
30. Foucault focuses on the 'police', broadly construed, and emphasises (2000: 415–16) that by the end of the eighteenth century 'the aim of the police is the permanently increasing production of something new, which is supposed to foster the citizens' life and the state's strength . . . The true object of the police becomes . . . the population; or, in other words, the state has essentially to take care of men as a population . . . and its politics, therefore, has to be a biopolitics.'
31. Cf. Chatterjee (1993: 12–13), Duara (1995: 65–9), Mallon (1995: 65) and particularly Gramsci (1971: 52–3) who notes that 'among the subaltern groups, one will exercise or tend to exercise a certain hegemony through the mediation of a party; this must be established by studying the development of all the other parties too, in so far as they include elements of the hegemonic group or of the other subaltern groups which undergo such hegemony'.
32. Giddens emphasised the 'coding of information' as an essential step in the formation of the 'nation states'. For Giddens, a 'nation' 'exists only when a state has a unified administrative reach over the territory over which its sovereignty is claimed' (1985: 119). This emphasis on 'administrative reach' renders cultural and lingual uniformity and territorial unity instrumental but not necessary (see especially 172 and *passim*).
33. I used James W. Redhouse's dictionary (1890) to translate the usual Ottoman titles such as 'eminent (*rif'atlu*)'. Such titles were common in this period, similar to 'honourable', 'esquire', and so on, in the British Empire.
34. That is, either Hacı Ömer Beğ himself decided to step down due to extenuating circumstances or a more powerful notable or officer demanded his resignation directly. This, however, does not change the outcome: leaving only a single candidate for the seat of a Muslim member.

35. The suffix –*zade* translates as 'son of'. Thus Ma'ruf Ağazade would mean 'son of Ma'ruf Ağa'.
36. There were four candidates for the administrative council in each of the four years; in 1872, a fifth candidate was added after the resignation of two others. This makes a total of seventeen candidate positions. For the council of appeals and crime, there were twenty-two candidate positions.
37. Ahmed Beyzade Mahmud Beğ, a candidate for clerk in 1871, for example, appears to have been the son of Ma'rufzade Ahmed Beğ. Also Hacı Ömer Efendizade Remzi Beğ, another member candidate in 1874, may have been the son of the twice-resigned candidate Hacı Ömer Beğ.
38. In addition to the names of those employed in the provincial administration, the yearbooks provide statistical information regarding the number of soldiers, local population, forests, rivers, bridges, lakes and the like. Their local publication and continuous nature render these yearbooks a useful source. I used all ten of the published yearbooks for the Danube Province for Table 3.3.
39. Petrov (2006: 93) notes that it was the 1871 regulation that reduced the number of elected members in the administrative council from six to four. This is not supported by the evidence in the yearbooks which list four members for the administrative council from 1868 to 1877. Petrov does not indicate if the same reduction applied to the judicial councils.
40. The local registers I use contain the copies of reports that were sent to Ruse; the registers themselves were not sent to Ruse or Istanbul. As I discuss below, they served a purpose other than merely informing the centre about the provinces. Their significance was at the local level. This, however, does not mean that the original reports were not drafted to inform the imperial centre. That, indeed, was their main function. This was also the case for the provincial yearbooks. They provided valuable information for the imperial centre; thus they were imperial records. Their significance was at the imperial level.
41. Each examining clerk could serve for two years in a single term.
42. After the relatively long-lasting administration of Midhat Paşa, the mastermind behind the empire's provincial reforms and the first governor of the Danube Province (1864–8), the governor of the province changed almost every year. Only Mehmed Asım Paşa served longer than a year – from April 1874 to October 1876 (Kuneralp 1999: 41).
43. There is no conclusive evidence that these members worked for a salary. The preface to the Regulation of the Danube Province notes that 'they' should be paid sufficient wages; however, it does not clarify whether 'they' refers to the appointed and/or the elected members (*Düstur-ı atik* 2nd ed.: 517). Sedat Bingöl, Beshara Doumani and Mahmoud Yazbak, scholars who worked on similar councils, noted (in my correspondence with them) that they did not come across any reference to administrative councils' elected members' salaries in this period. There is information on the salaries of appointed members of the councils. While the elected members might have been compensated

to cover expenses – for their work-related trips, for example – lack of any reference to their salaries and the fact that they had to be among the wealthier members of the society suggest that their salaries (if they were paid at all) were not very significant with respect to their accumulated wealth. BOA, İ. MVL, no. 24362 notes that the elected members of the municipal council were not paid. BOA, İ. MVL, no. 24971 notes the same thing for the elected members of the commercial courts. The clerks and appointed members in both organisations were paid regular salaries. An appendix from 1880 listing salaries of government officials in Adana included in a general report, (NA PRO 30-29-348: 198–9) recorded no payments for the administrative court members. The members of the judicial court received some money but it was paid irregularly and was about the same as the amount received by the clerks employed at the council (NA, FO 424-106: 537). I would like to thank Avi Rubin for sharing this information with me.

44. This draft is from a partial draft book of reports (NBKM, VD 98/13) sent by the administrative council to the provincial centre at Ruse. Since it is a draft book, its shape and structure differ from the other two registers I used to analyse the candidate lists; it has several corrections marked for the final report, yet its content is similar.
45. Clearly, a face-to-face meeting would lead to different dynamics in the decision-making process.
46. The 1873 yearbook (166–71) lists fifty-nine different villages within the district of Vidin. Teplov (1877: 173–4), who made use of the same yearbook, lists forty villages around Vidin. A 1945 catalogue of Bulgarian geographic names lists fifty-eight villages for the district (*okolia*) of Vidin (*Spis'k na naselenite*: 20); all but two match the list in the yearbook.
47. Hacı İliya's family members, his son and his son-in-law, were also on the candidate lists for the same council a number of times in the following years.
48. Based on the yearbook of 1873, Slanatruna (modern-day Slanotrŭn) was located three hours' distance from Vidin; it had a non-Muslim population of forty households and 140 people and a Muslim immigrant population of fifty-five households and 225 people. Helvacı (Khalvadzhi, or modern-day Maior Uzunovo) was two hours from Vidin and had a non-Muslim population of thirty-nine households and 143 people. Bregova (modern-day Briagovo) located six hours' distance from the centre, was the most heavily populated village of Vidin according to both the yearbook of 1873 (*Salname Tuna*) and the 1945 book of place names (*Spis'k na naselenite*): 561 households and 5,455 people. This is probably why a resident of this village was able to become a representative. The representatives from Slanatruna and Helvacı were perhaps there to support the candidates from their villages.
49. '*Kogo da obvinyavame? Koi e kriv?*' *Svoboda*, 8 January 1872. *Svoboda* began publishing in 1870; interestingly, in one of its earlier editorials (4 January 1870) it praised Midhat Paşa for the general reforms but noted that the effect of those reforms had 'evaporated' (Petrov 2006: 10).

50. Milena Stefanova (1998: 152) lists Sevastaki Ağa's as a local notable in 1856.
51. Vidin State Archives, ф. 17 К оп 1 л 30 гръб.
52. BOA, İ.DH. 13733 (15 February 1851).
53. Such as Tseko Vanchov, who represented Vidin in the Second General National Assembly (Obiknoveno Narodno Subranie) of the newly established Bulgaria in 1881 (Vulchev 2003: 624).
54. Rubin (2011: 27) considers separation of administrative and judicial powers as a 'distinguishing feature' of the *nizamiye* court system. Similar to the administrative councils, this system had a hierarchical structure. The judicial councils at the provincial level served as courts of first instance and constituted the 'backbone' of the system (Rubin 2011: 32–7). Rubin's book contains the most comprehensive treatment of this court system.

4

Once Inside the Chamber . . . Participation in the Politics of Local Administration

The elections for the council of our city are at last at an end, and the new members have finally, this week, commenced convening. But this time, the matter was not terminated as simply as it used to be. For, ten days after the ballot boxes were opened the citizens of our city were still eagerly looking forward to see which side the balance would tip. And this is the matter: among our Muslim citizens there are two aristocratic families, whose genealogy goes back to the days of the establishment of Islam in the country, the families of Ḥusaynī and Khālidī. And from olden times the competition among them is great, while the power of one of them is supreme, most important offices go to its sons, and it rules, while the other becomes weaker, until the balance is redressed in the opposite direction. And in our days now for many years the first family has the upper hand and the headship of the city council has been in the hand of its members almost from the day the municipality was established . . . But this time, when the time has come for the head of the council to leave his office, the second family gathered all its strength and put up for election one of its most distinguished elders, and the other family nominated as candidate the son of the outgoing mayor, and one of its distinguished men. After a severe campaign, which lasted for a month and a half, all the three were elected, and along with them also one Muslim and one of our nation [Jewish], who is the son of the permanent Jewish member of the council . . . and so there remained only the question of the nomination of the head of the council which by law is at the hand of the city governor . . . and so the list was sent to His Highness the Paşa, and all the great men of our city were looking forward to his decision. And after much contemplation he at last decided in favour of the Khālidī family, and as head of the council he appointed Yāsin Efendi al-Khālidī. (Haim Gerber [1985: 117] quoting David Yellin)

As the above account of the Jerusalem municipal elections of 1898 and my analysis in the previous chapter indicate, the election process in the local judicio-administrative sphere was a charged process that was impossible to untangle from the provincial power dynamics. Elections reflected the ever-changing power balance among the local notables and had an impact on how the elite participated in what Michael Meeker (2002: 185) has referred to as a 'single government of state officials and local elites' that reported/reconstituted the provincial reality to the higher levels of the Ottoman administration. Local notables' ability to maintain official involvement in the judicio-administrative sphere as elected members depended on the provincial power structure. Once elected, they engaged in political negotiations, as all agents within Ottoman governmentality did, yet members were able to use their position as a strategic asset. This chapter explores the members' involvement with the council, trying to identify the patterns in member participation. Because most local administrative and judiciary issues were handled by (and reported from) these councils, and because they did not have proper meeting minutes, their copy registers serve as the most important source on the members' participation in the politics of Ottoman administration. While the abstract nature of the copy registers reveal little about how the meetings took place in these councils, a focused analysis of some of the anomalies, when combined with a study of the county's representation in provincial yearbooks reveal that members of the council did not participate in the meetings regularly and equally. What appears to be political groupings among the members shaped their involvement with the council's meetings. Furthermore, this chapter also argues that the higher echelons of the provincial administration in Ruse knew about the inconsistent participation patterns of the council members. The provincial centre knew that the administrative council was the peak organisation of a connected web of political offices staffed by the local elite and extended out to the districts. With its connected offices, Vidin's judicio-administrative sphere operated as a hierarchical organisational structure operating in sync with local political networks and provided an opportunity for local notables to utilise provincial governance to negotiate for more prominence.

Seals: Images of Participation?

There is very little information about what happened in these councils following the elections or who attended their meetings. Although council members were not paid a salary, some members' dominance in the judicio-administrative sphere suggests that getting elected must have been important to the local notables.[1] The mere fact of election did not necessarily mean that all members held equal standing: sitting together, in other words, did not imply working together in harmony. Consider the following 'interesting spectacle' from the memoirs of Stanislas G. B. St Clair and Charles Brophy (1869: 380–1):

> A very interesting and edifying spectacle is a debate of the village [council], or Rayah 'Conseil Communal'; the 'Mairie' is the Tukhan [dükkan] or public-house, and 'M. le Maire' is a being remarkable by the dirt with which he is thickly encrusted, and who is, moreover, three-quarters tipsy; he is as uneducated as the rest of his colleagues, who differ from him in physical appearance only by being a little more or less unwashed, and a little more or less inebriated.
>
> The whole council is seated on the ground *alla Turca*, or lying about in any attitude they find convenient; smoking and drinking go on uninterruptedly, for a Bulgarian [council] is always thirsty, and the Bakal steps over the bodies of prostrate honourable members to fill their glasses and give his opinion on the subject in question.
>
> The case undergoing discussion is as follows: an honest Turk has caught a horse-thief in *flagrante delicto*, and as the horse belongs to the village of Derekuoi he has delivered up thief and stolen property to the 'authorities' of the village; the culprit is sentenced in a corner of the Tukhan, drinking his mastics, and occasionally joining in the debate, as do also the village witch and various other women whom the gravity of the occurrence has attracted in the door of the public house. [In a footnote the authors add: 'This scene is related as it really occurred.']
>
> 'What were we talking about?' says M. le Maire, who has taken off his old sheepskin cap, and is engaged in a minute investigation of its recesses.
>
> 'Kto snaje?' ('Who knows?') answers Vassili, pausing for a moment in his occupation of washing his feet with a penknife.
>
> 'You are an idiot, Vassili!' cries Nikolaki, his political opponent, an advanced Liberal who detests the old-fashioned Conservatism of Vassili.
>
> Vassili replies by some strictly unparliamentary language, and Nikolaki continues –
>
> 'An idiot and nothing else! We were talking about the horse, and you are too great a fool to recollect even that!'
>
> Hereupon ensues a free fight; but as everybody has been drinking too freely to be able to hit out, not much damage is done . . . finally, order and harmony are restored.

This account by St Clair and Brophy should be taken with caution since the purpose of their book was 'to show the falseness of accusations of Turkish misrule' (Todorova 1997: 101). The book was published in the midst of a heated debate on the role of Victorian Britain in the world and was written primarily for British readers.[2] Despite the authors' bias against (if not racism towards) the non-Muslim population, their depiction of the 'harmony' within the councils is not unfounded.[3] St Clair and Brophy's contemporaries also note that the provincial councils were marked with disputes and fertile grounds for abuse of power (Baker 1877: 442–8; Newton and Colnaghi 1865: 73–8). The Ottomans, aware of the problems regarding harmony in the councils, issued an imperial decree on members' duties in the tax-collection councils (which served as a prototype for the councils established in 1864), asking the elected members to debate all issues 'without any resentment or difficulty'.[4] Despite the explicit instructions on council discussions in the 1864 regulation, the state felt the need to issue a special 'regulation concerning the precedence of the [elected] members over one another' in the late 1860s (*Düstur* 1:719).

In the new regulation, the emphasis was on the hierarchical civil rank of the members. When the members' ranks were equal, opinions of those who had served on the council longer carried more weight. The purpose of the regulation was to disassociate a member's religious affiliation from his participation in the council meetings. The opening of the text indicates that religious differences were causing council members' hierarchy to be non-uniform in different parts of the empire. The government issued such a regulation 'because matters of precedence among the ... non-Muslim members of the council' were handled differently everywhere, and there was 'endless talk and complaints [arising] from this lack of regularity and order' (*Düstur* 1:719). Such a regulation serves as a reminder that an elected member's participation in the politics of the local councils had its limits. Nevertheless, our understanding of the discussion environment in these councils remains incomplete because these organisations did not have official minutes of their meetings.

The registers that contain copies of the council's correspondence with the province and the other districts provide the most important source of information about the county administrative council and the council of appeals and crime in Vidin. Unfortunately, these copy registers are mostly quiet about the interaction among the council members. Since the councils did not have to send these registers to the provincial capital, Ruse, their members were not required to add their seals to each report.[5] When a member of the higher councils at the imperial level – such as the Supreme Council of Judicial Ordinances or the Council of State – did not attend the meetings, or if he disagreed with the majority decision on an issue, his seal would not be present but his title would appear with others' titles and a note explaining his absence or noting his disagreement.[6] Yet Vidin's administrative council did not follow this practice for the copy register. This makes it impossible to know who was there or who disagreed with the general decision of the council. The copy registers examined here are examples of generic, abstract documents of modern governance.

Participation in the Politics of Local Administration

Such modern registers, as Brinkley Messick (1993: 240–1) observed, contrast starkly with pre-modern 'official' documents:

> Like the sale instruments of the period, old registers bore the personal mark of a particular [clerk] and displayed the artistry of his scribal craft. The text was suffused with the human presence, the *haiba*, the prestige, dignity and awe-inspiring quality of specific men who concretely embodied the state ... While the *haiba* of such a register was highly personalized, the authority of new bureaucratic texts is relatively de-personalized. Like that of the nation-state to which it pertains, a new register's authority rests on its diffused formal abstractness, implemented through the standardized printed forms now available for all official acts.

The administrative council members remain anonymous for most of the available registers (from 24 March 1871 to 4 August 1873) because each report lists only their titles (the circled area in Figure 4.1).[7] Members of imperial and provincial administration used their seals in official correspondence to establish authenticity of their relation to documents and linking the titles with the name inscribed on the seals.[8] Yet this was not a requirement for the copy registers.[9]

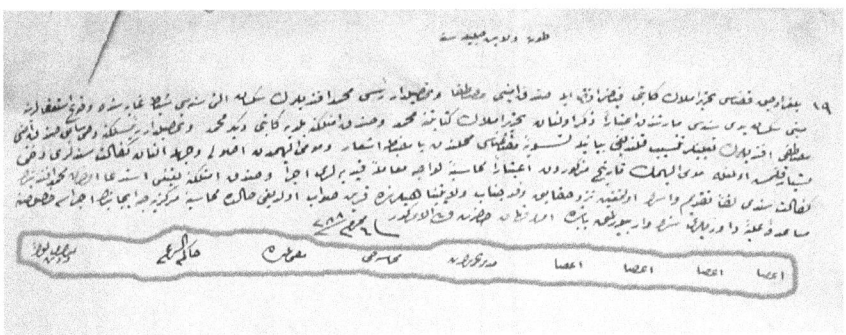

Figure 4.1 Vidin administrative council members' titles
Source: NBKM, VD 107/16.

Reports in the Vidin administrative council's copy register would have a row listing the council members. The subgovernor (*mutasarrıf-ı liva-i Vidin*), the council head, appears in the leftmost position in the row, followed by (from left to right) the titles of the *shar'i* judge (*hakim el-şer'*), the region's Muslim cleric (*müfti-i belde*), the accountant (*muhasebeci*), the director of correspondence (*müdür-i tahrirat*) and the four 'elected' members (*a'za*).[10] Of note here is the absence of a religious leader for the non-Muslim population. In fact, with the exception of the candidate list

Nineteenth-century Local Governance in Ottoman Bulgaria

of 4 April 1871 (discussed further below), non-Muslim religious leaders' titles are mostly missing from the reports. At the bottom of this candidate list, the titles 'the metropolitan' (*metropolit*) and 'the chief rabbi' (*haham başı*) appear along with other members' titles, evidently because the 'nominating committee' (*meclis-i tefrik*) included these religious leaders, whose titles do not appear in the council's copy registers from 24 March 1871 to 4 August 1873.

THE RATIONALE FOR THE SEALS

On 4 August 1873, the members began applying their seals under their titles (see Figure 4.2). This change coincided with the departure of the subgovernor. A deputy subgovernor, *vekil-i mutasarrıf-ı Vidin*, took charge of the council; the leftmost title under the reports reflected the change (the lower circled area in Figure 4.2). A note at the top of the report indicated that this was the 'term of the director of correspondence', who acted as the deputy subgovernor of Vidin (*der zaman-ı mektubcu efendi vekil-i mutasarrıf-ı Vidin,* the upper circled area in Figure 4.2). The register is silent about why the deputy decided to require seals in the local register – perhaps the subgovernor requested such a change due to his temporary absence. The use of seals stop on 23 September 1874 without any explanation; the subgovernor appears to have resumed his tasks on 23 July 1874, yet the use of seals continued. The impersonal, almost impenetrably

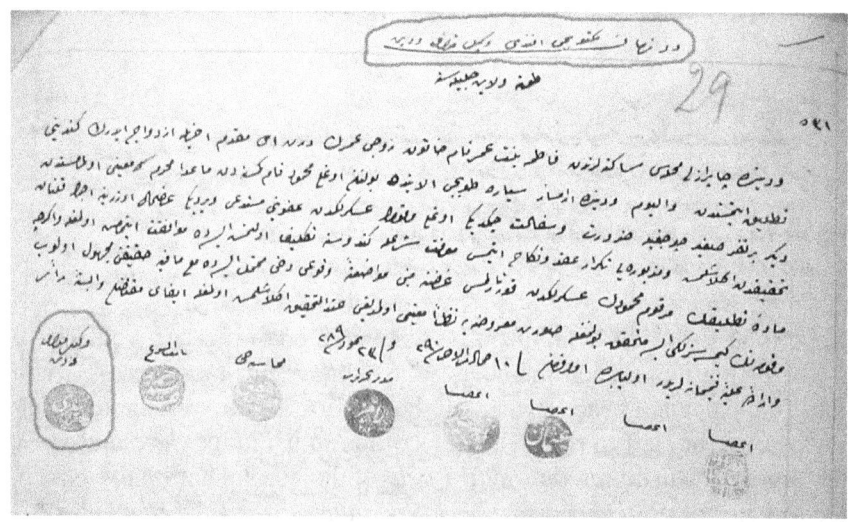

Figure 4.2 Report of 4 August 1873
Source: NBKM, VD 96/41.

Participation in the Politics of Local Administration

abstract nature of the reports in the copy registers becomes more personal with the seals. The seals' composition – from the way they were carved (in Cyrillic or in Arabic) to the particular order in which their impressions were left at the reports' end – provides insight into the politics of power within the council, a perspective that cannot be easily acquired from the yearbooks. An overview of the patterns and inconsistencies in the application of members' titles and seals in the copy registers provide some insight about the dynamics within Vidin's administrative council.

There are three noteworthy features on the first report (4 August 1873) containing seals – aside from the note identifying the beginning of the deputy subgovernor's term. The title of the *shar'i* judge is *na'ib el-şer'* rather than *hakim el-şer'*, the titles seals of the (Muslim and non-Muslim) religious leaders are missing and the seal of one of the four 'elected' members is missing.

Na'ib means a deputy of a *shar'i* judge, or *kadı* (Ayalon 'Na'ib'). The presence of a deputy serving in place of the actual judge (*hakim el-şer'*) in Vidin has to do with the general transformation of Ottoman judiciary. *Na'ib*s' roles and responsibilities in the provincial judicial system changed significantly after 1839. First, judges were banned from delegating their duties to *na'ib*s. Following that, an 1855 imperial decree accusing the *na'ib*s and *kadı*s of excessive fee collection, and regulating their conduct marked the beginning of more significant institutionalisation of *na'ib*s as a cadre of judges appointed from the centre (Akiba 2005: 45–51). A regulation – also from 1855 – organized *na'ib*s into five classes, related these classes to the size of the counties and districts, and defined their term limits (*Düstur-ı atik* 1st ed., 225–8). This regulation explained how one could become a *na'ib* – through examination at the headquarters of the religious establishment (Bab-ı Meşihat), or through apprenticeship in the *shar'i* courts (articles 11 and 12) – and related them to the provincial administration by defining investigation procedures for complaints against *na'ib*s in the local tax collection councils (articles 9 and 10).[11] The 1864 provincial regulation made the *na'ib*s salaried *ex officio* members of the provincial administrative and judicial councils. *Na'ib*s serving at the county- or district-level operated under the supervision of an inspector of judges (*müfettiş-i hükkam*) and a chief *na'ib* (*merkez na'ibi*) until 1871. Due to financial difficulties a single office, the *na'ib* of the provincial centre, replaced these two offices after that date (Akiba 2005: 45–51). Thus, after 1864, the judge of the *shar'i* court (*hakim el-şer'*) in Vidin was a *na'ib*. All the yearbooks of the Danube Province list a *na'ib* for the Vidin County while the copy registers appear to use the titles *hakim* and *na'ib* interchangeably.

The second irregularity in Figure 4.2 is the absence of the religious leaders' titles. The Muslim religious leader (*müfti*) Hamdi el-Seyyid Mustafa's title, which is consistently listed with the other titles, disappears on 26 October 1872 and remains absent until (and after) the report bearing seals beginning of the second register (4 August 1873). His title and seal reappear after eight days; then, after a couple of months the seal disappears again for fourteen days while his title remains.[12] Such intermittent disappearances recur a few more times during the year, each lasting one to two weeks. Four-and-a-half months before the end of the second register his seal disappears together with all the others, yet his title remains until the end (10 March 1875). There seems to be no obvious explanation for the missing title of the Muslim religious leader for the ten months after October 1872. Nor is there any explanation for Hamdi el-Seyyid Mustafa's missing seal.

The *müfti*'s title and the seal is not the only one that appears and disappears irregularly; those of the other religious leaders, as well as the metropolitan or the chief rabbi rarely make an appearance.[13] When such titles do appear, it is very difficult to connect them to the content of the reports. For example, a memorandum sent to the provincial capital on 27 September 1873, on a certain Anika and Angel's conversions to Islam prior to their marriage includes the metropolitan's title (but not the seal). The content of this particular memo might explain why the metropolitan's title was there because to convert, individuals had to 'prove their sincerity' in front of the council and their religious leaders. However, other conversion cases in the copy registers are missing the title of the Christian religious leader. On 14 September 1873, the title 'despot' appears at the end of a report on the transfer of the previous year's animal tithe to the provincial centre. Procedure required the administrative council to supervise such transfers and the first copy register includes a number of other similar reports, but none include the title of the despot. The Christian religious leader's title is absent from the following reports until 23 September 1873, when it appears (as *metropolit*) in a report regarding a district head official's (*ka'imakam*) appointment to the İvraca (Vratsa) District. The title remains a part of the reports until 9 October 1873, when, in another routine administrative case, metropolitan Kiril's seal appears for the first time, in Arabic letters (كرل), only to disappear in the next report – written following the subgovernor Rıf'at Paşa's return to his post on 14 October. After the subgovernor's return in mid-October, the title 'metropolitan' appears consistently between those of the *na'ib* and the *müfti* until 14 May 1874, when it disappears until the register's end (10 March 1875). The copy registries reveal very little about the rationale for the presence/absence of the titles in these records.

Participation in the Politics of Local Administration

The third irregularity in Figure 4.2 is the missing seal of the elected member. The missing seal imprint belongs to Marin Novinov, ('Dye Maker (*Boyacı*) Marin Ağa' as it appears on the candidate list of 1873) and it has been missing since 5 August 1873. His seal appears for the first time together with that of the subgovernor. It is difficult to say why these two seals appeared together. The subgovernor's return is noted in the same way as his departure (a brief note just above the very first report with his seal); however, nothing in the reports suggests why Marin Ağa did not use his seal in these records until the return of the subgovernor. On 31 March 1874, almost half a year after the subgovernor's return, the seal of an *ex officio* member, the director of correspondence Ramiz Efendi, disappears. While there was no explanation regarding Marin Ağa's seal's absence, a note under the title 'director of correspondence' explains that Ramiz Efendi was sent to Berkofça on a special duty.[14] The director himself was absent, not just his seal. There are other seals missing in the same report: those of the subgovernor, the judge of the *shar'i* court and the metropolitan, yet no similar note explains why those are missing. The note explaining Ramiz Efendi's absence disappears after six days. In fact, for the first couple of days, the note is inked over what appears to be an erased version of Ramiz Efendi's seal (see below).

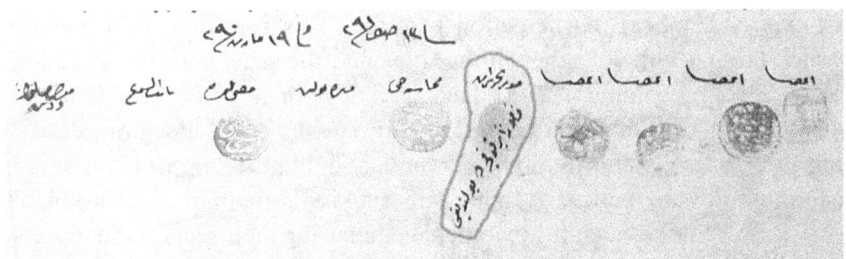

Figure 4.3 Report of 31 March 1874
Source: NBKM, VD 96/41.

That there was a need to explain the absence of Ramiz Efendi's seal for six days while the absence of other seals could go unexplained suggests that there might be a difference between the seals in the register and in the report sent to the province. It is possible that the explanation regarding Ramiz Efendi's absence was also noted as such in the actual report sent to the Danube Province, whereas the other seals were absent only from this register but not from the actual documents sent. Whatever might have prompted the explanation in the report, its presence points to the significance of noting the absence of a council member and suggests that explained absences of the seals need to be considered as different from the unnoted ones – such as the missing seal of Marin Ağa. In addition, the presence of the semi-erased imprint behind the note suggests the possibility that the pressing of the seals may not have been done at the time of the report's writing or by the member himself. It appears that the reasons behind the use of titles and seals in the copy register was not related with the content of the reports. The inconsistency in their application suggests that these reasons might be relevant to the council's internal dynamics which are not readily visible on the abstract nature of the modern copy registers.

THE FREQUENCY AND SYNCHRONICITY

Changes in the seals coincide with changes in the council's composition. Members' use of the seals began with the deputy subgovernor Ramiz Efendi's term. After the subgovernor's return (18 October 1873) all but the chief rabbi's seal are present until the report that includes the new candidate list (7 March 1874). Following the election, the subgovernor's, the *na'ib*'s and the metropolitan's seals disappear. The first report of the new administrative period notes that the *na'ib* had served honourably and resigned, but it does not explain why nor discuss his replacement. The elections replaced some of the elected members and caused a shift in the *ex-officio* members' participation patterns. This is visible in Table 4.1 which tabulates the changes in the titles and the seals between 1873 and 1874. The first column lists the dates of change in the titles or seal impressions. Each row marks a change in the council's composition; changing titles or seals are highlighted. The last column is the row's number. Missing titles are marked as 'none'; missing seals are marked with a blank cell. Line 1 marks when the members began using their seals at the reports, and Line 43 marks when they stopped doing so.

The composition of the titles and seals does not change much until 1 March 1874 (Line 10) except for intermittent disappearance/reappearances of the metropolitan's title and continuous absence of Marin Ağa's seal. Following the subgovernor's return, the reports between 18 October 1873 (the subgovernor's return) and 1 March 1874 (Lines 9 and 10) bear all the members' titles and seals. This seems to be a very stable period in the copy register; for 133 days the seals and the titles do not change. It is not clear why the council continued using the seals after the return of the subgovernor. The 6 March report with the candidate list has only two candidates because elections were being held to replace the other two. This report (Line 11) precedes the report of 1 March (Line 12) in the register, although chronologically the former should have come after the latter.

Table 4.1 List of changes in titles and seal impressions in Vidin administrative council's copy register

Date	Subgovernor	Shar'i Judge	Metropolitan	Müfti	Accountant	Director of Correspondence	Member	Member	Member	Member	Line no.[a]
4 Aug	Remzi Beğ (Deputy)	Ahmed Rıf'at Efendi	none	none	Mehmed Tevfik Beğ	Ramiz Efendi	Ahmed Ağa	Osman Beğ		Seko Ağa	1
17 Aug	Remzi Beğ (Deputy)	Ahmed Rıf'at Efendi	none	Mustafa Hamdi Efendi	Mehmed Tevfik Beğ	Ramiz Efendi	Ahmed Ağa	Osman Beğ		Seko Ağa	2
14 Sep	Remzi Beğ (Deputy)	Ahmed Rıf'at Efendi	(Despot)	Mustafa Hamdi Efendi	Mehmed Tevfik Beğ	Ramiz Efendi	Ahmed Ağa	Osman Beğ		Seko Ağa	3
15 Sep	Remzi Beğ (Deputy)	Ahmed Rıf'at Efendi	none	Mustafa Hamdi Efendi	Mehmed Tevfik Beğ	Ramiz Efendi	Ahmed Ağa	Osman Beğ		Seko Ağa	4
17 Sep	Remzi Beğ (Deputy)	Ahmed Rıf'at Efendi		Mustafa Hamdi Efendi	Mehmed Tevfik Beğ	Ramiz Efendi	Ahmed Ağa	Osman Beğ		Seko Ağa	5
27 Sep	Remzi Beğ (Deputy)	Ahmed Rıf'at Efendi	none	Mustafa Hamdi Efendi	Mehmed Tevfik Beğ	Ramiz Efendi	Ahmed Ağa	none	none	Seko Ağa	6
27 Sep	Remzi Beğ (Deputy)	Ahmed Rıf'at Efendi	(Metropolit)	Mustafa Hamdi Efendi	Mehmed Tevfik Beğ	Ramiz Efendi	Ahmed Ağa	Osman Beğ		Seko Ağa	7
18 Oct	Rıf'at Halil Paşa	Ahmed Rıf'at Efendi	(Metropolit)	Mustafa Hamdi Efendi	Mehmed Tevfik Beğ	Ramiz Efendi	Ahmed Ağa	Osman Beğ	Marin Ağa	Seko Ağa	8
18 Oct	Rıf'at Halil Paşa	Ahmed Rıf'at Efendi	Kiril Efendi	Mustafa Hamdi Efendi	Mehmed Tevfik Beğ	Ramiz Efendi	Ahmed Ağa	Osman Beğ	Marin Ağa	Seko Ağa	9

1873

Table 4.1 Continued

Date	Subgovernor	Shar'i Judge	Metropolitan	Müfti	Accountant	Director of Correspondence	Member	Member	Member	Member	Line no.[a]
1874											
1 Mar					Mehmed Tevfik Beğ	Ramiz Efendi	Ahmed Beğ	Osman Beğ	Seko Ağa	Zayko Ağa	10
6 Mar				Mustafa Hamdi Efendi	Mehmed Tevfik Beğ	Ramiz Efendi					11
15 Mar				Mustafa Hamdi Efendi	Mehmed Tevfik Beğ	Ramiz Efendi	Ahmed Beğ	Osman Beğ	Seko Ağa	Zayko Ağa	12
31 Mar				Mustafa Hamdi Efendi	Mehmed Tevfik Beğ	On duty at Berkofça	Ahmed Beğ	Osman Beğ	Seko Ağa	Zayko Ağa	13
31 Mar				Mustafa Hamdi Efendi	Mehmed Tevfik Beğ	On duty at Berkofça	Ahmed Beğ	Osman Beğ		Zayko Ağa	14
6 Apr				Mustafa Hamdi Efendi	Mehmed Tevfik Beğ	On duty at Berkofça		Osman Beğ		Zayko Ağa	15
15 Apr				Mustafa Hamdi Efendi	Mehmed Tevfik Beğ	Ramiz Efendi	Ahmed Beğ	Osman Beğ	Seko Ağa	Zayko Ağa	16
20 Apr				Mustafa Hamdi Efendi	Mehmed Tevfik Beğ		Ahmed Beğ	Osman Beğ		Zayko Ağa	17
21 Apr				Mustafa Hamdi Efendi	Mehmed Tevfik Beğ	Ramiz Efendi	Ahmed Beğ	Osman Beğ	Seko Ağa		18
23-Apr	Ramiz Efendi (Deputy)			Mustafa Hamdi Efendi	Mehmed Tevfik Beğ			Osman Beğ	Seko Ağa	Zayko Ağa	19

Date	Subgovernor	Shar'i Judge	Metropolitan	Müfti	Accountant	Director of Correspondence	Member	Member	Member	Member	Line no.[a]
2 May	Ramiz Efendi (Deputy)			Mustafa Hamdi Efendi	Mehmed Tevfik Beğ				Seko Ağa	Zayko Ağa	20
2 May	Ramiz Efendi (Deputy)			Mustafa Hamdi Efendi	Mehmed Tevfik Beğ			Osman Beğ	Seko Ağa	Zayko Ağa	21
7 May				Mustafa Hamdi Efendi	Mehmed Tevfik Beğ	Ramiz Efendi		Osman Beğ	Seko Ağa	Zayko Ağa	22
9 May				Mustafa Hamdi Efendi	Mehmed Tevfik Beğ	Ramiz Efendi	Ahmed Beğ	Osman Beğ	Seko Ağa	Zayko Ağa	23
14 May			none	Mustafa Hamdi Efendi	Mehmed Tevfik Beğ	Ramiz Efendi	Ahmed Beğ	Osman Beğ	Seko Ağa	Zayko Ağa	24
18 May			none	Mustafa Hamdi Efendi	Mehmed Tevfik Beğ	Ramiz Efendi	Ahmed Beğ	Osman Beğ	Seko Ağa	Zayko Ağa	25
27 May			none	Mustafa Hamdi Efendi	Mehmed Tevfik Beğ	Ramiz Efendi	Ahmed Beğ	Osman Beğ	Seko Ağa	Zayko Ağa	26
31 May			none	Mustafa Hamdi Efendi		Ramiz Efendi	Ahmed Beğ	Hacı Tahir Ağa	Seko Ağa	Zayko Ağa	27
31 May			none	Mustafa Hamdi Efendi		Ramiz Efendi		Hacı Tahir Ağa	Seko Ağa	Zayko Ağa	28
22 Jun	Ramiz Efendi (Deputy)		none	Mustafa Hamdi Efendi		none		Hacı Tahir Ağa	Seko Ağa	Zayko Ağa	29

Table 4.1 Continued

Date	Subgovernor	Shar'i Judge	Metropolitan	Müfti	Accountant	Director of Correspondence	Member	Member	Member	Member	Line no.[a]
12 Jul	Ramiz Efendi (Deputy)		none	Mustafa Hamdi Efendi				Hacı Tahir Ağa	Seko Ağa	Zayko Ağa	30
17 Jul			none	Mustafa Hamdi Efendi		Ramiz Efendi		Hacı Tahir Ağa	Seko Ağa	Zayko Ağa	31
21 Jul	Ramiz Efendi (Deputy)		none	Mustafa Hamdi Efendi		none		Hacı Tahir Ağa	Seko Ağa	Zayko Ağa	32
30 Jul			none	Mustafa Hamdi Efendi		Ramiz Efendi			Seko Ağa	Zayko Ağa	33
2 Aug			(Deputy despot)[b]	Mustafa Hamdi Efendi		Ramiz Efendi			Seko Ağa	Zayko Ağa	34
5 Aug			None	Mustafa Hamdi Efendi		Ramiz Efendi		Hacı Tahir Ağa	Seko Ağa	Zayko Ağa	35
9 Aug			None	Mustafa Hamdi Efendi				Hacı Tahir Ağa	Seko Ağa	Zayko Ağa	36
10 Aug			None	Mustafa Hamdi Efendi		Ramiz Efendi		Hacı Tahir Ağa	Seko Ağa	Zayko Ağa	37
3 Sep			(Deputy despot)[c]	Mustafa Hamdi Efendi		Ramiz Efendi			Seko Ağa	Zayko Ağa	38

Date	Subgovernor	Shar'i Judge	Metropolitan	Müfti	Accountant	Director of Correspondence	Member	Member	Member	Member	Line no.[a]
5 Sep			None	Mustafa Hamdi Efendi		Ramiz Efendi		Hacı Tahir Ağa	Seko Ağa	Zayko Ağa	39
15 Sep			None			Ramiz Efendi		Hacı Tahir Ağa	Seko Ağa	Zayko Ağa	40
17 Sep			None	Mustafa Hamdi Efendi		Ramiz Efendi		Hacı Tahir Ağa	Seko Ağa	Zayko Ağa	41
22 Sep			None	Mustafa Hamdi Efendi				Hacı Tahir Ağa	Seko Ağa	Zayko Ağa	42
26 Sep			None								43

Source: NBKM, VD 96/41.

[a] Ln = line reference number for the table

[b] (Line 34) the 'deputy despot' title appears for a single report listed amongst the elected members

[c] (Line 38) the 'deputy despot' title appears for a single report listed amongst the elected members

Ahmed Beğ and Zayko Ağa replace Ahmed Ağa and Marin Ağa with the elections.[15] The seals of the new candidates appear before the candidate list was sent to the province, although they should not have begun their terms before being elected. Either the candidates placed their seals under this pre-election report by mistake, or the report was (written but) not sealed until the new members were elected. Both possibilities raise doubts about the chronological preciseness of the reports.

The general temporal disorderliness that seem to be typical of the council's record-keeping procedures suggest that these reports were not recorded during the meetings. The council's clerks kept rough draft books where the outgoing correspondence was drafted – to be edited later.[16] Once the editing was complete, the council sent the correspondence and kept a copy of it in the register. Thus, the time of recording in the copy registers differed from the time of the council meetings. When council clerks glued copies of the correspondence arriving from the districts to be forwarded to the province in the draft books, it would lead to chronological disorder.[17] It is likely that discordance in the copy register reflects this disorder in the draft register because the council clerks used original dates of such correspondence when copying from these draft books. Furthermore, the council's numbering system (for the correspondence it sent) did not match the numbers of incoming documents (from the districts) on the drafts. A report (3 July 1874) sent from the Rahovo District to Ruse was glued (without a number) between the drafts numbered 213 and 214 (7 July and 8 July respectively). Such disruptions and delays that arose from the editing of the correspondence must have caused the general temporal disorderliness in the council's register.

Another puzzling change in the copy register is the disappearance of the subgovernor's, the judge's and the metropolitan's seals after the elections (Line 10 in Table 4.1). This cannot be due to these members' official absence, which is marked differently. Consider the two brief periods in April and July of 1874 when the director of correspondence, Ramiz Efendi, served as the deputy subgovernor (Lines 19–21, 29–32). It is unclear why he was elected to serve as the deputy; neither the copy register nor a draft book (NBKM, VD 94/01) covering the dates when Ramiz Efendi served as the deputy offer any explanation. However, when he assumed that surrogate post, the title 'deputy' was written to the front of 'subgovernor' with a different-coloured ink, indicating a deliberate effort to emphasise the change. Like many of the other council members, the subgovernor's seal is intermittently absent before and after these dates, yet when there is a deputy (because the subgovernor is on official leave) it is marked at the title level. It appears that the application of seals in the copy register are independent from the titles that appear as part of the text. When the subgovernor was officially absent from his post, the titles at the end of the reports would reflect that. That is also why the deputy despot's title appeared for the reports that related in particular to the Christian community of the region (Lines 34 and 38). Particular issues such as conversion must have required the presence of a metropolitan or despot as a member of the council.[18] Because the metropolitan was officially absent from 14 May onwards (Line 24), the deputy despot title was added among the others at the end of the reports on relevant issues. The application of seals in the copy register might have had a different purpose than reporting attendance to the meetings. While it is not possible to discern the exact motivation from the register, it is clear that the imprints connect individual members with particular reports.

Seeing the dates when such seals appear/disappear in the records allows us to speculate about the dynamics behind the movement of the members in and out of these councils. Following the elections in March 1874, Zayko Ağa replaced Marin Ağa while Ahmed Beğ replaced Ahmed Ağa (Line 10). The seals of the two non-Muslim elected members, Zayko and Seko Ağas, are a more consistent feature of the register than that of Ahmed Beğ, whose seal appears intermittently at the end of the reports only until the end of May, three months after the elections, when it disappears permanently from the register. The disappearance of his seal coincides with another unusual change: Hacı Tahir Ağa's seal replaces that of the other Muslim member of the council, Osman Beğ (Lines 27 and 28). Although Hacı Tahir Ağa's name was on the final candidate list (6 March 1874) together with Ahmed Beğ's (Table 3.1), the governor did not select him as a council member. It is not clear what made Osman Beğ quit his post. However, following his departure, Hacı Tahir Ağa became a member of the council and served for the rest of the year. The 1875 provincial yearbook lists Hacı Tahir Ağa, not Osman Beğ, as an administrative council member for 1874 and 1875 (Table 3.3).

The yearbooks (*Salname Tuna* 1868–77) list Osman Beğ for two years in Vidin's judicio-administrative sphere (an administrative council member in 1873 and head of the municipal council earlier). His election to the administrative council was due to the resignation of Hacı Ömer Beğ (Table 3.1). Hacı Tahir Ağa, on the other hand, appears to have served for five years in the administrative council and two years in the council of appeals and crime. In addition, he also was the municipal council's head for four years. Although Hacı Tahir Ağa was not elected to the administrative council (the governor preferred Ahmed Beğ over Hacı Tahir Ağa in 1874), due to Osman Beğ's resignation he became a

Nineteenth-century Local Governance in Ottoman Bulgaria

council member. Ahmed Beğ, even more visible than Hacı Tahir Ağa in the yearbooks, served for nine years in the most significant two councils in Vidin (Table 3.3). Interestingly, Hacı Tahir Ağa's arrival seems to have coincided with cessation of Ahmed Beğ's seals in the copy register from the end of May through to the end of September 1874. Both members continued to be listed as members of the council until the last volume in 1877 (Table 3.3), yet we do not know why the arrival of one led to disassociation of the other from the reports included in the copy register.

RIGHT SIDE UP?

In addition to the frequency of their application and synchronicity among them, the appearance of some of the seals is informative. Table 4.2 lists the seals that appear in the register. With one exception, each member has a single seal. Neofit Tseko (Seko Ağa), one of the two members with a Cyrillic inscription seal, changed his seal on 27 September (1873) to one that was carved in Ottoman. The other member with a Cyrillic seal was Marin Ağa, whose seal does not appear in the register until 18 October 1873 (Line 8 in Table 4.1).[19]

On 22 October 1873, only six days after its initial appearance, Marin Ağa's seal appears upside down (Figure 4.4). The seal generally appears in this form until the election.

Figure 4.4 The seal of Marin Novinov, upside down
Source: NBKM, VD 96/41.

Participation in the Politics of Local Administration

Table 4.2 Titles, names and seals of the administrative council members in Vidin in 1873

Title	Name	Seal 1	Seal 2
Subgovernor (*Mutasarrıf*)	Rıf'at Halil Paşa		
Deputy subgovernor (*Vekil mutasarrıf*)	Remzi Beğ		
Deputy subgovernor (*Vekil mutasarrıf*) See also: Director of correspondence	Ramiz Efendi		
Judge of the *shar'i* court (*Hakim el-şer'* or *Na'ib el-şer'*)	Ahmed Rıf'at Efendi		
Metropolitan (*Metropolit* and Despot)	Kiril Efendi		
Director of surveys (*Müdür-i tahrirat*) See also: Deputy subgovernor	Ramiz Efendi		
Muslim religious leader of the region (*Müfti-i belde*)	Mustafa Hamdi Efendi		
Accountant (*Muhasebeci*)	Mehmed Tevfik Beğ		

Title	Name	Seal 1	Seal 2
Elected member (*A'za*)	Osman Beğ		
Elected member (*A'za*)	Ahmed Efendi (Duhani Derviş Ahmed Efendi)		
Elected member (*A'za*)	Marin Ağa (Marin Novinov)		
Elected member (*A'za*)	Seko Ağa (Neofit Tseko)		
Elected member (*A'za*)	Ahmed Beğ (Ma'ruf Ağazade Ahmed Beg)		
Elected member (*A'za*)	Tahir Ağa (Hacı Tahir Ağa)		
Elected member (*A'za*)	Zayko Ağa (Tseko Vanchov)		

Source: NBKM, VD 96/41.

It is not very likely that someone would insist on affixing his seal upside down. The register's pages were big enough to fit several reports; if Marin Ağa were to have affixed his seal upside down by mistake, he could have noticed this irregularity in another report on the same page. The continuous use of the seal upside down indicates that this was not the case. It is possible that it was not Marin Ağa who affixed the seal on these reports. Furthermore, whoever did, either did not know the Cyrillic alphabet or did not care as much.[20]

The application of the seals by a clerk rather than the members does not imply that the clerks actually possessed these seals. As much as they were signs of participation in the politics of local administration, the seals were not used solely for that purpose. They served as official representations of individuals in many transactions, such as payment of salaried state officials, soldiers, teachers, and so on; weekly subsistence payments to immigrants; or assignments of benefices in land (*tımar*) and shares of annuities sold by the Ottoman treasury (*esham*).[21] Sample impressions (*tatbik mühürü*) of local officials' seals would be sent to the provincial centres and to Istanbul in order to inform the centre of the link between the names and the seals.[22] Their importance made seals attractive to thieves, and losing one was a significant matter. It is therefore unlikely that the members of the Vidin administrative council were not present when the clerks placed their unique seals' impressions under the reports. However, the upside-down seal of Marin Ağa suggests that they probably were not paying much attention to how they were affixed.

The practice of using seals in this register ends by 26 September 1874, and there are no seal impressions through to the end of the register (10 March 1875). Unlike its beginning, when a deputy replaced the subgovernor, the end of the practice is not marked by a cadre change. The curious disappearance of impressions marks a point when the practice of using seals was re-evaluated and found unnecessary by the then-dominant group in the council. That is, either the hegemonic power composition of the council changed or the institutional configuration that necessitated the use of the seals did. Regardless, as this analysis indicates, being a council member did not guarantee undisputed participation in the local decision-making process. Participation was related to but not solely explainable in terms of 'election'. As in the replacement of Osman Beğ with Hacı Tahir Ağa, at times the election results were challenged by factors uncontrolled by the state rules and apparatuses. This was the nature of local politics of administration.

Yearbooks: Reflections of the Judicio-administrative Sphere

The administrative and judicial councils were not the only organisations that the notables used to conduct politics. A brief analysis of the provincial yearbooks reveals the two councils' wider functioning environment. Each county's judicial, administrative, financial and military offices – that the yearbooks' editors considered worthy of listing – occupied exactly three pages in the Danube Province's yearbooks. The district-level organisational structure, following the counties, occupied only one or two pages. These pages fail to convey the judicio-administrative sphere's intricacies, but they are the government's official acknowledgement of its personnel and when read in conjunction with the registers they provide a better picture of local governance.[23]

The official publishing house of Danube Province in Ruse published the yearbooks for ten consecutive years (*Salname Tuna* 1868–77). The opening page of the first volume explains their intention to publish the yearbooks in the first month of the lunar calendar (Muharram). However, it was a challenge to collect and organise the relevant statistics of the province immediately at the beginning of the year, and this task was finished a few days into the first month. The editors request that the readers report the errors to ensure that the second volume is 'better and more perfect' (*Salname Tuna* 1:2). The yearbooks present structured information and contribute to the creation of a 'public sphere of state administration' (Giddens 1985: 179). Through their pages, they provide the names of people involved in provincial government and contextualise those names in a visual hierarchy.

The page design of the volumes visibly improves throughout the decade. Page borders become more ornate, clear lines separate sections, typeface becomes cleaner. Besides this, however, the content's organisation does not change much. An annual calendar in the first part of the yearbook lists prayer times for each day. Some anniversaries and significant dates are specially marked – like 'the eighth military campaign of Sultan Süleyman', or dates for 'flooding of the Nile River', or 'shearing of the sheep'. In all volumes after the fifth one (1872), a new table lists the sultans' birth, enthronement and death dates. In the later volumes, various fact tables provide lists of foreign monarchs, Ottoman provincial governors, hierarchy of honorifics and list of forms of address in written correspondence.

Following the general practical information in the first part, the yearbooks contain more specific content about the provincial offices and staff. This second part opens with a hierarchy of people working in the provincial centre, Ruse, with their rank, and decorations (*nişan*). The list starts with the administrative council headed by the provincial governor and includes various judiciary and municipal councils, officials and clerks appendant to the administrative structure, such as the council of education, offices of accounting, or forest, river and transportation administration. Following these are the offices and staff, not appendant to the administrative council: various military branches; the Danube shipyard, telegram office, and the ferry and railroad companies operating in the province; and foreign consulate officials.

A third section lists the judicio-administrative sphere's elected and appointed members for each county and district. There were seven counties (forty-eight districts) in the Danube Province. Vidin is the second district in all volumes after the head district of the province, Ruse. In a similar pattern, these pages provide a hierarchy of officials involved with Ottoman governance reflecting a many-tiered organisational structure.[24] The administrative council and the council of appeals and crime, the judicio-administrative sphere's core organisations, occupy the first page listed right after the subgovernor, the *shar'i* judge, the accountant and the director of correspondence. A note right below the *ex officio* (*tab'i*) and elected members of the administrative council, on the right side of the page, explains that the clerks of the administrative council function under the authority of the director of correspondence. The council of appeals and crime's clerks and the interrogators (*müstantık*) are right below its elected members (*mümeyyiz*), followed by the clerk of the *shar'i* court. (In the last three volumes, there are at least three *shar'i* court clerks separate from those of the council of appeals and crime.)[25] Concluding the first page are the commercial court's head, permanent and temporary (*da'imi* and *muvakkat*) members, and the clerks.

The provincial commercial courts were established with a regulation on 30 April 1860 (*Düstur-ı atik* 1st ed.: 185–217). While the regulation required a primary and a deputy head (*re'is-i evvel* and *re'is-i sani*) there were no deputies for the Danube Province's counties. In addition, county commercial courts would have two permanent and four temporary members; the subgovernors would appoint the head of the council and the permanent members for an indeterminate period (the ministry of trade's approval was necessary on these appointments). The employees of the council were required to have a superb understanding of commerce and according to article 11 they would be paid 'an appropriate amount of salary'. A council of the local merchants would elect the temporary members to serve for a single year without pay.

Table 4.3 lists the members of the commercial court – the yearbooks do not consistently include the first and the second clerks. Most of the merchant members of the council, listed as permanent and temporary members, seem to have served for two to three years, with a maximum of four years. However, I cannot comment more on the council members' tenure due to lack of means to verify the yearbooks' accuracy. There are a few names in Table 4.3 that are familiar from the administrative and judiciary councils: Persiyado Efendi, Derviş Ahmed and Hacı Todor Ağas. All three appear to have served in the commercial court prior to

Table 4.3 List of Vidin's commercial court members in the yearbooks

	1868	1869	1870	1871	1872	1873	1874	1875	1876	1877
Head	İsmail Ağa	İsmail Ağa	İsmail Ağa	Matyaş Efendi	Matyaş Efendi	Mamuriat (مامورية) Efendi	Mamuriat (مامورية) Efendi	Zare (زاره) Efendi	Zare (زاره) Efendi	Zare (زاره) Efendi
Permanent Member 1	Mehmed Efendi	Mehmed Efendi	Mehmed Efendi	Cafer Efendi	Cafer Efendi	Hafız Hüseyin Efendi	Hafız Hüseyin Efendi	Boşnak Mustafa Ağa	Hafız Osman Efendi	Hafız Osman Efendi
Permanent Member 2	Kanço Ağa	Kanço Ağa	Kanço Ağa	Vanko Ağa	Vanko Ağa	Kanço Ağa	Boyacı Kanço Ağa	Boyacı Kanço Ağa	Boyacı Kanço Ağa	Boyacı Kanço Ağa
Temporary Member 1	Derviş Ahmed Ağa	Derviş Ahmed Ağa	Derviş Ahmed Ağa	Mehmed Efendi	Abdülrahim Efendi	Ibrahim Efendi	Ibrahim Efendi	Edhem Efendi	Abdurrahman Ağa	Hacı Hasan Ağa
Temporary Member 2	Mutiş Ağa	Mutiş Ağa	Mutiş Ağa	Ali Molla	Hacı Kaşif Efendi	Kaşif Efendi	Other Ibrahim Efendi	Other Aziz Efendi	Hacı Hasan Ağa	Yako Kapon
Temporary Member 3	Çako Ağa	Çako Ağa	Çako Ağa	Hacı Yovanço Ağa	Hacı Todor Ağa	Şekerci Yovan Ağa	Şekerci Yovan Ağa	Rufa'il Efendi	Yako Kapon	
Temporary Member 4	Persiyado Efendi	Persiyado Efendi	Persiyado Efendi	Bahur Kohen	Yako Efendi	Yasef Denlore	Yasef Denlore		Aleksandri Ağa	
First Clerk	Ömer Efendi	Ömer Efendi	Ömer Efendi	Ibrahim Efendi	Ibrahim Efendi				Ibrahim Efendi	Ibrahim Efendi
Second Clerk									Yusuf Efendi	Yusuf Efendi

Source: *Salname Tuna* 1868–77.

the administrative and judiciary councils. There might be some upward mobility from this council to the higher councils.

The second page lists the financial/scribal units that functioned in close connection with the core councils. The accounting and correspondence departments in the top row are supervised by the accountant and the director of correspondence – members of the administrative council. The rest of the departments on this page, the municipal council (*meclis-i da'ire-i belediye*), commission of surveys (*tahrir komisyonu*), land office (*arazi kalemi*), survey office (*tahrir kalemi*), Agricultural Credit Funds (Menafi'-i 'Umumiye Sandığı), and Orphans' Funds (Emval-ı Eytam Sandığı) all had their own directors. Such offices were all part of the larger judicio-administrative sphere and served as negotiation platforms for different agents using Ottoman governance to advance their strategies. If we assume that members of these smaller offices functioned in a way similar to their colleagues in the core councils it becomes clear that the Ottoman provincial government, represented by the offices and the practices integral to this sphere, was far from being a monolith entity. Rather, it represented a complex matrix of interests pursued by different council members who did not necessarily get along with each other. As I point out in the later chapters, all of these institutions and offices constituting Ottoman governance, connected population control technologies to the economy – essential for the creation of political economy defined 'as knowledge of processes that link together variations of wealth and variation of population on three axes: production, circulation, consumption' (Foucault 2007: 450). This complex structure was staffed by members of the local elite and connected local economy to imperial governance.

The municipal council of Vidin, another second-tier council, presents a member turnover pattern similar to that of the commercial court. The first Ottoman municipal councils were established for the imperial capital Istanbul in 1857.[26] A decade later, with a decree in 1867, the imperial centre ordered the establishment of these councils in every city (*Düstur* 3: *Düstur* 1: 491–7). Article 7 of this decree defined municipal councils' primary function as overseeing the cleaning and organising (*tanzifat ve tanzimat*) of the urban living space. These councils were to operate with their own funds, which would come from construction fees and a portion of the annual taxes, and were to bank their excess revenues with the provincial Agricultural Credit Funds to collect interest (articles 5 and 9). While the funds for the Vidin municipal council are not included in the first three volumes of the yearbooks, the remaining seven volumes list an average of 300,000 *guruş* per year. The last five volumes indicate that a fixed amount of 200,000 was invested in Ottoman treasury bonds. The decree of 1867 defined the municipal councils as consisting of a head, an assistant (*mu'avin*) to the head and six elected members; furthermore, an engineer, a doctor and the police force would be at their service. The town alderman councils would elect the councils' six members to serve for two years. Each year half the members would be replaced in a process similar to the administrative and judicial council elections.

Table 4.4 lists the Vidin municipal council members. Again, we see names familiar from the administrative and judicial councils: Hacı Tahir Ağa and Osman Beğ. While Hacı Tahir Ağa served as the municipal council's head and an administrative council member between 1868 and 1870, Osman Beğ resigned from the same municipal council post in the middle of his two-year term to switch to the administrative council (Tables 3.3 and 4.4). The names common to both the administrative and the judicial council remain limited to the two heads appointed by the subgovernor. None of the municipal council members served longer than four years. This seems to be a common feature of the less significant offices: no one seems to have served in a particular organisation as long as Zayko Ağa or Ahmed Beğ did.

The only apparent exception to this is the commission of surveys, which also included members who served in the administrative and judicial councils (Table 4.5). They were introduced at the provincial level in 1860 in connection with the empire-wide population, property, and income surveys (*Düstur-ı atik* 2nd ed.: 889–903). They became a part of the provincial government six years later with an amendment to the regulation of 1860 (*Düstur-ı atik* 2nd ed.: 904). The commission was responsible for registering wealth and people, playing a crucial role in producing knowledge connecting wealth and population on the axes of production, circulation, consumption. It was to operate in accord with similar bodies at the county, district and village levels to guarantee the just appraisal of surveyed property, the correct numbering of houses and appropriate distribution of the tax burden on households. The county commissions had six members (with one acting as the head), the subgovernor, the *shar'i* judge, and the Muslim religious leader would elect three Muslim and three non-Muslim members, and each year one-third of the members were to be replaced (*Düstur-ı atik* 2nd ed.: 894). The first provincial yearbook does not contain any information about this commission (Table 4.5).

It is clear from Table 4.5 that members of the commission served, for the most part, longer than a year despite the regulation. Furthermore, the yearbooks do not contain a name for the fifth member after the third volume. Aside from such irregularities, there appears to have been a significant change in the composition of the commission circa 1870 – those

Table 4.4 List of Vidin's municipal council members in the yearbooks

	1868	1869	1870	1871	1872	1873	1874	1875	1876	1877
Head	Hacı Tahir Ağa	Hacı Tahir Ağa	İsmail Ağa Hafız	Hacı Tahir Ağa	Hacı Tahir Ağa	Osman Beğ	Mehmed Efendi	Hacı Yusuf Ağa	Hacı Yusuf Ağa	Hafız Mehmed Efendi
Member 1	Hüseyin Ağa	Hüseyin Ağa	Halim Ağa	Salih Ağa	Salih Ağa	Mahmud Beğ	Mahmud Beğ	Mahmud Beğ	Mahmud Beğ	Mustafa Ağa
Member 2	Mehmed Efendi	Mehmed Efendi	Minko Ağa	Minko Ağa	Minko Ağa	Minko Ağa	Yahya Efendi	Yahya Efendi	Yahya Efendi	Hacı Ömer Ağa
Member 3	Vanko Ağa Hacı	Vanko Ağa	Cercis Beğ	Cercis Beğ	Cercis Beğ	Cercis Beğ	Abdülrahim Efendi	Abdülrahim Efendi	Çelebi Ağa	Çelebi Ağa
Member 4	Yovanço Ağa	Yovanço Ağa	Flore Ağa	Aslan Efendi	Aslan Efendi	Aslan Efendi	Savo Ağa	Savo Ağa	Nako Ağa	Yovan Ağa
Member 5	Yako Efendi	Yako Efendi	Rufel Efendi	Gorge Ağa	Gorge Ağa	Gorge Ağa	Vulço Ağa	Vulço Ağa	Hacı Niko Ağa	Nako Ağa
Member 6		Mustafa Beğ	Mustafa Beğ	Mustafa Beğ						

Source: *Salname Tuna* 1868–77.

Nineteenth-century Local Governance in Ottoman Bulgaria

Table 4.5 List of Vidin's commission of surveys members in the yearbooks

	Head	Member 1	Member 2	Member 3	Member 4	Member 5
1868	—	—	—	—	—	—
1869	'Ali Beğ	Hacı Ali Beğ	Mahmud Beğ	Nako Ağa	Marin Ağa	'Aşir Efendi
1870	'Ali Beğ	Hacı Ali Beğ	Mahmud Beğ	Nako Ağa	Marin Ağa	'Aşir Efendi
1871	Hurşid Efendi	Mutiş Efendi	Molla İsma'il	Hacı Petko Ağa	Boyacı Marin Ağa	
1872	Hurşid Efendi	Mutiş Efendi	Molla İsma'il	Hacı Petko Ağa	Boyacı Marin Ağa	
1873	Hurşid Efendi	Mutiş Efendi	Molla İsma'il	Hacı Petko Ağa	Boyacı Marin Ağa	
1874	Hurşid Efendi	Mutiş Efendi	Molla İsma'il	Hacı Petko Ağa	Boyacı Marin Ağa	
1875	Hurşid Efendi	Derviş Ağa	Molla İsma'il	Hacı Petko Ağa	Boyacı Marin Ağa	
1876	Hurşid Efendi	Molla Ibrahim	Hacı Ahmed	Şükrü Efendi	Boyacı Marin Ağa	
1877	Hurşid Efendi	Molla Ibrahim	Hacı Ahmed	Şükrü Efendi	Boyacı Marin Ağa	

Source: *Salname Tuna* 1868–77.

who served that year were listed in the yearbook of 1871, which includes a new set of names for the commission.[27]

If the names listed in the yearbooks are accurate, such a drastic shift might indicate a shift in political power within the judicio-administrative structure. The same volume indicates also that two other influential names who were involved in choosing the members of the commission, the sub-governor and the *shar'i* judge of the county, changed that year, although the new subgovernor served for two years and the new judge for only a year. Following this shift, we see a relatively stable composition dominating the organisation, which was supposed to verify the structured information regarding the inhabitants of Vidin County. Familiar people such as Boyacı Marin Ağa or Hacı Petko Ağa (both were administrative council members for a year) seem to have served quite a long while in this commission. As I pointed out in the previous chapter in discussing the core council members (Table 3.3), we see a similar pattern in the administrative and judiciary councils: their members did not change until 1870 while staff in other offices of provincial government in Vidin did change.

The parallels between the change patterns in core councils and the commission of surveys are suggestive of a shift of power from one possible network represented by the members of the singular government of state

Participation in the Politics of Local Administration

and society before 1870 to another one after that date. In the absence of any other documents, this only remains as a speculation but, if correct, this might explain why the seal of Ahmed Beğ disappeared from the copy register after Hacı Tahir Ağa's seal appeared. Ahmed Beğ was a member of the judiciary council between 1868 and 1870 while Hacı Tahir Ağa served as a member of the administrative council. In 1870 the latter lost his position in the administrative council as the former became a member of it. After a two-year break, Hacı Tahir Ağa was elected to the judiciary council and two years later moved up to the administrative council following the resignation of Osman Beğ. We know from the seals that once Hacı Tahir Ağa replaced Osman Beğ, Ahmed Beğ's seal disappeared. Regardless of the speculative suggestions regarding local networks, the dynamism of members' names and seals in the yearbooks and copy registers indicate that Vidin's local government was a domain of negotiation among its members.

The last of the three pages designated for each county usually lists the members of the artillery battalion council (*kal'a topçu taburu meclisi*) and the police battalion council (*zaptiye taburu meclisi*) at the top. Right below them are a few less significant offices such as the office of customs, telegram and quarantine. Especially in the later years, the teachers of the advanced primary school (*rüşdiye*) are also listed on this page. The school in Vidin opened its door to new students on 13 December 1859; however, its personnel information is included only in the last four yearbooks (1872–7).[28] Information regarding each county is concluded by a list of the foreign nationals working in either consular or commercial (such as the ferry administration) posts.

This significant delay in relating information on the *rüşdiye* schools proves two related points regarding the yearbooks' design: first, the pages devoted to Vidin did not necessarily reflect all the offices in Vidin; second, there was a conscientious decision-making process behind the order in these pages. It was decided in 1872, one year after the significant shift in the core councils and the commission of surveys, the textual representation of Ottoman provincial administration should include the schools. Studying the composition of the yearbooks year by year is similar to tracing the public image that the modern Ottoman state sketched for its provincial expanse. Provincial year books replicated the role played by the imperial yearbooks (discussed in Chapter 2), providing a dynamic time–space convergence at the local level. They rendered what local administration meant and how it evolved textually visible.

Following the list of offices and their staff, we find information about the province's administrative structure: a table of the counties and districts and another of subgovernors and district head officials and their salaries, and so on. Also included are some financial tables: the summary balance sheets of the Agricultural Credit Funds and Orphans' Funds in the districts, the province's overall budget and practical tables, including a list of ferry terminals along the Danube, descriptions of railroads, roads, mines, manufactures and textiles, bathhouses, forests, rivers, and a list of newspapers published in the province with their annual subscription rates. Some volumes include unique tables reflecting surveys conducted in previous years. The most significant of these are detailed tables included in the sixth volume (1873: 106–309) that list all the villages, the number of households and the demographic composition, animals owned by inhabitants and the total taxes paid by these villages. The inclusion of such statistical detail in these yearbooks reaffirms their purpose as providing a representation of the 'public sphere of state administration' and practical information regarding the province.

Conclusion: a Better Vision of the System?

Participation in Vidin's judicio-administrative sphere required more than merely being elected. What began as a curious practice of leaving impressions of the members' seals on the administrative council's copy register following the county's subgovernor's departure on 4 August 1873, creates a limited opportunity to examine the participation of the members in the report-writing process. With a pattern common to its contemporaries in different organisations, the copy register was a uniform bureaucratic document that bore no personal traits. While there is nothing particularly unique about the registers' design, the titles and seal impressions (as analysed in this chapter) indicate that not all members attended the council meetings, some remained absent for extended periods, and sometimes significant changes in the council's composition (such as a member's resignation) were not reflected in the yearbooks. The politics of participation continued after the elections to the administrative and judicial councils, and while council meetings may not have been the cacophony described by St Clair and Brophy, there is little doubt about the presence of polyphony. This polyphonic structure's orchestration becomes more audible through the yearbooks that reveal shifts in how the local elite staffed the provincial administration.

Despite their limits in reflecting the dynamic nature of the local politics of administration, the provincial yearbooks relate valuable information regarding the general organisation of the local judicio-administrative sphere through the offices of the modern Ottoman state. The display of councils, courts, commissions and other organisations in the three pages

Participation in the Politics of Local Administration

that were devoted to the county of Vidin gives a sense of the bureaucratic hierarchy designed for the local judicio-administrative sphere by the Ottoman Empire. The cadres of provincial administration were rank-ordered properly in these pages. The names of the individuals were matched with their honorifics and decorations.[29] In a detailed fashion, the yearbooks categorised the information regarding the provincial judicio-administrative sphere.

Most importantly, the yearbooks demonstrate the interrelated nature of some of these offices. It is evident that some men served on the municipal council, commercial court and the commission of surveys in addition to the administrative council and the council of appeals and crime in Vidin. This gives us a better idea about the interconnected nature of the judicio-administrative sphere and helps us understand how certain local notables remained important figures in the modern Ottoman state and its production of official information regarding its provinces. While serving on the administrative and judicial councils of Vidin was very significant for the politics of local administration, this was not the only opportunity for the members of the local population who were willing and powerful enough to become a part of the modern Ottoman state. It is in this context that we need to understand how Vidin's administrative council and the council of appeals and crime functioned and wrote their reports to the province.

The reports sent from the organisations within the judicio-administrative sphere of Vidin were inevitably shaped by the politics of administration in Vidin. Reporting from the countryside was a highly politicised act; thus the letters that the provincial administration received from the judicio-administrative sphere in Vidin reflected the negotiations and conflicts among those who had the privilege to draft them. As I discuss in Chapter 5, the distinction between 'reality' and 'unfounded allegations' was often a very thin line in such correspondence. Still, the registers used by the councils provide valuable insight into the politics of administration at the local level. While we cannot establish the veracity of all the details included in the documents, the political language and the silences used in official correspondence can help us understand Ottoman governance better.

Notes

1. Notables' dominance in these councils was not limited to Vidin. The few monographs on the topic points to similar occurrences in other places such as Haifa (Yazbak 1998), Jerusalem (Gerber 1985), Bosnia (Gölen 2010: 174–80) and different parts of Anatolia (Bingöl 2004: 238–43).

2. The debate about the role of Great Britain in the world revolved around the so-called 'Eastern Question' among other things (from Britain's involvement in Ireland to the colonisation of India). 'The Bulgarian atrocities' of 1876, Richard Shannon notes (1975: 14), 'provoked the most convincing demonstration of the High Victorian public conscience; and the agitation can be understood only in relation to the development and refinement of that public conscience'. For more on this, see (Shannon 1975: 202–38) and (Long 1980: 198–209).
3. Ludmilla Kostova (1997: 116) summarises their message as 'fairly clear: everywhere else in Europe at least a modicum of progress has been achieved; the Bulgarian alone have been left out of History's grand scenario because of "racial" deficiencies and general inferiority'.
4. (*Düstur-ı Atik* 1st ed.: 484). *A'za*, generally stands for the 'elected' members as opposed to the 'appointed' ones. For the latter, the term clerk, or *me'mur*, is used.
5. The actual letters that were sent to the provincial centre or to the districts would contain the seals of the members who were present at that meeting.
6. See for example BOA, A. MKT. ŞD. 13/78, where some members are noted as 'absent' (*bulunamadı*), BOA, A. MKT. ŞD. 3/27, where a member is noted as 'sick' (*namizac*) or BOA, İ MVL. 23909, where a member is marked as 'in Istanbul' (*Dersa'adet'de*). Even in the provincial councils there seems to have been a concern to note if a member was absent for a particular reason. In a letter from the Danube Province Administrative Council (chaired by Midhat Paşa) to the Supreme Council of Judicial Ordinances, one member is marked as having 'passed away' (*vefat eylediği*) (BOA, İ MVL. 24680).
7. The dates for the first and last records in the Vidin administrative council register (NBKM, VD 107/16) that I use.
8. Seals were used for identification purposes. At the provincial level they represented individuals' presence in official documents as signatures would do in the modern sense. Sample seal imprints of government employees (or subcontractors) would be kept at the relevant offices to verify their identities. People also used their seals to prove that they collected a sum of money, or that their statements were included properly in an interrogation protocol, or to show that they agreed with the decision of council as a member and so on. To prevent fraud and forgery, the engravers were required to keep a register with the imprints of the seals that they sold to their customers (Kütükoğlu 'Mühür').
9. In some of the imperial councils, such as the Council of State (Şura-yı Devlet), such reports would be accompanied not only by the seals of the members who participated in the meeting but also a note under the seal if the member disagreed with the decision.
10. The titles are ordered according to rank: the highest-ranking member, the subgovernor, is on the left side of the row of titles, and the elected members

are on the right (Kütükoğlu 1994: 33). Mahmud Yazbak (1997: 73) uses 'jurisconsult' in translating mufti; however, that translation does not seem proper to use here as the judicial functions of a mufti was fairly limited in this time period.

11. Sultan Mahmud II established Bab-ı Meşihat in 1826. Bernard Lewis ('Bab-ı Mashikhat') argues that 'this step, taken simultaneously with the creation of an Inspectorate of *Waqf* to centralize the supervision and control of *waqf* revenues, prepared the way for the bureaucratization of the *ulema*'.
12. All the reports with seal imprints belong to the second register, NBKM, VD 96/41.
13. The titles 'metropolit' and 'despot' seem to be used interchangeably in these reports. Both are of Greek origin, and in Modern Greek both refer to the same position (metropolitan bishop).
14. '*Me'muren Berkofça'da bulunduğu*', NBKM, VD 96/41 report dated 31 March 1874.
15. See the last row Table 3.1 in the previous chapter for the full list of candidates.
16. NBKM, OAK 88/01, VD 94/01, VD 96/35, VD 96/53, VD 98/13, VD 100/7, VD 101/18 and VD 107/15 are some examples of the rough draft books.
17. For example, there are three reports placed between the reports Nos 213 and 214 in NBKM, VD 94/01.
18. This was not unique to Vidin or the Balkans but was also practised in places like Ankara (BOA, DH.HMŞ 1329-12-21). Many thanks to Zeynep Türkyılmaz for this information.
19. Marin Ağa was on the candidate list for the elections of 1874 but was not re-elected. He was replaced by Zayko Ağa (Tables 3.1 and 3.3).
20. Most of the seals with Arabic letters include the date of carving below the name. The date of Marin Ağa's seal, 1862, is above his name. In contrast, in his old Cyrillic seal, Seko Ağa had the date, 1846, carved below. Seko Ağa's seal does not appear upside down at all. Having the date carved below the name, following the pattern of the seals carved in Arabic, might have led to the proper application of the seal in this case.
21. The head of each 'family' would apply his seal on a register in order to verify that he had received a weekly allowance. See NBKM, VD 98/10. In the case of benefices and annuities, the recipients would send their personal seals' impression. Should they lose the seal they used to receive their payments, recipients had to pay a fee proportional to their payment. See report No. 891 in NBKM, VD 107/16.
22. See for example BOA, Maliyeden Müdevver Defterler No. 9016, a register of the names and the seals of the administrative council members and the district head officials in different provinces.
23. Yearbooks contain a wealth of information that Ottomanists utilise extensively (Palalı 2010). Duman's two-volume work (2000) provides arguably the most comprehensive list on what yearbooks are available. Among other things, scholars have used them for demographical information (Karpat

1985; Karpat 2002) or for identifying organisational structure and salaries of bureaucratic cadres (Findley 1980, 1989).

24. Recently, Christine Philliou (2011: xxiii) provided a concise definition for governance as 'the project of keeping a political order in place, including the formal state apparatus but also the many relationships in society involving institutions, networks, individuals, customs and beliefs that contribute to upholding that order'. Governance, in these perspectives, does not involve a questioning of the legitimacy of governmental action. Foucault (2008: 16) makes this very clear: 'There will be either success or failure ... rather than legitimacy or illegitimacy, [that became] the criteria of governmental action. So, success replaces legitimacy.' The information included in these yearbooks is not there to legitimise the government, but to showcase the working government, to prove that it is doing what it is supposed to be doing.

25. This seems to be the case for Vidin County alone. Other counties list only one clerk for the *shar'i* courts.

26. (*Düstur-ı Atik* 1st ed: 436–41). Up until the nineteenth century, control of the urban space in the Ottoman Empire was closely associated with the control of the market place (*ihtisab*) and prices (*narh*). *Ihtisab* was an Islamic office (*muhtesib* was the office holder) with functions that overlapped (and exceeded) those of municipal governance; yet *muhtesib*s operated under the authority of the *kadı*s (Saraçoğlu 2015: 62–5). Following the destruction of the Janissary forces in 1826 the empire increased the authority of the *muhtesib* over the urban space in the capital first, and eventually in other towns. In 1855 an imperial decree transferred the jurisdiction of the *kadı*s on urban governance affairs to a new office, *şehremaneti*, which became the basis for Ottoman municipalities (Ergin 1995: 325–43; Akgündüz 2005: 44–5). While a series of imperial regulations continued to tweak and alter the organisational structure of the municipalities in the second half of the nineteenth century Midhat Paşa was one of the earliest governors who experimented by establishing municipal authorities and councils at the local level in 1860s (Petrov 2006: 99).

27. That is, if we consider Marin Ağa and Boyacı Marin Ağa were different people. Even if these two names referred to the same person (a thesis supported by the information listed in Table 3.1; Boyacı Marin Ağa was a 'candidate' for the administrative council in 1872 and Marin Ağa was mentioned as a 'former member' in the candidate list of 1874), the change is rather significant: while the number of members on the commission is reduced by one, all but one of the members have changed.

28. Report No. 1110 (12 February 1872) in NBKM, VD 107/16 responds to the request by the provincial government for the dates that county and district high schools were founded and their personnel hired. The county high school did not begin its operation with full staff. According to the report, in its first year a certain Şakir Efendi from the town of Vidin was the only educator at the school, which typically employed two or three teachers and a special

instructor for writing (who would generally focus on the *rik'a* style that was being used in most of the official correspondence). A *rik'a* instructor did not begin working at the Vidin high school until nine years after its founding. In Vidin the availability of teaching faculty seems to have imposed limits on the success of the educational reforms. Similar schools were established in Vidin's districts several years later: first in Lom (1868), then Belgradcık (1870), and then Rahova, Berkofça and İvraca (1871). Among all the teachers employed in these schools only the highest-ranking teacher in the Vidin high school had former teaching experience; the rest were hired as teachers for the first time. The difficulty in finding teachers might have been related to the fact that their salaries were not paid regularly. In fact, the above report from 1872 concludes by noting that the clerks and the teachers in the Berkofça and İvraca high schools and the writing instructor in Belgradcık had not received a salary since their official paperwork had yet to arrive at the time of the report.

29. We learn, for example, that Ahmed Beğ and Sevastaki Ağa had the title *kapıcıbaşı*, which did not have a high rank according to the table of titles included in the provincial yearbooks (1877: 26–8). Although the candidate lists did not include their titles, these gentlemen were referred to as 'eminent' (*rif'atlu*) in those lists (see Table 3.1) – a reference used only for a limited group of titles including *kapıcıbaşı*.

5

Writing Politics: Ottoman Governmentality and the Language of Reports

> What would need to be studied now, therefore, is the way in which the specific problems of life and population were raised within a technology of government. (Foucault 1997a: 79)

On 2 May 1872 Vidin's administrative council concluded a lengthy report on the administrative council members of Berkofça (Bergovitsa) District.[1] The report levelled some serious allegations against the district head (*kaymakam*) Mustafa 'Ali Beğ, including negligence in a case involving the local police (*zaptiye*) beating several villagers, verbal harassment of council members and the sodomising by force of a shampooer in a public bath. The extended report, explaining how the case was handled, provides insight into this chapter's two interrelated themes: the administrative councils' procedures and the politics of administration.

Unlike the former chapters which focused on the context in which Vidin County's councils were formed, their election procedures and regular functions within the provincial judicio-administrative sphere, this chapter focuses specifically on the reports that the administrative council wrote to the provincial capital, Ruse. I discuss the official reports on the events in Vidin County as components of the political processes centred on the local judicio-administrative sphere, arguing that the politics of local administration influenced the way these reports were written and thus our understanding of the events in Vidin County. The writing of reports and petitions and other provincial administrative/judicial practices (such as interrogations) constituted the Ottoman government at the local level. That is, following İslamoğlu's conceptualisation, I consider the government as a 'hegemonic environment' that is constituted through administrative and legal practices (İslamoğlu 2004a: 278). To maintain authority, the dominant groups must continually reconstitute the environment through negotiations that order social reality (such as laws that regulate access to and allocation of resources).

Ottoman Governmentality and the Language of Reports

The first case I examine is an extensive one focusing of the malfeasance of the Berkofça District's head official. A detailed summary of this lengthy case in the first section is followed by an analysis of other sources on the district to provide a better understanding of the parties involved in the case. In the third section, I examine some structural aspects of the same case focusing on Ottoman governance to explore how the single government of state officials and local elites functioned in Vidin. The judicio-administrative sphere in Vidin operated with the provincial elite's participation, and reflected the local power relations. This conceptualisation of governmentality as a form of power follows Foucault's discussion of the concept (2008: 65; 1980: 141–2) and transcends the state–society binary, defining the practices of the judicio-administrative sphere as negotiation spaces open to a wide array of agents, including peasants, notables and government employees. This particular case not only illustrates, in general terms, how different actors in the judicio-administrative sphere referred to their official duties while serving their personal interests, but also demonstrates how their actions were reflected in the official correspondence.

Sections four and five expand the analysis beyond people directly involved with the judicio-administrative sphere. I provide examples of how local people participated in, and at times challenged, Ottoman governance. To do this, I analyse cases from the council's copy register together with petitions written by the peasants and sent without the involvement of the council. For the purpose of comparison, I also look at other cases in the same copy register to get a better understanding of the council's language and to explore politics of local administration in Vidin.

'Several Times He Had Been Given Well-intended Reminders': a Case of Local Antagonism

The lengthy report that Vidin's administrative council wrote on 2 May 1872 explains and summarises the correspondence on the allegations made against the Berkofça District head, beginning with two telegrams that Halid Ağa, an elected member in the district's administrative council (*meclis-i idare*), sent on 25 November and 1 December 1871.[2] In these, Halid Ağa intended to inform the Vidin County administrative council of Mustafa 'Ali Beğ's wrongdoings. The first telegram reported that Mustafa 'Ali Beğ had ordered two representatives from the village of Draganiçe (Draganitse) out of the administrative council, where they had come to complain about the local police bastinadoing them; the second reported that he had reprimanded Halid Ağa, threatening him with incarceration for some 'warnings' he had given to the district head.

In response to the pleas of Halid Ağa in his first telegram, the administrative council in Vidin reportedly discussed the matter and decided to send Matyaş Ağa, an elected examining clerk of the council of appeals and crime, to investigate the issue further, as 'the beating of the village inhabitants by the police is abominable conduct, almost like torture'.[3] Matyaş Ağa returned from Berkofça with a 'memorandum from the council of administration and litigation' (*meclis-i idare ve de'avi hey'eti mazbatası*) that had the same date as the second telegram from Halid Ağa (1 December 1871). According to the Vidin administrative council's report, this memo indicated that Mustafa 'Ali Beğ's current position was his first official post. To help him in his first assignment, 'several times he had been given well-intended reminders, and when necessary, he had been directed to the regulations and details of legal articles'. Nevertheless, Mustafa 'Ali Beğ apparently considered such suggestions 'disagreeable'; instead, he relied mostly on the opinions of the district metropolitan, Dorotheus Efendi, who, it seems, was not only a spiritual leader but also a significant member of Berkofça's judicio-administrative sphere.[4]

After establishing the relationship between the novice district head Mustafa 'Ali Beğ and the veteran metropolitan Dorotheus Efendi, the memo from the 'council of administration and litigation' focused on the bastinadoing case, which served as an example not only of Mustafa 'Ali Beğ's partiality but also of his negligence. According to the report's summary of the memo, rumours about what happened in Draganiçe had circulated for a month; however, village inhabitants did not complain to the administrative council until the two village headmen came to the council on behalf of the bastinadoed. Apparently, Mustafa 'Ali Beğ listened to the village headmen only to insult and order them out before letting the other council members express their opinions on the case. When some members emphasised the need to investigate the matter further by sending the second lieutenant of the police forces 'in a mild-mannered way', Mustafa 'Ali Beğ brushed aside the issue (referring to the complainants' arguments as provocations) and dismissed the meeting of the council. When the issue was reportedly raised again in a meeting four days later, Mustafa 'Ali Beğ threatened a council member, Halid Ağa, with imprisonment.

These remarks in the memo delivered by Matyaş Ağa explained the two telegrams received from Halid Ağa in the last two months of 1871 and also contained more accusations against the district head. Allegedly, Mustafa 'Ali Beğ made excessive payments for firewood purchased from remote villages when wood was available for a fraction of the cost in the local market. Furthermore, he and the district tithe officer failed to answer questions regarding the number of people employed in tithe collection and the delay in collection. In its report, Vidin's administrative council notes that, on 11 February 1872, they sent the relevant correspondence to Mustafa 'Ali Beğ demanding an explanation.

Mustafa 'Ali Beğ responded with a detailed report composed of several sections, each responding to an accusation, and this response is summarised in detail in the administrative council's report. In the first section, he repudiated the allegations made against him in a telegram from Hasan, the keeper of the local bathhouse, who charged that Mustafa 'Ali Beğ had forced a shampooer into sodomy. The district head claimed that 'he did not perpetrate such actions that would mar the government'. He insisted that this nonsensical claim was solicited by Nureddin Ağa, an elected member of the Berkofça administrative council. Moreover, the local bathhouse keeper had admitted in front of two witnesses (Ahmed Efendi and İbrahim Ağa) that he had been manipulated.

In the second section of his response, Mustafa 'Ali Beğ defended himself against the accusations of negligence made by the two representatives from the village of Draganiçe. According to him, the events unfolded in a different way. During the month of Ramadan, two 'elected administrative council members, Nureddin and Halid Ağas, came to the council meeting room' and reported that the local police had beaten two villagers from Draganiçe with cudgels and bastinadoed them 'for tax collection'. Upon this, 'it was decided' that the complainants should be summoned to the council to write an official petition, and that the deputy chief of the police forces (*bölük ağası mu'avini*) should be sent to the village to investigate the matter. The district head maintained that despite these decisions, Nureddin and Halid Ağas insisted that the policemen should be dismissed from service. Their persistent demands, however, had gone unanswered due to the impending investigation of the matter.

Mustafa 'Ali Beğ then discussed the motives behind the two members' insistence on discharging the policemen. Apparently, Halid Ağa's brother, Hacı Salih Ağa, had been lending money to the villagers through *selem* contracts.[5] Their persistence in demanding the dismissal of the local policemen was 'founded solely on the purpose of collecting their loans' from the peasants. It was a 'lie' that the peasants had been ordered out without being heard.

In the third section, Mustafa 'Ali Beğ denied the allegation that he threatened to imprison Halid Ağa, claiming that the latter had inveighed against giving meal allowances to the local police and had insisted that the 'policemen were not paying for their provisions while on duty anyway'. Furthermore, Mustafa 'Ali Beğ counter-charged that Halid Ağa had verbally harassed a policeman sent to invite him to the administrative council for official business.

In the fourth section, the district head claimed that the council members' accusations regarding excessive payments for firewood were a manifestation of their hostility toward him; this issue should have been brought up at the district level before a complaint was made to the county. Unfortunately, such a complaint had not been brought to his attention. Mustafa 'Ali Beğ added that complaints regarding the delay in tithe collection were unfounded, as well. The administrative council members were simply unhappy about the replacement of the chief tithe collection clerk (which he had ordered), and accused him of being easily influenced by the metropolitan on government affairs, including tithe collection. This was untrue, the head insisted, and it was common knowledge that Nureddin and Halid Ağas 'hated' the metropolitan.

Furthermore, according to Mustafa 'Ali Beğ, not everyone in the administrative council was competent. Other than the district head, only the *shar'i* judge (*na'ib*), the finance office director (*mal müdürü*) and the head secretary (*tahrirat katibi*) knew how to read and write. The judge's inadequacy was obvious from his paperwork, often returned from the county, while the head of the finance office and the head secretary were drunk 'day and night'. Their incompetence had not kept the administrative and judicial council members from 'conjointly announcing' a lower vineyard and hay tithe rate than in previous years, just 'to further their esteem and popularity' among the people.

Vidin's administrative council noted that Mustafa 'Ali Beğ concluded this fourth section of his response by claiming that Nureddin Ağa had attempted to abuse his powers as a member of the council. Someone allegedly had reported to the district head that Nureddin Ağa wished to build a granary on his farm for a fraction of the normal cost by 'forcing the peasants' in the local village to provide free labour. Subsequently, Nureddin Ağa asked for a policeman to be sent to this village to facilitate the construction. The district head refused to grant permission, explaining that such business could be done only by mutual consent. Besides, he added, this request did not comply with the member's former appeal to ban policemen from visiting these villages (with which Nureddin Ağa had *selem* money-lending contracts) to collect taxes.

In the fifth section of his response, Mustafa 'Ali Beğ reportedly focused on Matyaş Ağa, the investigator sent by Vidin's administrative council. Adopting a respectful tone, the district head noted that Matyaş Ağa had not discussed these issues with anyone but the elected members of the administrative council. Consequently, he had limited his report to the memorandum of the council – which was nothing but calumny. When Mustafa 'Ali Beğ suggested that Matyaş Ağa interrogate those who had made the bastinadoing allegations, the latter apparently refused, stating that 'interrogation [was] a judicial procedure'. Instead, he based his report solely on consultations (*müzakere*) with the members of the council. Furthermore, Matyaş Ağa allegedly dismissed the complainants' dissatisfaction with the *shar'i* judge as the result of their disagreement with the judge's decisions.

Curiously, the administrative council's report skips the sixth section without even mentioning it and moves on to the seventh (last) section. The district head ended his report on a positive note by adding, first, that due to the local administration's persistent efforts to improve the conditions of the Circassian refugees in Berkofça, they had been able to 'prevent evil from happening'.[6] Second, he noted that in order to expedite the collection of tithes and because of the continuation of bad weather that year, they had hired eleven additional officers and two scribes. Therefore, tithe collection for the year was completed in a timely manner.

The seven-section response from Mustafa 'Ali Beğ summarised in the administrative council's report caused the Vidin council to request an interrogation of the two men from Draganiçe who were allegedly beaten by the police. The interrogators from the judicial council met the villagers, Todor and Kirko, in the presence of Antimos Efendi (Antim I), the metropolitan of Vidin and the first Bulgarian exarch.[7] Apparently, when the peasants had come to Berkofça earlier in 1871 to borrow money from Halid Ağa's brother, Hacı Salih Ağa, the latter had advised them to visit Nureddin and Halid Ağas the following day and to state that they had been brutalised with cudgels and bastinado by the local policemen.

The police corroborated this version of events during their interrogation, and the Vidin administrative council summoned the *shar'i* judge, together with Halid and Nureddin Ağas, who refuted the claim that they had encouraged the peasants. When Todor and Kirko were brought face to face with the two Ağas, they reiterated their initial claim that the policemen had bastinadoed them. The council decided that the peasants were not credible and their case was sent to the council of appeals and crime in Vidin; the council also decided that Halid and Nureddin Ağas had been complicit with Halid Ağa's brother in manipulating the peasants.

After examining the interrogation of the council members from Berkofça, Vidin's administrative council acquitted Mustafa 'Ali Beğ of all charges but one: buying firewood from other villages at prices above the market price. The council also added that these accusations proved that the members of the Berkofça council could not handle their tasks professionally and efficiently because they allowed their personal disputes to impede their ability to accomplish their official duties. In submitting the case to the attention of the provincial government in Ruse, the council concluded that the firewood issue needed to be considered as a minor issue accentuated by this broader problem.

I am not concerned here with unravelling the truth behind this complicated case. Instead, my initial question is much simpler: why was the communication so complex? The confusing nature of the report partially reflects the impossibility of establishing the veracity of information transferred from one council in the district to the other in the county. Despite this problematic aspect, the report reveals several details regarding the ways different members of the community used the practices of the council to reach their goals. Learning more about the material resources and groups of local notables in Berkofça and Draganiçe is necessary to assess the case properly.

Land and Power in Berkofça

The modern-day town of Bergovitsa (Berkofça) and the village of Draganitse (Draganiçe) are parts of the district of Montana, not Vidin (USOG 1959: 20, 64). The village is approximately eleven kilometres (6.8 miles) north-west of the town. It appears that in the 1870s all the inhabitants of the village were Bulgarian. While the 1873 provincial yearbook (175) lists forty-four households and a population of 385 people, V. Teplov (1877: 197) notes that there were sixty-two households in the second half of 1870s. An 1897 survey (*Zemledelcheska statistika* 1902: 70–1) indicates that the village has approximately 312 hectares (771 acres) of farmland, 251 hectares (620 acres) of pastureland, very small tracts of vineyards, forested land and prairies, and no orchards. The survey reports a total of 173 proprietors in the village: seventy-nine actual inhabitants and ninety-four residents of other villages. The latter group's possessions were mostly small plots, and only twenty-one of this group of proprietors owned farmland – although fifty-two of them owned vineyards.[8] The resident proprietors were fewer in number than the non-resident ones; however, they owned larger plots of land (on average 8.8 hectares [twenty-two acres]).

One particular resident proprietor attracts attention in this survey: the church. The church owned sixteen hectares (39.5 acres) of forested land, approximately 36 per cent of the total registered forested land. This seems to be an unusually large amount of forest land owned by a single proprietor in this region, which would have made the church an influential actor at the local level. In the entire district of Bergovitsa, only 197 proprietors (roughly 2 per cent of the total) owned more than fifteen hectares (thirty-seven acres) of land; however, this relatively small group held 4,970 separate plots of land. The church owned its sixteen hectares as a single plot, which is significantly larger than the average plot size for the forest land in the district (3.6 hectares). According to the same survey, in all of Vidin County ninety-nine churches were proprietors, but only fifteen owned more than fifteen hectares. The land owned by the church was sizeable.

Available data do not clarify whether the church in Draganiçe actually owned this forest in 1872, when the reports discussed above were written. That it did twenty-five years later means that either the proprietorship was established before the Ottoman administration in the region de facto dissolved in 1878, or that the church acquired the forested land after 1878. Assuming that these sixteen hectares of land were a valued resource in the 1870s, both scenarios imply that in the last quarter of the nineteenth century the church had a considerable amount of power, either emanating from an already established proprietorship, or displayed by the ability to obtain this land after 1878.

An examination of the parcellisation patterns in Draganiçe can reveal the value of sixteen hectares (39.5 acres) in this region. The 1897 survey notes that, in Draganiçe, there was a total of 193 hectares (477 acres) of forested land that was divided into 444 plots. Excluding the church's forested land, each parcel would have been on average around 0.4 hectares (*Zemledelcheska statistika* 1902: 70–1). The high rate of parcellisation in these forested lands might relate to the importance of raw silk production to the regional economy in the 1860s and early 1870s (Palairet 1997: 190). In the 1850s the spread of pébrine disease among silkworms 'devastated' French cocoon production and forced 'French silk-raisers [to turn to] foreign, uninfected sources' (Quataert 1987: 286). This meant a short-lived boom in raw silk production in the region. By the end of the 1870s the same disease had devastated the Balkans (Palairet 1997: 185). According to Felix Kanitz (1882a: 284), who travelled in this region in the 1860s and early 1870s, raw silk production and leather tanning were important in the town of Berkofça. The presence of an economic sector that relied on mulberry trees could explain why small plots of forested land with mulberry trees would be economically attractive in this town and its surrounding villages.

Although it is not possible to estimate the density of mulberry trees in the forested lands of the village of Draganiçe in the early 1870s, the presence of a high rate of parcellisation in the 1890s implies that even a small amount of forested land had the potential to yield a decent income for the possessor.[9] The 174 resident and non-resident proprietors of Draganiçe owned 444 plots of forested land. Of the ninety-four non-residents, only nine owned more than five plots of land (of any kind), none owned more than fifteen plots and seventy-three of them owned farmland and/or vineyards (*Zemledelcheska statistika* 1902: 70, 589, 708). It appears to be the case that ownership of forested lands was more appealing to the residents of the village than to non-residents. In this context, the ability of the church to hold a large single parcel of forested land would be related to the political power of the local ecclesiastical organisation.

The metropolitan in Berkofça, Dorotheus Efendi – or 'Greek Dorotheij', as Felix Kanitz (1882a: 285) refers to him – replaced Metropolitan Joachim in 1860, when the latter left the town. (Kanitz refers to some tensions between Metropolitan Joachim and townspeople without giving any specific information.) Dorotheus Efendi remained in office until 1873. His long service may have been a factor that led novice Mustafa 'Ali Beğ, who began his career as a district head in 1871, to ally with him – if they actually did form an alliance. From the early decades of the nineteenth century until the Ottoman Empire's official recognition of the Bulgarian Exarchate in 1872, Greek bishops' relations with the Bulgarian-speaking community were strained (Faroqhi and Adanır 2002: 29; Glenny 2000: 114–15; Hupchick 2002: 242–6; Jelavich 1983: 56–7; Stavrianos 2000: 366–75). The alleged 'alliance' between the metropolitan and the district head therefore may have been no more than a politically expedient fabrication by a group of discontented local notables. Felix Kanitz (1882a: 287) notes that this 'reform-friendly' district head (that is, supporter of then-contemporary reforms, which Kanitz considered necessary to modernise the empire) was so preoccupied with local affairs that he complained of not having time to attend to matters in the surrounding villages.

According to the report of Vidin's administrative council summarised above, Halid and Nureddin Ağas were on the opposite side of this 'alliance'. The first two volumes of provincial yearbooks (*Salname Tuna* 1868–77, 1:59, 2:84) list Nureddin Ağa as a Berkofça municipal council member. While he is listed as an administrative council member in the fourth volume (1871: 59), his name is not included in the yearbook for the following year. Instead, Halid Ağa is the only Muslim administrative council member in the fifth and sixth volumes (*Salname Tuna*, 5:60, 6:61). Interestingly, in these two volumes (the only two years for which Mustafa 'Ali is listed as the district head), there are only two administrative council members: Halid Ağa and Petra Ağa.[10] According to the yearbooks, Nureddin and Halid Ağas served in councils for relatively brief periods and never simultaneously. The report, however, notes otherwise; they served and worked against the district head together.

Ottoman Governmentality

The majority of the accusations in the report asserted the inability of the other parties to understand and perform the tasks expected of them as members of the nineteenth-century judicio-administrative sphere: the initial accusation against Mustafa 'Ali Beğ was negligence in responding to the police brutality towards the villagers – described as 'abominable conduct, almost like torture'. The second accusation emphasised his inability, as an inexperienced officer, to handle administrative affairs properly, particularly in light of the other council members' superior knowledge of the applicable rules and regulations. It was the other members, the experts in provincial administration, who gave him 'well-intentioned reminders; and when necessary . . . referred [him] to the regulations and details of legal articles'.

The council members' language implies their familiarity with the governing practices of the empire. Their expertise rendered the members superior to others in administering a society that was located outside the sphere in which the members operated. As the summary of the case reveals, however, these people were hardly apart from the local society. In fact, it was their entanglement with that society that brought them to these positions of authority. As attested by their populist policies of lowering the tithe on certain products, these members cared about their legitimacy in the eyes of the 'society' to which they belonged. The modern Ottoman provincial government, by design and in practice, could not dissolve the connections between the members of its organisations and the populations they governed.

Those who were involved with the judicio-administrative sphere in the modern Ottoman state were often members of the local populace. Here, I would like to return to Anthony Giddens's discussion of the 'enlargement of the sphere of the political'. What makes the modern state possible is not necessarily its ability to separate itself from society; more significant is the belief held by the members of the society en masse (including the members of the judicio-administrative sphere) that there is a separate 'sphere of the political' that organises the ways in which 'the state' relates to 'society'. According to Giddens (1985: 179), this belief is inseparable from 'textually mediated organisation' (the 'regulations and details of legal articles' that Mustafa 'Ali Beğ was directed to by the elected members who were supposedly 'illiterate') and from the 'intertextuality of exchange of opinions and observations'. In all the accusations mentioned above, textually mediated organisation's validity or necessity was never questioned. In other words, the actual separation of society from the state is not as necessary as the discourse of a modern state (disseminated through the practices of agents in the sphere of the political).[11]

These intertextual exchanges of opinions and observations, I would argue, constituted a domain for the politics of local administration. The agents involved in this process (including the peasants who claimed that they were bastinadoed) had the power to use such exchanges and practices to attain their particular goals so long as they used the specific language of the state. In this context, knowing the language and procedures of these intertextual exchanges becomes essential, and the inability to read and write, drunkenness 'day and night', and unfamiliarity with the textually mediated organisation of the modern state become factors detrimental to the procedures of local administration.

Such sets of exchanges and practices constituted the building blocks of an Ottoman governmentality that, as a 'complex form of power', targeted the population and was not simply confined to the government. Because the target of this power was the population, its politics became 'biopolitics' conducted in a complex web of education, surveys and taxation, among many other ways.[12] Imposing on the population the idea that they, as subjects of an empire, needed to be taxed and surveyed was a technology of this power. A petition from the villagers complaining about abuse of power in tax collection became another part of Ottoman governmentality, as well. This is because the peasants, as agents themselves, got involved in a 'dialectic of control' (Giddens 1985: 10–11) with the Ottoman government by intertextually referring to the nature of Ottoman governmentality. Thus, the case of bastinadoing was vehemently criticised as 'abominable conduct'.[13]

Once allegations of such an odious crime had been made, an investigation was inevitable. Certainly, there was a set procedure for such an investigation, which was itself an aspect of the 'biopolitics' of Ottoman governmentality. Interestingly, each party in this debate accused the other of trying to prevent such an investigation. On the one hand, Halid Ağa claimed that when he asked 'in an appropriate way' to send the second lieutenant of the police forces to investigate the matter, he was threatened; on the other, Mustafa 'Ali Beğ claimed that Halid Ağa had insisted on not sending the second lieutenant. Also, in his seven-section report, the district head accused the elected members Halid and Nureddin Ağas of contempt for the policemen and hatred of the metropolitan. Accusations such as these implicated the other(s) by portraying them as behaving improperly or being unqualified, and as impeding the proper functioning of the system. Foucault, in concluding his seminar in 1980, draws attention to the relationship between obedience, examination and confession: 'the verbal manifestation of the truth that hides in the depths of oneself appears as an indispensable component of the government of men by each other' (Foucault 1997b: 84).

It is not coincidental that all the elements of this 'ensemble' constituted the responsibilities of the individuals involved in this case. The allegations made by the involved parties focused on the first two elements while the county administrative council in Vidin demanded the third element, namely, an exhaustive confession. This proved difficult to achieve, hence the complexity of the case. Interestingly, the first attempt, the dispatch of Matyaş Ağa, resulted in failure as this long-time member of the judicio-administrative sphere failed to gather adequate information on the case.[14] The administrative council therefore felt the need to interrogate people from Draganiçe and Berkofça by summoning them to Vidin. Regardless, the involvement of Matyaş Ağa renders the case all the more revealing with regard to the politics of local administration.

Matyaş Ağa's assignment to the 'investigation of the matter' brings together two layers of the administrative structure described in Chapter 3: the county and the district. However, there is only limited information about what this member of a county council did in the district. The county administrative council's report notes only that he went there and brought back a memorandum from the district council which confirmed the accusations of the council members in Berkofça against the district head. Mustafa 'Ali Beğ, however, notes in the fifth section of the lengthy response that Matyaş Ağa had limited his investigation to the elected members of the administrative council. Furthermore, when Mustafa 'Ali Beğ suggested carrying out some interrogations, this elected member of Vidin's judicial council declined, referring to the procedure as a 'judicial procedure'.

Someone coming from the county with the charge to investigate the matter should not have avoided interrogation, which, in this case, was clearly limiting his investigation. Being a member of the judicial body at the county, Matyaş Ağa was obviously familiar with the interrogation procedure. What is more puzzling, perhaps, is the silence in the Vidin administrative council's report to the provincial capital about Matyaş Ağa's reluctance in investigating the matter.

The need to interrogate all parties involved in these serious allegations of odious crimes is obvious. A little less than a year earlier Matyaş Ağa had been among the members of the council of appeals and crime who had interrogated several people in another scandalous case. That case (No. 452, in NBKM, VD 107/16) involved an appraiser in the customs office in Vidin who stole the seal of another customs clerk, while the latter was intoxicated and unconscious at a gathering, in order to forge some documents. To resolve the case, Vidin's judicial council summoned several individuals from different locations.

Such interrogations were common procedures. Indeed, Vidin's administrative council eventually did conduct interrogations in Mustafa 'Ali Beğ's case. Matyaş Ağa must have had other reasons that kept him from interrogating all parties despite the district head's request – reasons that might have related to the fact that in this instance he was investigating a case that involved other elected council members. I cannot claim that his political interests as a local notable serving in the judicio-administrative sphere of Vidin would have connected him directly to the members of the council in Berkofça. Nevertheless, it is clear that he did not follow the usual procedure and failed in his juridical role. Certain issues brought up by Eric Paras (2006: 104–5) in his discussion of human subjectivity might help put Matyaş Ağa's behaviour in context:

> In relation to juridical will, interest . . . constituted an irreconcilable element. *Homo economicus* and *homo juridicus* represented distinct forms of political subjectivity; that is to say, they posed wholly different questions to the power that would govern them. [T]he subject of interest did not respect contracts because they were contracts; he respected them because it was in his interest to do so.

The agents within Ottoman governmentality – including tax paying subjects, the bureaucrats and the police – *referred to* their contractual obligations so long as doing so was in their interest. At the local level, an agent's economic interests must have been relatively obvious to those with whom he interacted (as opposed to a historian who attempts to understand them more than a century later). Perhaps Mustafa 'Ali Beğ or the elected council members understood Matyaş Ağa's intentions very well (or vice versa). In this context, the district head's plea to Matyaş Ağa to interrogate others in order to find out the truth also served as a reminder to Matyaş Ağa that he was supposed to be a *homo juridicus*. Matyaş Ağa was also referring to his role when he reminded that an interrogation was a 'judicial procedure' and thus would not be appropriate.

While Matyaş Ağa reminded the district head of the distinction between administrative and judicial procedures, he appears not to have challenged the conflation of administrative and judicial councils in the memorandum that he submitted. Recall that he returned from Berkofça with a memorandum of the 'council of administration and litigation', which could not have existed, for at the district level, there were separate councils for administrative and judicial issues. This did not prevent the members of the council from working together, not only to draft the memorandum, but also apparently to insist on a tax cut.[15] None of the members refuted the structural framework introduced by the provincial regulation (separate judicial and administrative councils) or their official duties; however, they worked around them to serve their own interests.

One would expect Vidin's administrative council at least to have raised questions about Matyaş Ağa's allegedly unsatisfactory methods of investigation. After all, the council had sent him to the district and, based on his report, decided to accuse Mustafa 'Ali Beğ. Unsatisfied with this, Vidin's administrative council ordered interrogation of almost everyone mentioned in Mustafa 'Ali Beğ's response except for Matyaş Ağa. While the council obviously took Mustafa 'Ali Beğ's lengthy answer seriously, it is not clear why the council did not do anything about Matyaş Ağa. Nor is it clear why one section was omitted from the administrative council's summary of 'Ali Beğ's response.

Mustafa 'Ali Beğ responded to all the allegations in the first four sections. He then used the fifth section to outline problems in Matyaş Ağa's investigation and the seventh to reflect on how some of the general problems in the district had been resolved during his term. Based on the flow of the text, the omitted sixth section most likely focused either on Matyaş Ağa's investigation techniques, or on the nature of the resolved problems discussed in the seventh section. In either case, Vidin's administrative council seems to have chosen not to reveal certain aspects of the case in its report to the province.

The decision to reveal or conceal information in these reports was linked to the politics of local administration. All the agents involved in this complicated case used the institutionalised practices of Ottoman governance. They did not do so merely out of respect for the institutions or fear of the state. They used these practices because it was in their interest to do so. That is why what they included in – or omitted from – these reports and the ways they did so reveal certain aspects of the politics of local administration. Just as the members of the judico-administrative sphere in the Berkofça district chose to exclude certain events from their memorandum, so the administrative council in Vidin chose to remain quiet about Matyaş Ağa's inadequate investigation. The omissions are explained by the prominence of the elected members on Vidin's administrative council and the local political dynamics within that council.

Utilising Ottoman Governance

So far, I have focused on Ottoman governmental practices. These practices are a result of institutions that constituted the modern Ottoman state.[16] Governmentality is more of an aspect of a 'conjuncture' – in the Braudellian sense – that coincides with the development of a liberal-capitalist social formation.[17] Textually mediated information, including the reports of the councils and the petitions of the peasants, was a part of Ottoman governmentality; it was *one* of the means that people used to protect their interests either as part of the local judicio-administrative sphere or as part of the governed population. Such practices were constitutive of the Ottoman modern state, and provide insight into the hegemonic politics of local administration.

Submitting petitions through the offices of the local judicio-administrative sphere was one of the means the governed populations use governmentality to protect their interests. It is important to note that scribes of the council edited these petitions when incorporating them into the registers of the councils. The administrative council forwarded the original petitions that came to the council together with their reports. While the copy registers I utilised do not include these petitions, the summaries provide a glimpse of the governed populations' language.

Consider the following case regarding the pasturelands outside Vidin's fortress. In 1871 the Vidin administrative council responded (Case No. 269 in NBKM, VD 107/16) to a request from the provincial capital (Ruse) for clarification regarding a pasture's official status. Town inhabitants referred to the pasture as 'Müşriye' and used it for grazing their animals and for occasional strolls. The capital's request, which had arrived in Vidin two years before, in 1869, was a follow-up to the inhabitants' petition forwarded by the administrative council in 1868.

This initial petition had apparently asked that the imperial forces relinquish this pasture, which they had appropriated from Vidin's inhabitants 'a while before'. This petition had been forwarded by Ruse to the Council of State (Şura-yı Devlet), which asked for further investigation of the matter (BOA, ŞD 2080/27 and 2081/2). After receiving this request, the council did not respond for two years, and finally sent this report in 1871.

The report does not provide any evidence regarding the status of the land in question but states that the issue was investigated by a 'great multitude of experts' from different villages who 'had no personal interest whatsoever' in the matter. A mention of prior correspondence on the issue from the previous three years is followed by a brief history of the Müşriye pasture based on the findings of the 'experts' mentioned.

Apparently, the land was used solely by the inhabitants until 1834, when a new governor, Ağa Hüseyin Paşa, arrived in the town with abundant horses and livestock.[18] To assist the governor, some of the town's 'landowners' encouraged him temporarily to use other, possibly more distant, pastures. Eventually, Ağa Hüseyin Paşa returned to using Müşriye to graze his animals. The governor and his successors, however, limited their use of this pasture and took turns with Vidin's townsfolk.

This symbiosis persisted until the eve of the Crimean War. In 1853 the imperial forces appropriated Müşriye, calling it a 'state pasture'. From then on, it appears, the pasture was a continual source of tension. The first complaint mentioned in this report, from 1868, triggered a response a year later from the Council of State asking for 'evidence' that Müşriye was a communal pasture. The report failed to provide any proof and related the lack of evidence to a regional practice of not issuing title deeds for pastures, adding further that 'from days of old' (*min el-kadim*) this land had been regarded as a pasture 'and had been reckoned so for centuries'. In this case evidence, it seems, was irrelevant in the face of traditional practice verified by experts.

Preference for 'custom' over evidence, however, appears to have been in conformity with the law, since the Land Code of 1858 determined use rights over pastures based on established practices 'from days of old' rather than title deeds. Article 97 of the law, for example, notes that 'in a pasture that has belonged to a village *from the days of old*, only the animals of that particular village can be pastured, and inhabitants of another village cannot lead their animals to that pasture'. Article 98 established that the boundaries of a pasture, determined 'from days of old', could not be altered later (Karakoç 1924: 231–2). The inhabitants were in fact within their legal rights when they made what appears to have been a claim without evidence.

The 1871 report by Vidin's administrative council on this matter was not sufficient to resolve the issue. A year later, on 24 June 1872, the same council wrote another report (Case No. 423 in NBKM, VD 107/16), which, for the most part, repeated the 1871 report verbatim. The new report responded to the provincial capital's repeated request for further investigation, which the council had apparently received only nine days prior to its response. After confirming receipt of the request from Ruse, the council copied the results of the earlier investigation from its 1871 response and briefly noted that its new investigation had yielded the same results.

Sixteen days later the provincial administrative council in Ruse forwarded this response to the Council of State. This time, however, the Council of State responded in a different manner. In a decree sent in the autumn of 1872, the Council of State asked the governor of the Danube Province and the Second Army field marshal to end the occupation (BOA, ŞD 2081/2). Although Vidin's administrative council did not provide any new information on the matter, the Council of State took a different course of action. The reason for this apparent inconsistency is not obvious in the council's register. The similarity of the two reports conceals what might have happened between 29 May 1871, when Vidin's administrative council sent the first report, and 24 June 1872, when the same council wrote a very similar second report.

What is not mentioned in the second report is that some Vidiners who used this particular pasture wrote a petition (BOA, ŞD 2080/27) to the Council of State before the council demanded further investigation. This petition, written in May 1872, did not go through the administrative council in Vidin, although this does not necessarily mean that the administrative council was unaware of it. In it, the inhabitants explained the matter in different terms. They claimed that the governor's and the residents' joint use of Müşriye did not end in 1853. For 'five to ten years' following the death of governor Ağa Hüseyin Paşa (d. 1849), the pasture was left to the Vidiners, who used it until 'four years prior' to the petition, when the armed forces' intervention began.

'For the last four years', the residents complained, the soldiers had prevented the Vidiners from entering Müşriye from the beginning of the hay season until the hay was harvested and sent directly to the armed forces. According to the petitioners, this was 'absolutely disrespectful of the pasture status' of the land. The locals added that they had taken their case to the local government, which reported on the matter to the imperial offices in Istanbul. 'For unknown reasons', however, the soldiers were not prevented from impeding the inhabitants. This year, prior to their intervention, the soldiers had allegedly ousted the security guards that the townspeople had hired for the pasture.

There are many possible reasons why this problem emerged 'four years ago', in 1868. Available information leads to no definitive conclusion. According to the provincial yearbooks, the commander of the battalion in Vidin changed almost every other year between 1868 and 1877. As the first four lines of both sections of Table 3.3 (in Chapter 3) indicate, the composition of Vidin's administrative and judiciary councils was rather stable between 1868 and 1871. The local membership changed in the fifth year: while all the members retained their posts for the first three years recorded in the provincial yearbooks, none of them were listed in the fifth volume. A particular member of these councils, or a number of them, might have been behind this change in policy toward the pasture.

Regardless of who caused the change in policy regarding the use rights over Müşriye, the slight difference between the report of the council and the earlier petition – regarding the date of policy shift – gives the impression that Vidin's administrative council was unaware of the petition, and hints at the contrasting political agendas of the administrative council members and the petitioners. While the council members' report explains the matter as the consequence of an upsurge in the number of armed forces on the eve of a war, the petitioners distance themselves from such an explanation. They report the incident as completely independent from the war – an event that is hardly negligible but that is seemingly exogenous to local politics. Based on the petition, the change in practice seems to relate primarily to local politics.

The soldiers' actions were not without consequence. Several impoverished residents apparently relied on what they could earn from the milk cattle that they had been grazing in this particular pasture. The soldiers' behaviour, the petitioners explained, 'not only inevitably led to different sorts of cruel acts, but [was] also in complete contradiction to the article on pastures of the [1858] Land Code'. The petitioners added that 'in this age consecrated to the justice of His Imperial Majesty the Sultan', such actions were clearly unacceptable. The inhabitants employed a language that not only reminded the government of its duties but did so in the context of the rule of law. They were aware and making use of the necessary regulations to prove their case.

Towards the end of their petition, the residents revealed another bit of information not mentioned in the administrative council's report. Apparently, the local administration's recent confiscation of some 'arable land' (*mezra'a*) that had been 'reserved for the inhabitants since the days of old' further worsened the residents' conditions. This particular 'pasture' (*mer'a*) within the town of Vidin's boundaries, known as Yukarı Ova, was 'sold [to pay] for the steamers of the river administration'. Because of this, the residents had been 'in desperate need of pastureland (*mer'a*), and the pastureland had become very scant'. The interchangeable use of 'arable land' (*mezra'a*) and 'pastureland' (*mer'a*) is confusing. The legal status of Yukarı Ova is obscured in the petition; however, the implications of its appropriation are clear. The residents who used Müşriye argued that appropriation of Yukarı Ova had harmed them, albeit indirectly.

This particular case regarding Yukarı Ova is not mentioned in the administrative council's reports on the Müşriye pastureland. Nevertheless, there are two separate reports (Case Nos 200 and 752 in NBKM, VD 107/16) on Yukarı Ova in the administrative council's register for May and October 1871. According to the first report, certain 'Muslim and

Christian' inhabitants of the town had protested the appropriation (for sale) of Yukarı Ova three years before, claiming that they had farmed the land 'for more than thirty or forty years'. The sale was based on an investigation by an official sent from Ruse, who discovered that 'somehow, the land was occupied unlawfully without title deeds'. Therefore, this arable land was taken back from its occupants and some part of it was sold through auction while the official from Ruse was still in Vidin.

A December 1872 report by Ahmed Hamdi Paşa, governor of the Danube Province, to the Council of State noted (BOA, ŞD 2081/29) that the land initially sold in 1868 totalled 3,000 *dönüm*s (696.32 acres). A significantly larger parcel of 8,000 *dönüm*s (1836.84 acres) of land was appropriated but not sold immediately. This larger part of Yukarı Ova was eventually surveyed and sold to the residents of the town. While the October 1871 report by Vidin's administrative council concerning this land recommended that the land be offered to the Vidiners for a price of twenty-five to thirty *guruş* per *dönüm*, the provincial governor's report noted that this land had already been sold to the very same villagers who had been demanding a price of fifteen *guruş* per *dönüm*. There appear to have been negotiations that lasted for over a year. The residents had refused to buy the land for the price that the administrative council initially suggested; consequently, the provincial administration and the Council of State agreed on fifteen *guruş* per *dönüm* instead of letting the land remain idle (BOA, ŞD 2081/29).

In addition to the negotiation process, another interesting detail of the Yukarı Ova case concerns the signatories to the letter from among the residents who purchased the land. The letter is stamped with the purchasers' seals, several of which can also be found in a petition that some Vidiners, including village headmen and some neighbourhood imams, had sent regarding the Müşriye pasture. In this petition, Yukarı Ova is again defined as 'pastureland'; in the purchase agreement submitted to Vidin's administrative council, in contrast, it is defined as 'land' (*arazi*) and 'arable land' (*mezra'a*). It is difficult to believe that the choice of different words to define Yukarı Ova's status was accidental, particularly in view of the fact that the legal status of arable land differed from that of pastures. Whereas ownership of arable land (idle or harvested) had to be proven by title deeds, that of pastureland was established based on customary use of the land by the residents. Therefore, following the Land Code of 1858, the Ottoman government was able to collect money through the sale of arable state lands. At the same time, peasants who had been using state lands for extended periods could maintain their use rights once they proved that the land they had been using was pastureland. As argued in Chapter 2, control over the means of production (and land in particular) becomes very significant in the legitimation crisis of the traditional social order and the formation of the modern/capitalist one.

Yukarı Ova is only one of the many similar land dispute cases reported in this register. Several reports by Vidin's administrative council point to the prevalence of this type of tension in the county. In the spring of 1871, the administrative council responded (Case No. 77 in NBKM, VD 107/16) to an imperial order it received from the provincial capital the previous year demanding that districts report on the winter and summer pasturelands' locations and sizes and indicate what proportion was owned by deed holders. The Ottoman government was concerned about measuring the land it could potentially claim. As in the case of Yukarı Ova, the money collected from such sales could be used to meet the expenses of the local governments.

In a similar case (Case No. 308 in NBKM, VD 107/16), the council focused on approximately twenty-seven acres of land that had been 'idle for several years' on Kerkenez Island in the Danube. In response to another 1870 imperial order, the council reported that all but four acres of the land in question was indeed arable. Vidin's administrative council offered these four acres (eighteen *dönüm*s) to the 'owners' of the land for a price determined by 'those who are knowledgeable': twnety-five *guruş* per *dönüm*. 'The owners of the land', the report concluded, 'considered it appropriate to assume [the ownership of the arable land] at the mentioned price.' For the remaining twenty-three acres, defined as 'just meadowland', they agreed to pay 5 per cent of the estimated value to cover the 'expenses' of registration.

The wording of the report suggests that these 'idle' lands were somehow 'owned' by the inhabitants who, for some reason, agreed to 'buy' them back for a price determined by the experts.[19] That the inhabitants agreed to pay twenty-five *guruş* per *dönüm* – almost 70 per cent higher than what the Vidiners had agreed to pay at Yukarı Ova – for lands they were 'not using' shows that they were interested in keeping these lands for themselves. Perhaps this is why they are referred to as 'owners' in the report.

The difference in what residents agreed to pay for land in these places might have been related to differences in the quality of land. Regardless, in both cases the reports clearly note that the exchange involved a group of assessors who measured, evaluated and monitored the sale of lands. In the case of Yukarı Ova, the administration formed a special commission to measure the land and to keep a register of the individuals who bought the land, the amounts they purchased and how much they paid. Most likely this was the case for Kerkenez Island, as well. The register prepared by the experts' commission in Yukarı Ova was among the files that were sent to the Council of State. Among the members of the commission were Zayko Ağa and Marin Ağa, two prominent members of Vidin's judicio-administrative sphere. The former was not a member of the administrative council or the council of appeals and crime in that particular year, but that did not prevent him from becoming involved as an expert in a significant case like this.

The involvement of local notables in a case like this makes it difficult to frame these disputes simply in terms of 'state vs society'. The lines of alliance within the judicio-administrative sphere were rather fluid. It is difficult (and perhaps unnecessary) to see where 'the state' ends and 'society' begins. What is clear, however, is that such governmental practices served as negotiation domains among agents within this sphere. Marin and Zayko Ağas served on these commissions because they were prominent actors. Their position served perhaps as an advantage to groups who were on good terms with them at the moment and contributed to their ongoing prominence in the judicio-administrative sphere. Differences in the language and the logic of the reports on Yukarı Ova and Kerkenez hint at different compositions of power among the agents involved, including the residents, the local government and the assessment commissions. Ottoman governmentality, with its target the Ottoman population, served as a 'surface of contact on which the way of conducting individuals and the way that they conduct themselves [were] intertwined'.[20]

Staying Out: Challenging Ottoman Governmentality

It is difficult to ascertain if all agents within the society were willing participants in this 'surface of contact'. Here, I would like to focus on Foucault's (1980: 141–2) emphasis on the omnipresence of power: 'One is never "outside" [the power]', he noted in an interview. This key aspect of power is essential for a proper understanding governmentality, which he defines as a form of power. Foucault elaborates further on this general statement by adding six qualifications:

1. Power, occupies the same space with the social structuration; no segment of the society has some form of primal liberty.
2. Other relations like that of production, or sexuality are interwoven with power relations. They condition and at the same time they are conditioned with power relations.
3. Power, and other associated relations, take many forms, including, but not limited to punishment.

4. The interconnections of power and other relations discursively define general conditions of domination, a somewhat coherent, global strategic form (governmentality). However, the social structuration is not divided into two distinct groups ('the dominated' and 'the dominators'); rather, diverse agents utilise 'dispersed, heteromorphous, localised procedures of power' for their various strategies – all discursively conditioning/ conditioned by governmentality.
5. Because of this discursive formation and the openness of power to all, power relations are useful not only because they serve the dominant economic interests (economic determinism), but because agents use them for various strategies of domination and resistance.
6. Power relations, as utilised in diverse strategies of domination are always accompanied by multiple forms of resistance, which can be incorporated to strategies.

This particular nature of power shapes how different agents' strategies become visible in the Vidin administrative council's reports. In the land disputes discussed, registration through commissions and surveys constituted an essential procedure in which administrators, local notables and other inhabitants participated. In a similar way, local governance served as a domain in which different groups could articulate different responses. Two separate cases from the administrative council's register illustrate how this happened. The first case is from the 'Adliye District. According to a report (Case No. 544 in NBKM, VD 107/16) from the summer of 1871, the district head imprisoned several Tatar refugees and their animals. Vidin's administrative council sent Matyaş Ağa, the same examining clerk at the council of appeals and crime who investigated the cases against Berkofça district head, to investigate the reasons for his actions.

Apparently, the 'Adliye district head official ordered the arrests to punish the Tatars who had refused to lend their horses for wheat-tithe collection from another refugee group, the Circassians.[21] (I discuss the refugee settlements further in the next chapter.) The tithe, collected in kind, needed to be ground before it could be sold. The Tatars reportedly had enough beasts but refused to comply with the head official's request. Matyaş Ağa described the town as composed of three neighbourhoods, each keeping their threshed grain in different places. 'Because of this', he reported, 'each neighbourhood should be considered a [separate] village' and it was 'an old principle and ancient tradition' that each neighbourhood took care of grinding its own wheat tithe.

Matyaş Ağa deemed the district head's high-handed attitude as 'quite inappropriate' and noted that it reflected his unwillingness to follow the precepts of the administration in Vidin County. Thanks to his punitive and aggressive attitude, the district head was making ordinary matters unnecessarily difficult. In closing its report on the matter, Vidin's administrative council noted that interrogations were being carried out in the district to determine who might have provoked the alleged crimes committed by some Circassians against a notable from the Circassian community, Hacı Mirza Beğ. Perhaps this obscure allegation was part of Matyaş Ağa's attempt to underscore the district head's incompetence, as it hints at the district head's probable involvement and seems to be included in support of Matyaş Ağa's account, which resembled the charges he levelled against Berkofça's district head.

There is no reason to consider Matyaş Ağa's or the Vidin administrative council's report as accurate accounts of events in 'Adliye. In fact, some details do not match other sources: a mid-1870s survey of the town (NBKM, VD 96/44) identifies eight neighbourhoods, not three (one Tatar, one Circassian and six Christian). However, the report is an interesting example of how opposition to a particular fiscal organisational logic (represented by the head official's actions) could come from within the judicio-administrative sphere (represented by Matyaş Ağa and the administrative council). The head official's alleged actions imply that he valued effective tax collection over norms associated with the 'traditional' organisation of society along ethnic lines and considered himself entitled to use the available resources of the community to accomplish tax collection.[22] However, neither the refugees nor Matyaş Ağa approved of this particular vision of proper government.

The way this report problematises the dispute is a good example of how 'specific problems of life and population were raised within a technology of government' (Foucault 1997a: 79). This snapshot of the negotiation process (focusing on the use of economic resources such as beasts of burden) exemplifies how different agents engaged with each other on issues of governing practices. The county administrative council, only one of the spaces in which such negotiations took place, was part of the judicio-administrative sphere in Vidin. That Matyaş Ağa and the district head official were closely associated with the administrative complex at the centre of this sphere does not imply that they should have adhered to the same governing principles.

The last case that I would like to analyse is related to lands belonging to a monastery in Roman, a village in the İvraca (Vratsa) District. According to a June 1871 report (Case No. 380 in NBKM, VD 107/16), the assistant administrator of the monastery, Father Yovanço, requested (for a second time) that the council prevent the village's inhabitants from taking illegal possession of forested, arable and pasturelands that the monastery owned by title deed. After Father Yovanço's first request, the council had reportedly inquired into the status of the lands with the head of the office of land registry (*defter-i hakani*) in the provincial capital. The official from Ruse, Hacı Tahsin Efendi, had explained that the land in question belonged not to the monastery but personally to Father Bartina, the former administrator of the monastery. Hacı Tahsin Efendi knew this because of an earlier adjudication between Father Bartina and the villagers, which had resulted in a decree banning the villagers from interfering with the land.

Apparently, following Father Yovanço's first petition, the local administrators remeasured the disputed property and found it to be larger than previously estimated. Although evidence and Tahsin Efendi's report invalidated the peasants' claims, Father Yovanço agreed to offer some of the disputed land to the peasants. The peasants, however, refused this and demanded all the land. Vidin's administrative council then recommended that the issue be resolved through peaceful negotiations at the local level. This attempt proved useless, as the peasants insisted that the land was theirs and that they would not relinquish 'even the smallest bit of it'. The peasants' insistence seems to have triggered Father Yovanço's second petition, which accompanied the council's report to Ruse in 1871. In concluding their report, the members of Vidin's administrative council added that they did not see the peasants as having any evident rights over the land in question.

Another report (Case No. 182 in NBKM, VD 107/16), written in the spring of 1872, reveals that the issue remained unresolved for almost another year, and that the attitudes of the parties involved only worsened. Apparently, the peasants sent a petition directly to the provincial administration, requesting the release of four villagers imprisoned as a result of the dispute and demanding Vidin's administrative council to reconsider their pleas. The administration in Ruse forwarded this petition to Vidin and asked for an explanation. In response to the request from Ruse, Vidin's administrative council explained the reasons behind the imprisonment of the four villagers.

Reportedly, by reassessing the land, the district council had narrowed the focus of the dispute to an approximately thirty-five-acre arable plot that was not used for agricultural production. The district council formed a commission to assess the value of the plot and Vidin's land registrar was dispatched to the village to offer the plot first to the monastery administrator, and – if he declined – then to other buyers willing to pay the determined price. Father Yovanço agreed to pay the price, but the peasants insisted they would not vacate the land. When Father Yovanço, accompanied by several farmers, went to till the land under the protection of police, the peasants attacked, severely injuring two people. The priest and the police fled for their lives and reported the incident. Soon afterward the police arrested four villagers for the attack.

Even after their arrest, however, the culprits remained 'resolute on their claims'. Nothing in this second report (or in any other report in the register) indicates who won this dispute. According to the 1897 survey of the region (*Zemledelcheska statistika* 1902: 48–9), the monastery owned 121 acres (forty-nine hectares) of forested, pasture and arable land (combined) in the village. The amount of land 'owned' by the monastery, according to both the 1871 and 1872 reports, totalled 153 acres (sixty-two hectares). The difference between the figures (thirty-two acres) is roughly equal to the amount claimed by the peasants (thirty-five acres), but it is not possible to reach a decisive conclusion regarding how this dispute was resolved.

What is interesting about this case is the way Vidin's administrative council chose to report the peasants' resistance. In these reports, Roman's peasants are not depicted as claiming the pasture on the basis of ancient rights. Instead, they are presented as defiant, stubborn and violent. They appear to be claiming ownership of land without any valid documentation, a position deemed 'unacceptable' by the administrative council. When confronted with the rules of property, the peasants took a radical stance, 'rejecting' negotiation – according to the council. Their unsuccessful attempt to appeal to the provincial centre with a petition indicates that some among them may have chosen to act within the confines of Ottoman governance. However, their resistance – the structure and logic of which are not described in the reports of the council – indicates that certain members of their community chose to oppose the organisations and institutions of Ottoman governmentality. In writing their report – one of the primary practices of Ottoman governance – the administrative council labelled the peasants' opposition illegitimate and irrational. While the imprisoned refugees and their livestock in 'Adliye could challenge the practices of Ottoman governmentality, the peasants of Roman could not. This, I would argue, had to do with the particular political configuration at each place. While the refugees in 'Adliye could get the support of a significant part of the local judicio-administrative sphere against the wishes of the district head, the peasants of Roman did not have similar support against their church.

Conclusion

The reports of the administrative council examined in this chapter reflect the complex matrix of factors and the diverse interests of the parties involved in their formation.²³ Through its 'authorial language' (Bakhtin 1981: 271–2), the judicio-administrative councils organised the complex arguments of different groups into unitary reports. They reiterated the pleas of administrators, who wished to defend themselves against the accusations of council members, or townsfolk who wanted access to their pasturelands, or priests who wanted to keep peasants away from their lands. This was a political process. The council members, who had various connections to different political and economic networks in Vidin County, had to negotiate among themselves in order to produce an official document describing the social and historical complexity of Vidin County with a single, authorial voice. By choosing to include and exclude certain details, council members formatted the local disputes into textually mediated representations of reality. Other sources reveal information on the missing parts of the administrative council's reports and the political composition of power in the region. The glossed-over segments of Mustafa 'Ali Beğ's report regarding Matyaş Ağa's failure to conduct a proper investigation, for example, might concern Matyaş Ağa's relative prominence as a long-serving member of the judicio-administrative sphere of Vidin County. The same Matyaş Ağa described Berkofça's district head as insensitive. By failing to mention the reasons behind the resistance of the inhabitants of the village of Roman, Vidin's administrative council rendered their resistance insignificant. By using their vested authority in handling and reporting the local events – an essential practice of Ottoman governance – certain members of the administrative council were able to protect their own interests. The councils did not occupy a homogenous environment; on the contrary, members of the council were operating in a hegemonic environment that was reflected, to a certain extent, in the heteroglot nature of some of their reports. Thus, these reports mirror the environment in which they were created more than the reality they claim to represent.

The ambiguity of terminology in these reports – for example, the residents of Kerkenez 'buying' the land they 'owned', or confusion over the nature of pasture/arable land in Müşriye and Yukarı Ova – reflects the hegemonic nature of Ottoman governance. There is no 'massive and primal condition of domination' in which the homogeneous body of the modern state confronted rebellious groups resisting reforms that it was trying to introduce. Instead, different agents were able to use the 'surface of contact' that was Ottoman governmentality in devising their own strategies for a hegemonic environment at the local level.

It is essential to understand the complexity of the environment and the processes that generated these reports. Those involved in the

Nineteenth-century Local Governance in Ottoman Bulgaria

investigation and writing of the reports performed within the confines of a *homo juridicus* so long as it suited their interests. Those who were 'subjects' of these reports, or who wrote petitions that appeared outside of these councils' correspondence, chose either to adopt practices that were commensurate with the institutional repertoire of Ottoman governmentality (such as the peasants 'buying' the lands that they 'owned'), or to challenge that repertoire. Some of those who chose to challenge, as did the refugees in Berkofça, introduced new practices slightly at odds with the principles of Ottoman governance. Some fought longer, like the villagers in Roman, but were left out of the hegemonic power structures of the judicio-administrative sphere, as they were rendered mute in the official correspondence.

The writing of these reports and petitions (which informed the imperial centre about the provinces) constituted a part of the politics of local administration. As with the other procedures of governance, the writing of these documents contributed to the constitution of the Ottoman state through practices that involved various agents. Despite the wide range of these constitutive practices (from the purchase of firewood in Berkofça to the arrest of beasts of burden in 'Adliye), they all shared a common concern about establishing the limits of how much one should govern. Analysing how this 'single government of state officials and local elites' (Meeker 2002: 185) imposed limits on its practices reveals a certain core concern: a liberalist understanding of how the economy ought to function. In Chapter 6, I examine this core, which determined the contours of Ottoman governmentality, by focusing on the particular problematic of refugee settlement in this region in the second half of the nineteenth century.

Notes

1. Case No. 202, dated 2 May 1872 (23 S 1289), in NBKM, VD 107/16.
2. I discuss these communications in the same order in which the administrative council introduced them in their report: the two telegrams followed by a memo from an examining clerk, followed by an inquiry from Vidin and a lengthy response to that inquiry, and so on.
3. The Ottoman ban on the use of torture for interrogation, punishment or abuse of power began with the 1840 penal code just after the Gülhane imperial decree. While there was some ambiguity in the 1840 and 1851 penal codes, the 1858 penal code banned such practices in no uncertain terms (Kalkan 2017).
4. The metropolitan's name does not appear in the report's summary of the memorandum from Berkofça, but it does appear in the first six provincial yearbooks, published between 1868 and 1873, where Dorotheus Efendi is listed

following the names of the district head, the judge (*na'ib*), and the Muslim religious leader (mufti) at the top of the single page devoted to the district. That his name is listed as the metropolitan in the first six volumes of a total of ten suggests that he was a relatively stable figure in the district. (He might have been serving as metropolitan even prior to the publication of the first yearbook in 1868.) In contrast, the district head and the judge had changed four times between 1868 and 1873. Dorotheus Efendi's replacement is not named in the later four volumes (1874–77); in fact, the title 'metropolitan' disappears from the page devoted to Berkofça District – most likely a consequence of the reorganisation following the Bulgarian Exarchate's formation in 1872.

5. The defining principle of selem (*salam* in Arabic) money-lending contracts is prepayment by a purchaser for an object of sale to be delivered to the buyer on a predetermined future date. It allows a farmer to borrow money for sale of the coming season's produce at a certain risk (Latham 'Salam').
6. The official correspondence sent from the Danube Province to the imperial capital includes several cases accusing the Circassian refugees of animal theft. See for example, BOA, ŞD 2078/16, 2078/39, 2080/2, 2080/18 or A.MKT.ŞD. 11-66 (2 and 3). The concern regarding such thefts and their relation to this refugee community is obvious in these discussions. This is discussed further in the next chapter.
7. The Bulgarian national church was officially established following Sultan Abdulaziz's decree on 27 February 1870 as subordinate to the Patriarchate of Constantinople. Two years later, the Provisional Exarchic Council elected Antim I (Atanas Mihaylov Chalakov) as the first Bulgarian exarch. The sultan rejected another candidate, Ilarion of Lovech, before considering Antim I. Later that year, 'the Patriarchate of Constantinople, which was opposed to the establishment of a Bulgarian church, declared the Bulgarian Exarchate schismatic' (Detrez 1997: 74).
8. Eighty of the ninety-four owned fewer than two hectares (five acres), with an overall average of half that amount (*Zemledelcheska statistika* 1902: 312–13). One-third of all vineyards were owned by non-residents (*Zemledelcheska statistika* 1902: 706).
9. A recent unpublished study on biodiversity in the region (conducted by the Berkovitsa local branch of the Regional Environmental Center (REC) for Central and Eastern Europe) notes the abundance of mulberry trees. As part of a trans-boundary project, 'West Stara Planina', that covers the Balkan ranges in Bulgaria and Serbia, REC is trying to reintroduce silk production as a sustainable non-timber source of income for the inhabitants of the region. I would like to thank Ors Szilard Marczin, General Project Manager for the Environmental Policy Program at REC for Central and Eastern Europe, for sharing this study.
10. Petra Ağa is listed as a municipal council member in the fourth volume as the only non-Muslim council member in the fifth and sixth volumes, and as one of two non-Muslim members in the tenth volume.

11. As Florencia Mallon (1995: 6) notes: 'A discourse is a political as well as an intellectual process, because human struggles over power and meaning are intimately interconnected. Even if meanings are multiple and relational, hence always changing, people struggle with uneven access to power and knowledge in order to construct and tell their stories.' Based on the information included in the provincial yearbooks, the Ottoman state was aware of the fact that the members of society were in fact a part of the state at the local level.
12. According to Foucault (1997a: 73; 2008: 317), biopolitics is 'the attempt, starting from the eighteenth century, to rationalize the problems posed to governmental practice by phenomena characteristic of a set of living beings forming a population: health, hygiene, birth-rate, life expectancy, race . . .'
13. In the formulations of the 'circle of justice', prevention of oppression (*zulm*) has always occupied a significant place in defining the sovereign's responsibility towards his subjects. As Ergene (2001: 58) notes, however, 'by its very definition, justice was expected to govern only a portion of what the "circle of equity" was thought to encompass, that is, the relationship between the sovereign ruler and the taxpaying *reaya*. According to various definitions of the circle of equity, the system could not function without other separate (albeit interdependent) variables, including the sharia, the capacity of kingship, military power and wealth.' What we see here is a subtle shift in the definition of torture as 'abominable' not because of condemnation of oppression in the traditional sense but in the sense that Talal Asad (2003: 100–27) explains as a violation of the sacredness of the human body.
14. According to the yearbooks he was a five-year member of the council of appeals and crime and had been a member of the commission of surveys for two years before that.
15. Compare this with the fluidity of boundaries between the administrative and judicial councils in the context of the politics of election discussed in Chapter 3.
16. Douglass C. North (1997: 113) defines institutions as: 'the humanly devised constraints that structure human interaction. They are made up of formal constraints (rules, laws, constitutions), informal constraints (norms of behaviour, conventions, and self-imposed codes of conduct), and their enforcement characteristics. Together they define the incentive structure of societies and specifically economies.'
17. Braudel (1992: 71). Habermas (1975: 20–1) argues that the principle of organisation in the 'liberal-capitalist social formation, is the relationship of wage labour and capital, which is anchored in the system of bourgeois civil law'. As I discussed in Chapter 2, this definition presumes a state–society split (where the former is a necessary establishment to oversee the functioning of a separate domain of economy through laws and regulations); however, it correctly emphasises the relationship between forces of production and legitimation.

18. While the report gives the *hijri* year of 1250 as the beginning date of Ağa Hüseyin Paşa's term, H. A. Reed ('Agha Husayn Pasha') notes that the Paşa's first governorship began on 4 August 1833 and lasted until early February 1844. Ağa Hüseyin Paşa assumed this post again in October 1846 and served until his death on 25 April 1849. In addition to his lengthy service in Vidin, as Reed points out, this important statesman was 'noted for his leadership in the suppression of the Janissaries in 1826'.
19. The inhabitants are defined as 'owners (proprietors) of the land' (*eshab-ı arazi*); however, they agree on 'assuming the fiscal responsibility' (*der'uhdeye ru-yı muvafakat gösterdiklerine*). Such assumption of responsibility has been described as a phenomena pertaining to villages or communities (McGowan 1981: 168–9; Adanır 2006: 173); however, it is clear that in this case the responsibility refers to smaller individual plots.
20. Frédéric Gros (2005: 548n30) quotes this as the way Foucault defined his concept of governmentality in the first unpublished version of the 1981 lecture.
21. Sequestration of animals was not unique to the Ottomans. Pinson (1970: 26) notes that one of the abuses of local gentry in nineteenth-century Russia was to hold 'the peasants' draft animals as security for the payments; while holding the animals, the lords also worked them'.
22. Clearly, 'traditional' here cannot refer to a long time span for the refugee community who, as I discuss in the next chapter, settled here around the middle of the nineteenth century. The refugees used this term because it had a legal function – similar to the term 'the days of old' discussed above – and it fitted their strategic goals.
23. My discussion here is influenced by Mikhail Bakhtin's definition of 'heteroglossia'. According to Bakhtin (1981: 428), the meaning of any utterance is determined through a set of conditions – historical, social, and so on – that bind a word uttered in a particular place and time to a specific meaning. Any utterance, therefore, reflects the complex matrix of historical, social and other forces that generate its meaning. Bakhtin refers to this nature of historic time as 'heteroglossia' – and hence any utterance is 'heteroglot'.

6

'Cattle Thieves': Refugee Settlement, Ottoman Governmentality and Biopolitics

> Only when we know what . . . liberalism was, will we be able to grasp what biopolitics is. (Foucault 2008: 22)

This chapter focuses on governmental practices regarding different groups of refugees, particularly Circassians, who came to Vidin in the second half of the nineteenth century. It explores their problematisation in official correspondence as an example of how different agents handle specific matters related to life and population by governmental technologies. The efforts of the Ottoman state in settling the refugees has been examined in several different works (Chatty 2010; Rosser-Owen 2007; Shami 2000; Cuthell 2005; Pinson 1970). It is commonly accepted that this was a major challenge to the state and was a very painful process for the refugees. 'Problematisation, in this context, refers to the processes through which certain acts, practices, and thoughts emerge as "problems" for politics' (Foucault 1984). This is an attempt to conceptualise the dispute I discussed briefly in the last chapter involving the Tatar and Circassian refugee groups, Matyaş Ağa and the district head in 'Adliye (Case No. 544 in NBKM, VD 107/16). The two groups were in a dispute about the district head's use of his powers to force the Tatars to lend their horses to carry the wheat tithe of the Circassians. I discuss this case as an example of biopolitics.

Foucault (2008: 317) defines biopolitics as 'the attempt, starting from the eighteenth century, to rationalize the problems posed to governmental practice by phenomena characteristic of a set of living beings forming a population: health, hygiene, birth-rate, life expectancy, race . . .'. Although Foucault's use of 'biopolitics' may not always have been 'consistent', as argued most recently by Lemke, his lectures devoted to the topic provide a consistent and connected group of meanings, for this particular technology of government.[1] Biopolitics, through the way that it operates, reaffirms the validity of a liberalist system where governing is a necessity defined and limited by the effort to avoid obstacles to market operations which are inseparable from the well-being of civil society.

Refugee Settlement, Ottoman Governmentality and Biopolitics

Following a brief elaboration on the difficulties in estimating the number of refugees coming in the region and the complexity of the situation that Ottomans faced, I discuss how refugees became a problematic in Ottoman governmentality. Because Circassians were often called 'cattle thieves', I analyse the significance of the cattle trade in the region to understand the underlying reasons for the increased significance attributed to these animals. Through an analysis of settlement practices, I examine how biopolitics served as an Ottoman governmental technology in problematising Circassians. In the last section, I focus on a regulation issued to prevent Circassian cattle theft as an example of Ottoman biopolitics.

The settlement of Circassians served as a problematic that both validated and imposed limits on the extent of Ottoman governance. This is a key concern in liberalism, which aims to establish just enough state intervention to protect civil society and the market economy; governing more than what is required to maintain the security of these domains is considered unnecessary and unproductive (Foucault 2008: 61–70, 318–20). The provincial judicio-administrative sphere and the issues it deliberated reflect a central process of defining governing practice through the setting of boundaries. Analysing the processes of problematisation regarding these refugees in the nineteenth-century Ottoman Empire can enhance our understanding of the place of biopolitics in Ottoman governance.

The Numbers

Donald Quataert (1997: 792–5) has estimated that 3.8 million Muslims emigrated from areas of Russian imperial expansion in the Crimea, the Caucasus and Central Asia in the 130 years between 1783 and 1913.[2] The destination for the overwhelming majority of these refugees was the Ottoman Empire. While many ethnic groups were involved in the process, the Tatars of the northern Black Sea littoral made up the bulk of the refugees during the early to mid-nineteenth century, and the Circassians of the Western Caucasus constituted the majority in the second half (Petrov 2006: 346).

Milen Petrov (2006: 352) puts the total number of 'Muslim refugees' in the Danube Province during the 1860s at somewhere between 140,000 and 150,000, of whom about 80,000–90,000 were Tatars and the rest mostly Circassian. Petrov's estimate is close to others' for the Danube Province. Mark Pinson (1970: 50, 75) notes that 'from 1862 on, until the mid-1870s there had been no sizeable emigration of Tatars from the Crimea' and estimates the total number of Tatars who settled in Bulgaria to have been somewhere between 70,000 and 100,000. Citing statistics accompanying an Ottoman imperial decree, Saydam (1997: 131) gives a more precise number for the refugees who had settled along the Danube by the middle of 1861: 142,852. In a confidential report from 1865, British consul John A. Longworth reported from the region that 'the number of Circassian emigrants . . . in Bulgaria [was], as nearly as [he could] ascertain, 50,000, about a third . . . of the whole surviving emigration'.[3] In another confidential report, British consul for the Danube Province R. A. O. Dalyell gave a higher estimate for the number of Circassians in 1869: 100,000.[4]

It is difficult to establish how many of these refugees were settled in Vidin. Existing works (Kanitz 1875: 313; Tsukhlev 1932: 415; Pinson 1972: 75) seem to agree on a number cited by Felix Kanitz (1875: 313): 13,000 families. However, Kanitz's information is based on official Ottoman newspapers from July 1864 and fails to reflect the change in numbers in the second half of the 1860s.[5] Dana Sherry (2009: 16) notes the intensification of Russian campaigns in the Caucasus in the first half of the 1860s; following Imam Shamil's capture in August 1859, 'stamping out resistance in the west became the final step in the "final conquest" (*okonchatel'noe pokorenie*) of the Caucasus as a whole'. This 'final conquest' officially ended on 9 June 1864: 'many villages were burned that day [8 June], and over the succeeding days troops reconnoitred the villages and burned buildings that remained standing' (Sherry 2009: 18). Clearly, statistics published in 1864 could not have captured the full size of the refugee influx from the Caucasus. Confidential correspondence from British consuls (NA, FO 97-424) and works on the immigration waves (Cuthell 2005: 209–11, Rosser-Owen 2007: 20–1) indicate that the waves continued into 1867. For example, Pinson (1972: 72) notes that 'the transportation of the emigrants in 1864–1866 was so large an operation that the Ottoman as well as the Russian government had to take a hand in it. (Even England became involved in various ways.)'

In determining the number of settlers, the narrower one's geographic focus is, the more difficult it becomes to reach a good estimate. A survey from the mid-1870s (NBKM, VD 96/44), for example, identifies the total number of male Tatar refugees in Vidin as 6,572 and Circassians one as 7,020. When adjusted with the proper sex ratio we end up with 26,585.95 refugees.[6] On the other hand, David Cuthell (2005: 170–1) points out that in 1861 the Refugees Commission noted the settlement of '10,000 families (50,000+ individuals)' in Vidin. It is difficult to reconcile such diverse numbers.

In a telegram (BOA, AMKT.UM 448-47) dated 13 January 1861, Vidin's seemingly confused subgovernor inquired whether he should prevent the refugees from settling along the river only or keep them out of the province entirely. He also appeared unclear whether he was supposed to be sending away all the refugees, including those who were 'not involved with evil', or only the troublemakers. By the mid-1860s a more organised settlement process must have replaced the initial confusion – primarily due to the efforts of the Refugee (*muhacirin*) Commission. However, it is difficult to determine the exact number of refugees who settled in Vidin. Different districts in Vidin were used as temporary settlements for refugees en route to somewhere else: on 26 May 1864, 2,500 Circassians, many of whom had smallpox, arrived in Vidin on their way to Nish (NBKM, 26/11885). The subgovernor decided to host them until they recovered and requested medical help from the provincial capital in Ruse. Pinson (1972: 74) notes that other refugees arrived in Lom before being transferred to Nish. Another document (NBKM, 26/11888) informs us of the subgovernor's plans to place Circassian refugees in the houses vacated by Tatars who had left the Berkofça District. We are, however, left in the dark as to the fate of those Circassians who were destined to go to Nish, or why the Tatars left Berkofça and where they might have gone. Alexandre Popovic (1991: 67) shares an equally pessimistic perspective on the number of refugees who moved across Bulgaria to be resettled elsewhere:

> We will never know the exact number of [Circassians] who arrived to Yugoslav territory since the figures quoted by various people, already incomplete and contradictory, are no more than rough estimates and impossible to verify ... According to a plan of 1864, 6,000 families were to have been sent to [Nish], but it is not known if the plan was actually carried out.

One thing seems to be certain: the refugees were not numerous enough to change the demographic composition of the county significantly. Based on some contemporary accounts on the Balkans, Pinson (1970: 141–3, 231–2) argued that these refugees were resettled along the north-western frontier of the empire in an effort to create a buffer zone against the Russians. Some evidence support Pinson's argument: according to a survey from the 1870s (NBKM, VD 96/44), the number of Tatar and Circassian settlers increased the percentage of Muslims in the region from 11 to 20 per cent, and in the second half of 1870s the local government in Vidin sent telegrams indicating that the 'refugees' *together with* the 'native' inhabitants (*ahali-i kadime*) were volunteering to serve in defending the empire (for example, NBKM, VD 92/7). However, in the second half of the 1860s an increasing number of refugees were being resettled in Anatolia (Cuthell 2005: 114; Habiçoğlu 1993: 138–42; Saydam 1997: 124).

If the intent of the Ottoman Empire was to 'Islamicise' Vidin against the Russians, then it would have made more sense to increase the number of refugees in the 1870s. A reductionist approach to these refugees simply as 'Muslims' ignores their diversity.[7] It cannot explain the official welcoming response to over 10,000 'Bulgarian Christians' who had left for Russia between 1862 and 1863, and returned soon after, noting their unhappiness with the conditions there (BOA, A.MKT.UM 478-86; NA, FO 97-424; NA, FO 78-1669, 128; NBKM, 26/889; Petrov 2006: 357; Tsukhlev 1932: 412–13; Şentürk 1992: 157–60). These Bulgarian 'returnees' were pardoned, given a free steamboat ride back to Vidin and were granted land and animals, tax exemptions and permission to stay in other villagers' houses for a year or more until they could get back on their feet (NBKM, 26/11979). So we cannot safely argue that the refugees were simply used to establish buffer zones in Vidin. Such tax exemptions and grants of land, animal and money appear to have been a part of the current Ottoman policy towards different refugee groups, including the Tatars and the Circassians (NBKM, 1/18593; BOA, A.MKT.MHM 476-41; NA, FO 881-2956: 16; Pinson 1970: 79, 134).

The most valuable information source for determining the numbers of the refugees in Vidin would be the records of the Refugee Commission. While researchers can access the summary registers of the correspondence of this commission, at the time of writing there was very limited, if any, access to the actual reports and correspondence. Due to the lack of sources and demographic flux in the region, any attempt to determine the religious composition of the refugees or their ratio among the population in a given region must remain speculative. However, focusing on the problematisation of the settlement process can provide insights into how the Ottomans governed.

The Circassian refugees came to Vidin during a period of rapid economic and demographic expansion. Michael Palairet (1997: 84) argues that '[while] the most rapid phase of [economic] expansion was probably concluded in the late 1860s, the output of the Bulgarian lands . . . was at or near its peak at the time of the liberation [1878] . . . Ottoman rule in Bulgaria was extinguished at the high tide of its prosperity'. In the midst of such economic expansion, further complicating the mosaic in Vidin after the mid-1860s were several thousand souls fleeing from Belgrade, Smederovo and other formerly Ottoman towns in newly independent Serbia (BOA, A.MKT.MHM 241-40; A.MKT.MHM 264-72; A.MKT. MHM 271-31; İ. HR 011-558). The provisioning of these four groups – the Tatars, Circassians, Bulgarians and Muslim refugees from Serbia – seems to have varied (Cuthell 2005: 115–16). Furthermore, within each group – particularly among the Circassians – there were differences based on a variety of factors, including their wealth and the time of their arrival.[8] The Ottomans seem to refer to 'Circassians' as a single group of refugees – in their correspondence at least – with the generic title of *muhacirin-i Çerakise* (Cuthell 2005: 155–6; Rosser-Owen 2007: 8, 21). The Russians appear to have had a more detailed categorisation – they used some tribes against others (Pinson 1970: 93–100). However, they used 'Circassian' as a collective ethnonym as well (Wixman 1984: 5, 45, 49–50; Pinson 1970: 87). As for settlement policies, certain essential provisions for the refugees were standard, but there does not appear to have been a particular method the Ottomans used consistently to resettle the refugees.

Housing for refugees exemplifies the discrepancy in provisioning practices. Pinson notes the construction of a new town, Mecidiye (in the Dobrudja region), for the earlier wave of Tatar refugees in 1856. The material and the labour for houses were to be provided by the inhabitants of the neighbouring regions, including Vidin County. Vidin's subgovernor volunteered some of the county's residents to build approximately 1,500 houses while government paid 500 *guruş* per house to cover the costs. (In comparison, the monthly salary of the highest ranking teachers in the *rüşdiye* schools was 600 *guruş*, the doctors responsible for treating the refugees earned 500 *guruş* and pharmacists, 700 *guruş* (NBKM, 26/8534).) This, Pinson notes (1970: 68–9), caused significant discontent among the Bulgarians who were volunteered to work for little pay. Eight years later, in 1864, the local government built 900 houses for Circassian refugees at almost half the per-house cost: 300 *guruş*. (More than 3,000 houses were built for the same cost at different places in the county (NBKM, 26/896 26/887, 26/880).) The decline in the cost of these buildings might be indicative of their quality; in some cases they were occupied not by Circassians but local poor and unmarried male squatters (NBKM, 26/880).

While the houses built for Circassians might have been less appealing than those built for the Tatars, the refugees from Serbia seem to have got a better deal. Not only were they, like the other groups, provided housing, but they were also compensated for the loss of their homes in Serbia. The payments for these houses ranged anywhere from the 400 *guruş* that Ayşe Hatun received for her single-room house (NBKM, 26/8572) to the 1,500 *guruş* that Saatçi Mustafa bin Mehmed received for his (NBKM, 26/5048).

While the centralised Refugee Commission oversaw the settlement process, the bulk of the responsibility lay with the local administrative offices. Because such councils reflected the local political–economic dynamics, it is probable that the diversity in the settlement policies were partly caused by the changes in the composition of these councils over time and space in the region. Processes of problematisation such as the debates around the resettlement of refugees were being carried out through the governmental practices that used biopolitics as a technology of Ottoman governmentality.

Cattle as Liquidity

Among the four main groups of refugees, Circassians appear to have been in the worst condition during these two decades. Their relatively bad condition (particularly as compared to the earlier wave of Tatar refugees) have been noted by several scholars (Cuthell 2005; Rosser-Owen 2007; Pinson 1970) and is reflected in official correspondence (BOA, A.MKT. MHM 203-61; A.MKT.MHM 476-41; Y.PRK.KOM 1-28; A.MKT.ŞD 10-76; Ayniyat 488-14; NBKM, VD 107/16). Owing to the fact that they were among the last group of refugees to an empire already in great financial distress due to earlier waves of immigration, they were frequently described in Ottoman and British official correspondence as not having enough food, shoes or clothing. Their migrations peaked in the mid-1860s, just around the time that Midhat Paşa became governor of the newly established Danube Province and a number of major infrastructural projects required state funds. The costs of settlement added to the existing budgetary strain on the province (Petrov 2006: 200–5). Perhaps that is why their settlement process constituted a charged issue for the provincial administration.

In order to analyse the narratives about the refugees properly it is necessary to examine some patterns in the settlement process. According to a survey from the mid-1870s (NBKM, VD 96/44), the Circassian settlements appear to have been more densely populated than the Tatar ones: 490 people per village or neighbourhood, compared to 367 among the Tatars.[9] Only 7 per cent of the Circassians appear to have been settled in urban quarters – compared to 34 per cent among the Tatar population. It appears as if the local government decided to push these latecomers outside of the urban area after flooding the towns with the Tatar refugees. Considering that the Muslim population in Vidin County was concentrated in the towns, this choice of location meant Circassians were mostly located in new villages close to Bulgarian Christian villages. The average Circassian household, according to the same survey, had 3.9 individuals whereas the same average for Bulgarian Christian households was 5.9, which led to an average of 126 houses per Circassian village vs seventy-nine per Christian one (NBKM, VD 96/44). This perhaps made their status as 'Muslim refugees' vis-à-vis 'Bulgarian natives' more apparent to Felix Kanitz, the famous Austrian geographer who travelled extensively throughout the region during the 1860s and 1870s and published the three-volume *Danubian Bulgaria and the Balkans* in 1875.[10] Kanitz argued that Tatar refugees adapted to Bulgarian culture much better than their 'more violent' Circassian counterparts. This is how he assessed their comparative impact on Bulgarian society (1882b: 58):

> From a political and economic viewpoint, the colonisation of Circassians was an error on the part of the Ottoman administration, one that drove the Bulgarians mistreated and exhausted towards the arms of Russia. When, in 1877, the Tsar's army appeared on the Danube they were enthusiastically accepted by the Bulgarians, who thought they were being saved from their Circassian oppressors. In actuality, while the Russians were bringing in their victorious armies, the Circassians were running away, and with them the peaceful Tatars. After spending fifteen years on Bulgarian soil, both groups have today completely disappeared. Their belongings, which the Bulgarians seized in their rightful return, were distributed with the help of local government.

While similar observations about Circassians as 'quite a different breed' who were 'freebooters' and 'hostile to agriculture' also commonly found in significant works published later (Pinson 1970: 137), as Rosser-Owen (2007: 55) points out, these were only stereotypes and the reality was more complex. The British Consul General Longworth's observations about the Circassian refugees included in his confidential report from Vidin add a further layer of complexity to the local politics of settlement. According to Longworth the government was able to resettle the poverty-stricken and malnourished refugees effectively and the local response to them had been favourable for the most part (Longworth to Bulwer, 15 July 1864, NA, FO 97-424). However, he added, a former member of the administrative council, Tchanko Ağa, was cooperating with the Russian consul in town to create feelings of resentment among the Bulgarians about the settlement policies. This particular member apparently had been removed from the council some time before because he was found guilty of encouraging the Bulgarians to migrate to Russia – again in cooperation with the Russian consul in town. As soon as he became aware of the intrigue, the sub-governor summarily exiled Tchanko Ağa to Constantinople, leaving the 'sinister' Russian consul without a local assistant.

Kantiz's and Longworth's discussion of the refugees provide clues about the formation of local and international discourses about the refugees and their resettlement and explains how the government comes into the picture. The various ways these refugees were settled became a topic of discussion (or problematised) in what Foucault referred to as the particular 'triangle formed by government, population and political economy'.[11] Political economy assumes its role in this triangle because, from the eighteenth century onwards, 'the relationship between population and resources can no longer be managed through an exhaustive regulatory and coercive system that would strive to increase the population by increasing resources'.[12] Liberal philosophy presumed that the economy 'obeyed and had to obey "natural" . . . spontaneous mechanisms' (Foucault 2008: 31), and this envisioned a particular role for the market: 'that of a "test", of a privileged site of experiment in which one can pinpoint the effect of excessive governmentality and take their measure' (Foucault 2008: 320). Thus, while political economy required governance to manage the population through biopolitics, the 'natural order of the market' became the gauge to measure excessive intervention. With respect to the dispute regarding threshing in the 'Adliye District, the efficacy of those who participated in the act of governing the local society was measured by their success in resettling the refugees with the least disturbance to the 'native' inhabitants and the political economy of the region. Given the variety of refugee groups, ranging from 'former inhabitants' returning after a period in Russia to 'exiled Ottomans' coming in from Serbia, to 'earlier (and relatively wealthier) Tatar' or 'recent Circassian' refugees, their rights and privileges had to be ranked against each other in cases such as the one that led to the arrest of the Tatar refugees' animals.

In that sense, the processes of settlement became a test of how well the local judicio-administrative complex 'governed'. This peculiar relationship between political economy and governance is key to Foucault's discussion of biopolitics, in which he argued (2008: 13) that, from the middle of eighteenth century, political economy became essential for the development of a self-limiting reason that shaped biopolitics as a technology of government. That is, modern governance (including biopolitics) and its associated scientific discipline, political economy, focused on determining what limits should be imposed on the state's involvement with the economy and society. An analysis of biopolitics becomes possible only when we understand the general regime of modern governance. This is why he notes that 'only when we know what this governmental regime called liberalism was, will we be able to grasp what biopolitics is' (2008: 21). In the particular case of the Ottoman Empire, the limits circumscribing governmental action become apparent in the way refugee resettlement was problematised. Most of the concerns of the Ottoman administration seemed to focus on a well-functioning market economy and the protection of property rights.

The settlements put an inordinate financial burden on the local economy and simultaneously increased economic activity in the region. A letter (BOA, A.MKT.UM 507-100) from the Supreme Council of Judicial Ordinances to Vidin, in 1862, designated the local treasury as responsible for paying two-thirds of the expenses incurred from the weekly allowance payments, construction costs and oxen/cart purchases for the refugees. Only in exceptional cases, such as a natural disaster, the share of the imperial treasury was to be increased to account for the part that could not be covered locally. If the designated funds for such expenses was not sufficient the local treasury was allowed to transfer funds from previous years' tax revenues (NBKM, 26/5032). Of course, Vidin County was not the only county to absorb refugees. But Vidin markets often supplied the animals and construction material (NBKM, 20/817) or otherwise shared the financial burden of the resettlement process in another county (NBKM, 20/819; BOA, A.MKT.MHM. 302-3).

In the context of this economic activity, livestock, particularly cattle, became more liquid assets. Cattle were significant even in the early migration process. Reporting in 1863 from the portal town of Kertch in Russia, British consul R. C. Clipperton noted the impending departure of 150,000 members of the Abazeck tribe for Samsun. The two town merchants responsible for the transport were charging five roubles per head, three to be paid by the Russian government and two by the refugees, either in cash or in cattle (Clipperton to Russell, 21 December 1863, NA, FO 97-424). Refugees in Vidin appear to have received a pair of cattle for every four households in addition to land during the resettlement process (BOA, A.MKT.UM 476-92). When a land dispute resulted in the resettlement of a group of refugees within the county in 1875, those with cattle received fifty-five *dönüm*s per animal while those without received only twenty-eight *dönüm*s (NBKM, VD 101/03).

The correlation of cattle provision with the settlement process must have increased the circulation of cattle within the region significantly. Cattle moved in and out of Vidin and its surroundings; they were bought from Vidin to be sent to Varna (NBKM, 20/817) or were bought in other markets to be brought to Vidin (BOA, A.MKT.UM 507/100; A.MKT.UM 476-92). Their association with the land distributed guaranteed an increase in the number of cattle as new waves of refugees were resettled in the region. However, not all could farm the land they were given. Among other reasons, the land reserved for the refugees was not always arable (NBKM, VD 101/03), contributing to the sale of cattle. The increased importance of cattle for economic exchanges combined with the harsh conditions contributed to cattle theft in the region, and local correspondence is replete with references to Circassian involvement with this theft. It appears to have been something the local administration wanted to end simply by punishing those involved, without inquiring into the reasons behind its growth. Prevention of cattle theft, in this context, constituted one of the primary reasons for governmental intervention.

'Security, Territory, Population' in Vidin[13]

It is clear that the influx of refugees presented the Ottoman state with a challenge. The twin tasks it faced were to alleviate the suffering of the refugees and to alleviate the suffering caused by them. By focusing on the ways in which the Ottoman state responded to these two issues we can better understand the technologies of Ottoman governance and the governmental reason within the judicio-administrative sphere.

The following case provides a good example of the constraints that the Ottoman government imposed on itself as it settled the refugees. In 1875 the headmen of the Midhat Paşa village in Vidin sent a petition (NBKM, VD 101/03) to the subgovernor of the county noting that approximately 100 houses comprising the refugee village needed to be moved because the land on which they had been built was not suitable for agriculture. Midhat Paşa was a village established specifically for the refugees. According to the 1873 yearbook, during the previous year the village had only Circassian inhabitants. The yearbook lists a total of 115 houses with 451 inhabitants living in this village located approximately fifteen miles north of Vidin (171). Four years prior to the petition, the inhabitants of the village were granted some farmland in another village, Gradets; however, that offer was not extended for more than a year. The subgovernor's initial response, indicated on the margins, was to request further investigation by the administrative council. The response to this request reveals the background of the case and the administrative logic of the local government.

Gradets is 8.4 miles north-west of Vidin, and according to the same yearbook (169) it had 164 Christian families (364 people). The permission to use the land in Gradets was revoked following a complaint from the village inhabitants, who noted that the land given to the refugees included forested, grass and farm land owned by them, and they had the title deeds to prove it. However, no further action was taken for three years. Vidin's administrative council wrote in its report it was not possible to find such large amounts of 'vacant land without deeds' (*hali ve tapusuz*). The solution promoted by the council would allow the refugees use of lands further west, on the border with Serbia, between the two villages of Rabrovo and Chernamasnice, (Rabrovo, in Bulgaria, is approximately eighteen miles west of Vidin; Chernamasnice, approximately four miles north of Rabrovo, is in modern Serbia), as long as it could be guaranteed that the land was not owned by anyone and that the arrangement was agreeable to the local administrative council members in the 'Adliye District where these villages were located. The fate of Midhat Paşa's refugees was to be determined in accordance with the ownership rights and the decision of the local administrative council. Today there are no other settlements between those two villages.

The care taken by the administrative council to prevent the settlement process from gaining priority over established norms and practices exemplifies the governmental reason within the judicio-administrative sphere. In fact, in several different cases, the government officials seem to have been both sympathetic to the needs of the Circassians but at the same time concerned about limiting the repercussions of protecting them. The local administration did not want others to claim the unused lands allotted to the refugees (BOA, A.MKT.NZD 420-52; A. MKT.MVL 144-39). Some of the Circassian refugees were resettled on land belonging to Bulgarian-speaking emigrants who had left for Russia. Upon the latter's return, the government requested that the Circassian refugees be removed to other 'vacant' slots. The returnees' claim to their abandoned land was considered to be more pressing then those of the refugees (BOA, A.MKT. UM 522-30). While the provincial administrators in Vidin praised the local effort to help the refugees (BOA, A. MKT.MHM 203-61, 209-99, 210-86, 211-79, 213-43; A.MKT.NZD 344-31, 345-93; A.MKT.UM 454-41), they also warned their district administrative councils not to allow people to force others to help the refugees (BOA, A.MKT.MHM 216-61; A.MKT.UM 444-2, 454-63). At times, they reimbursed some of the donors for their generosity, such as Ayşe Hatun and Fatma Hatun, who had given up some of their land in return for land from another village (A.MKT.MHM. 449-5). The Ottoman administrators, as exemplified in their response to the 'Adliye District head who had imprisoned several Tatar refugees and their animals, did not want to interfere too much with the local political economy unless it was absolutely necessary; when they had to interfere they seem to have made an effort to follow existing procedures that respected the rights of current inhabitants in the region.

Such individual cases reflect local practices and do not provide a full perspective on how governing was conceptualised at the imperial level. Imperial policies regarding the refugees can be more informative about the Ottoman 'government's consciousness of itself', which is important in understanding biopolitics and the domain it operates: governmentality.[14]

This is not to claim that what imperial laws, rules and regulations reflect is a homogenous, monolithic entity, that is, the state. The negotiated nature of 'administrative practices, rules and regulations' in the Ottoman context has been emphasised by İslamoğlu (2004a, 279 and *passim*). The omnipresence of governmentality, and therefore the possibility of biopolitics, is conditional on the presence of a 'civil society', which is 'a concept of governmental technology, or rather, it is the correlate of a technology of government the rational measure of which must be juridically pegged to an economy understood as a process of production and exchange' (Foucault 2008: 296). The inseparability of economy and civil society, therefore, defines a purpose for governance in liberalism: guaranteeing a properly functioning economy, or market, as a site of 'verification–falsification for governmental practice' (Foucault 2008: 31–2). Hence, eliminating the suffering caused by the refugees through limiting their disturbance of economic activity, became not only a task for the Ottoman state, but also a test of its efficient governance through biopolitics.

From Refugees to Cattle Thieves

> Unless there is a legitimate reason, Circassians should not travel from one village to another with or without a permit. (NBKM, 26/12101)

> Among the Circassians, like the ancient Spartans, the thief who exercises his profession with dexterity excites universal admiration; and you cannot insult a Circassian more than to tell him he did not know how to steal an ox. (Spencer 1839: 335)

In their analysis of political power, Rose and Miller (1992: 181) note that government

> is a problematizing activity: it poses the obligations of rulers in terms of the problems they seek to address. The ideals of government are intrinsically linked to the problems around which it circulates, the failings it seeks to rectify, the ills it seeks to cure.

Theft, particularly cattle theft attributed to the Circassians, quickly became a 'failing' or an 'ill' that the Ottoman government had to cure. In 1876 the office of the subgovernor in Vidin circulated a detailed regulation (NBKM, 26/12101) aimed at preventing this particular problem. The regulation imposed strict travel restrictions on the refugees and introduced several offices to monitor individuals, including non-Circassians. Such governmental oversight was justified by the threat that theft posed to civil society and the economy.

The regulation required the election of a council of elders – primarily in the refugee villages – composed of two village headmen, six members, and the village imam (*ex officio*). Depending on the size of the village, the number of elders could be anywhere from three to ten. Such councils were already an established part of the village administration. What differentiated them in this case was the issue of security. If there was an already existing council, its members could continue only if they were 'trustworthy'. If not, they were to be replaced through election. Following the election, the council was to require all village inhabitants (including themselves) to take an oath not to steal or let others steal and to report those who did – but to avoid wrongfully incriminating others. A member from the county administration was to witness this communal oath ceremony.

Utmost attention was paid to the reliability of the council. Similar to other councils, its members were expected to use identification seals in place of (or to accompany) their signatures in their correspondence, assuring the veracity of the official document. The new regulation required the members to acquire new seals and to keep all of them in one box that would be opened only in presence of the entire council. Perhaps as a measure of protection, the council was held exempt from investigating criminal allegations regarding non-refugees. If they suspected thievery by Muslim or Christian 'natives' (*ahali-i kadime*) they were expected to report directly to the county with the understanding that the latter would further investigate the case without revealing former council's role in the investigation.

Tension between 'natives' and refugees was also implied in other regulations, such as the ban on Circassians' right to bear arms: only 'trustworthy' refugees were allowed to carry weapons, and only as long as they were travelling to a different town with a permit that was issued exclusively for that trip. Another article ordered the councils to pay particular attention to native-born residents who committed theft while disguised as Circassians.[15]

In connection with their general surveillance mission, councils of elders in the refugee villages would issue permits to village inhabitants who wished to travel. To receive one, refugees had to explain the reasons for the trip as well as the itinerary. If convinced, the council would issue an official permit bearing the official seals and summarising the details of the trip. Travellers would have to present this passport to the administrative council at their destination. Undocumented refugee travellers were to be arrested and interrogated. In the event that travellers wanted to sell cattle in another town, their passports had to include a detailed description of the cattle. Circassians caught travelling with cattle but without a permit would be treated as thieves. The regulation clearly subjected the refugees' ordinary movements to the scrutiny of the councils (at the village or county level).

This regulation proposed to impose severe limitations on refugees' (and others') freedom. Such a sacrifice was necessary in face of the dangers posed by theft and 'animosity' between the Circassians and native-born citizens. What matters, for the purposes of this analysis, is not whether such a dangerous environment existed or not. Of interest rather is the problematisation of this 'danger' and how it constituted sufficient ground for government action. As such, this particular document exemplifies how 'the game of freedom and security [was] at the very heart of ... governmental reason' (Foucault 2008: 65) in Vidin during the nineteenth century. Within the framework of this complex form of power, biopolitics functions as a technology to maintain the proper processes of production and exchange. Liberalism, the ideology forming the basis for such strategies, helped establish limits to governance by balancing freedom against security: government becomes necessary only to ensure the smooth operation of general mechanics of behaviour, exchange and economic life. A constant threat of derailment becomes the *raison d'être* for technologies of government.

Conclusion

There is no liberalism without a culture of danger. (Foucault 2008: 67)

The resettlement of Circassians and other refugees was an obvious problematic for the local, regional and imperial political economy. As such, it had to be governed carefully and effectively; that is, the 'danger' created by the refugees and the necessity of its elimination contributed to the *raison d'être* of Ottoman governmentality.

The imperial policies of refugee-provisioning and overall economic expansion in the Vidin region meant that cattle served more and more as liquidity in the second half of the nineteenth century. This created a suitable environment for fomenting narratives of 'dangerous Circassians', adding strength to calls for effective government. One can question the veracity of reports of animosity between Circassians and other inhabitants in the region; however, it is more important, for the purposes of this chapter, to identify how these debates served as a base for power negotiations at the local level. Because different agents deployed narratives about refugees (which became available in the problematisation of settlement processes) strategically in their own negotiations within Ottoman governmentality, existing documents would naturally reflect the claims constructed in these particular settings.

For example, the quick decision of 'Adliye District's head official to imprison several refugees and their animals in the case discussed earlier was not perceived as the ideal solution for a situation that could have been resolved with less tension. This report, prepared under the authority of Matyaş Ağa (who was sent by the judicio-administrative complex in Vidin to investigate the case) preferred to limit the government's intervention in the local political economy over the effective collection of taxes for the state. We must, however, keep in mind that Matyaş Ağa was a (very) active agent in the judicio-administrative sphere. Over the ten-year course during which the provincial yearbook was published (1868–77) his name consistently appeared on the list of county administration members. During the same period, the head official of the 'Adliye District changed six times. The head official serving during the year of the incident, Hadi Efendi, was not in the same position the next year.

Perhaps more interesting is the fact that Hacı Mirza Beğ, the Circassian notable whose name was briefly mentioned at the end of the report as the victim of an attack, was listed as a member of the district administrative council in nine out of the ten yearbooks published for the province – his name was not listed in the 1876 yearbook, only to reappear the following year. Considering that the elected council members had a term limit of two years, Hacı Mirza Beğ's repeated election to the same position should mean that he was a prominent member of the local political structure. This is why Matyaş Ağa must have pointed out that the district head official was *still* interrogating the suspects. The details of this simple report point at a more complex set of relations between members of the local elite, who served in the judicio-administrative sphere for several years, and government-appointed officials, who were frequently replaced.

Biopolitics, as a technology of Ottoman governance, was shaped in the context of the problematisation of refugee-related matters. These debates, serving as platforms for power negotiations among various agents, were also instances in which the extent of government intervention was discussed – that is, they were debates of economic liberalism. Protecting the market from destructive effects of refugee settlement, like many other issues associated with proper governance (public hygiene, education, infrastructural investment), created a complex array of heteromorphous, localised power procedures (passport control, house construction, cattle allocation and other applications of biopolitics) and allowed different agents to engage with others to pursue their strategies. The debates about the efficacy of biopolitical power procedures determined the effectiveness of Ottoman local governance. The yardstick for that measurement, the base for the discursive formation of Ottoman governmentality was the belief in a spontaneous market order. The Ottoman response to the refugee crisis and functioning of the provincial judicio-administrative sphere in other case studies on property, corruption, and so on explored in the previous chapters all contributed to this discursive formation for which the Ottoman transition to the liberal-capitalist social formation – that began with the transformation of the social order (discussed in Chapter 2) long before the Tanzimat era – played a definitive role.

Notes

1. 'Foucault's use of the term "biopolitics" is not consistent and constantly shifts meaning in his texts. However, it is possible to discern three different ways in which he employs the notion in his work. First, biopolitics stands for a historical rupture in political thinking and practice that is characterised by a rearticulation of sovereign power. Second, Foucault assigns to biopolitical mechanisms a central role in the rise of modern racism. A third meaning of the concept refers to a distinctive art of government that historically emerges with liberal forms of social regulation and individual self-governance' (Lemke 2011: 34).
2. Reşat Kasaba (2009: 116) notes that 'as many as two million Muslims left Russia and the Balkans for Ottoman lands' in the after the 1877–8 Ottoman–Russian War. The focus on the post-1877 period is characteristic of much of the recent work on this devastating exile as exemplified in Blumi's (2013) attempt to contextualise them in development of global capitalism. Nora E. Barakat's recent dissertation on Jordan (2015) is a particularly noteworthy contribution on the dynamic relationship between the refugee populations and Ottoman governance at the local level.
3. 'Report by Mr Consul General Longworth on the Organisation of the Vilayet of the Danube' NA, FO 881-1393, p. 8. The report is about the new provincial organisation and the formation of the Danube Province. Consul John A. Longworth, was sent on a 'special service' to Circassia between 1855 and 1858 prior to this report and seems to have been particularly interested in the colonisation of the Circassians (Hertslet 1874: 132). His reference to the high mortality rates among the refugees is not exaggerated. Others claim even higher rates (Chatty 2010: 101–3).
4. 'General Report by Sir R. Dalyell on the Vilayet of the Danube' NA, FO 881-2956, pp. 3–4. Dalyell was appointed to his post in the province in 1865 (Hertslet 1877: 83–4). In the four years between his appointment and the report he must have had enough time to observe the settlement process. Petrov, Pinson and Saydam do not mention these reports in their works cited above, which might account for the discrepancy in the number of refugees.

5. Kanitz published these numbers first in an 1865 article (Kanitz 1865). The paragraph with the 13,000 figure (on p. 238 along with others for different districts) is one of the several that were reprinted verbatim in 1875.
6. I am using the ratio that Petrov (2006: 60) provides (100 male to 95.6 female). He develops this ratio based on the work of Nikolai Todorov (1983).
7. It is interesting to note what Louis Loewe mentioned (1854: 5–6) in the introduction to his dictionary: 'Since the appearance of Sheykh Manzoor the princes and nobles profess the Mookhamadan religion, and belong to the sect of the Soonites, but the mass of the people adhere faithfully to their former idolatrous worship.' What matters here is not how 'Muslim' the refugees were. It is well known that religious practices, even among the Sunni Muslims, varied significantly within the Ottoman Empire. It is unrealistic to assume that different refugee communities not only shared a common 'Islamic identity' but also that their particular religious understandings and practices would have been similar to those who identified themselves as 'Muslim' in the Balkans.
8. (Cuthell 2005: 155–6). Determining the wealth of the refugees was a particular concern for the Ottomans. The village headmen in Vidin, for example, were required to identify and report 'Circassian' refugees' wealth levels once they were settled (BOA, A.MKT.UM 556-45). This appears to have been the general concern wherever different refugees were settled (Saydam 1997: 128–9).
9. Unfortunately I did not come across enough data to establish how densely populated the Serbian Muslim and Bulgarian Christian refugee settlements were.
10. Kanitz, born in 1829 to an Austrian Jewish family that had moved to Budapest, was perhaps the epitome of the nineteenth-century encyclopedic amateur traveller to the 'Orient'. A freelance painter and self-taught geographer, art historian, ethnographer, archaeologist and classicist, Kanitz wrote well-received travelogues on Montenegro and Serbia, before embarking upon a series of journeys (1864–74) through the Ottoman Danube Province. The result was his important account, published in 1875 and reprinted a decade later and translated into different languages, including Bulgarian and French.
11. This particular relationship constitutes the main theme of Michel Foucault's lectures at the Collège de France in 1977–8, and serves as an introduction to the lectures of the following year devoted to 'the birth of Biopolitics'. Particularly in his 1 February 1978 lecture, where he introduces the notion of governmentality, he emphasises the centrality of political economy for the art of governing (Foucault 2007: 87–114).
12. (Foucault 2007: 366). Foucault argues that as a field, political economy emerged around the middle of the eighteenth century: 'The intellectual instrument, the type of calculation or form of rationality that made possible the self-limitation of governmental reason was not the law . . . starting from the middle of the eighteenth century . . . it is political economy' (Foucault 2008: 13).

13. The quoted segment is the title for the 1978 lectures of Michel Foucault. According to Michel Senellart, who wrote the course context, these lectures 'mark the opening of a new cycle in [his] teaching at the Collège de France'. Together with the lectures of the following year, The Birth of Biopolitics, these lectures 'form a diptych unified by the problematic of bio-power' (Foucault 2007: 369, 377)
14. 'I wanted to study government's consciousness of itself . . . to grasp the way in which this practice that consists in governing was conceptualized both within and outside government, and anyway as close as possible to the governmental practice . . . In short, we would call this the study of the rationalization of governmental practice in the exercise of political sovereignty' (Foucault 2008: 2).
15. In his recent article Omri Paz (2015: 242) explores how migrants/refugees were problematised in a similar manner in western Anatolia and argues that migration 'was, and still is, first and foremost a legal experience'.

7

Conclusion

In her work on Mosul, Dina Rizk Khoury (1997: 214) notes that:

> Mosuli urban and rural societies were better integrated into the Ottoman 'system' in the late eighteenth century, the century of decentralisation, than they were in an earlier period when state controls were said to be more stringent . . . This approach to the eighteenth century makes dealing with the modern period somewhat less problematic. Instead of viewing the Tanzimat reforms as a rupture with the old order and as an initiative coming from a central state bureaucracy inspired by European models, we now can look at the internal social and political bases of the modern period. To be sure, not all of Mosul's gentry and merchants were supportive of the liquidation of political households and the old order. Nor were they enthusiastic about the model for reform espoused by the stronger elements among the state elite. However, they were engaged in the political debates of the time, and offered their own agendas for reform.[1]

Khoury's framework provides a good starting point for the conclusions of this book. While the focus of the previous chapters has been mostly on the late nineteenth century, the changes that occurred in the period under study did not happen as a rupture from the previous century. In fact, as Donald Quataert (2005: 54) observed, the 'long nineteenth century' (1789–1922) 'continued processes of change and transformation that had begun in the eighteenth century and sometimes before'. The nineteenth-century transformation of Ottoman provincial administration took place in the context of 'the dynamics inherent in seventeenth- and eighteenth-century decentralisation, which can no longer be regarded as a manifestation of "Ottoman decline" and a precondition for proto-nationalism' (Faroqhi 2006b: 11).

Survival of Lower-tier Elites

State–society relations in the Ottoman Empire differed from their European counterparts. As Lisa Anderson (1987: 14) notes, 'the historical significance of corporate, lineage and tribal groups in exercising political authority alongside – *and sometimes within* – centralized bureaucratic administrations presents a starting point for state formation markedly different from that in Europe' (emphasis added). The historiography of the

Nineteenth-century Local Governance in Ottoman Bulgaria

Ottoman Empire is not the only one troubled by an overemphasis on the presumed rift between state and society. In studying the emergence of a Russian 'middle class', William Wagner (1991: 210) notes that such undue stress leads to the exaggeration of 'both the unity within the tsarist state and the extent of the state's isolation from educated society'. The analysis of the election results and rotation patterns in Vidin's judicio-administrative sphere in Chapter 3 points to 'a single government of state officials and local elites' (Meeker 2002: 210). Understanding how local notables were an integral part of this single government gives us a better perspective on the nineteenth-century transformation.[2]

The integration of local notables to Ottoman governance happened in various stages. The provincial regulation of 1864 and the infrastructure it introduced exemplify one of the later stages of communities' involvement in local judicio-administrative sphere. The 1864 reforms described a set of offices and practices that, in theory, allowed members of the local populace to participate in provincial governance, yet prevented them from gaining permanent powerful positions by limiting their terms of service to only two years. Midhat Paşa, who introduced this procedure, aimed to systematise local participation while preventing local administration from being an extension of the provincial notability. Midhat Paşa travelled, for six months, to Paris, London, Vienna and Brussels 'with a view to the study of certain points of European administration with which he desired to make himself acquainted' prior to submitting his plans for the provincial administration reform of 1864.[3] However, the main framework for the administrative reforms did not have its origins in those trips.[4] The changes in local governance and local participation were parts of a larger transformation associated with the Ottoman legitimacy crisis.

Provincial governance is closely related to the means of production and exploring the changing relationship between these reforms and the means of production contributes to our understanding of the evolution of this single government of officials and local elites over the long nineteenth century. That is why this book focused on reform and the means of production in Chapter 2. The gradual transformation of the provincial institutional structure in the seventeenth and eighteenth centuries indicates that changes in the way the local populace related to the means of production began much earlier than the nineteenth century. In his recent analysis of provincial notables prior to the Tanzimat era, Fikret Adanır (2006: 166–9) notes the following for the seventeenth century:

> The replacement of feudal forms of revenue distribution went hand-in-hand with the spread of the practices known as *mukata'a*, tax-farming techniques

that had previously been in use only on some larger estates ... [In this system tax was] levied not on a household basis ... [but was] calculated for each commune as an annual lump sum ... On the whole, the new regime had the effect of de-emphasizing differences in social status, religious affiliation and the urban or rural character of one's residence. The relationship between the state and the taxpayer became more fluid, and the land, the basic means of production in an agrarian society, became increasingly mobile, capable of being bought and sold.

This transformation coincided with population decline in the countryside and local notables' ascendancy to power at the provincial level (Faroqhi 1994: Hathaway 1998; Faroqhi 2006d). The fiscal pressure on peasants increased as the seventeenth-century population decline was reversed in the Balkans during the eighteenth century (McGowan 1994). This led to increased conflicts between the local dynasties and the imperial administration (McGowan 1994: 658–72; Zens 2004: 44–98; Adanır 2006: 170–85). Although such dynasties owed their positions to the imperial centre to a certain degree, they became more prominent in the eighteenth century (Faroqhi 2002: 366–7; Yaycioglu 2016: 65–115). As the prominence of these families increased, so did their connections with other regional families resulting in many-tiered elite networks that allowed high-ranking elite to exert their influence at the frontiers of their influence zone through lesser elites.[5] Recently Ali Yaycioglu defined this as the transformation of Ottoman polity 'from a vertical empire, in which the imperial elite sustained claims to power through a hierarchical system, to a horizontal and participatory empire, in which central and provincial actors combined to rule the empire together' (Yaycioglu 2016: 2). Thanks to the increased mobility of land, this transformation gradually led to accumulation of usufruct on land in the hands of these notables. The evidence from Vidin indicates that although the highest tier of the local dynasties, like Pasvanoğlu Osman Paşa, gradually lost their power vis-à-vis the imperial administration by the beginning of the nineteenth century, the lower-tier elite among the communities remained politically active and benefited from cooperation with the Ottoman administration.

Crisis and Means of Production

The nineteenth-century transformation of legal and administrative institutions was a response to the reconfigurations of Ottoman social integration during the late seventeenth and eighteenth centuries. Prior to the nineteenth century, local notables were prominent due to their involvement with tax collection, and extending funds to members of provincial communities in need. These dynastic local elites cooperated with the Janissary forces and, as recent studies underscore, the latter played a significant role in controlling access to funds in the provinces (Anastasopoulos and Spyropoulos 2017). Mahmud II's reforms gradually curbed the power of the local elite and the Janissaries and thereby transformed how individuals related to each other in the collection of taxes and availability of funds at the provinces. The provincial reorganisation of the nineteenth century followed this shift in power at the provinces. As I argued in Chapter 2, the transformation of Ottoman social integration was linked to the crisis of the traditional social formation.

Crisis in a social system occurs when 'the consensual foundations of normative structures are so much impaired that the society becomes anomic' and they lead to the disintegration of social institutions requiring an institutional reconfiguration to generate new consensual foundations (Habermas 1975: 2).[6] Because these transformations had to do with the way people related to means of production, the institutional readjustment of the system integration in the long nineteenth century focused on them as well – such as the transformation of tax collection methods, measures taken to prevent arbitrary confiscation of individuals' properties, the Land Code of 1858. While not *all* of the reforms associated with the Tanzimat era had to do with means of production, the reforms discussed in Chapter 2 indicate that the long nineteenth century, and the Tanzimat era as part of it, corresponded to the crisis of the traditional social formation, the institutional restructuring related to that crisis and the liberal-capitalist social formation in the Ottoman Empire.

These nineteenth-century revisions to the institutional structure focused on legitimating the imperial order, which was done through a series of reforms that led to establishing particular limits to the power of the state, to Ottoman governance. One of the more significant components of these reforms was the establishment of local councils as provincial extensions of a newly emerging modern state that increasingly relied on economic exchange as the dominant steering medium and sought to complement the functioning of the self-regulative market commerce with civil law.

Connected Offices

The establishment of local councils preceded the 1864 provincial regulation. Tax-collection councils (*muhassıllık meclisi*) established two decades prior to the administrative councils were their predecessors. What made the 1864 regulation unique was how it aimed to establish a more

Conclusion

complex structure that systematised the reach of Ottoman governmentality. The provincial judicial and administrative councils helped with the institutional transformation of the long nineteenth century in three significant ways. First, they provided an essential framework to which different offices of Ottoman governance were linked – such as the Orphans' Funds and other fiscal, military and scribal units discussed in Chapter 4. Second, they facilitated the dissemination of reforms and the textually mediated organisation of the modern Ottoman state at the provincial level – a process closely related to the growth of 'a public sphere of state administration' (Giddens 1985: 179). Third, they served as a means to facilitate participation of local notables in the Ottoman governance – which *might* have made the application of reforms less objectionable. Overall, these councils constituted a significant component of 'a single government of state officials and local elites' (Meeker 2002: 210).[7]

The provincial regulations of 1864 and 1871 organised the structure and the procedures of the Ottoman provincial judicio-administrative sphere in a systematic fashion. On the one hand, local notables were part of this framework as members of different provincial councils; on the other, the imperial administration sought to limit their influence by limiting their service on these councils to two years. This reflected the intentions of the state to establish a certain level of integration between the imperial administration and local populace as much as to curb the local politics' influence on administrative and judicial practices.

Despite the imperial centre's intentions, as the election results for the judicial and administrative councils in Vidin County demonstrate, certain local notables in Vidin secured their influence in these councils. The provincial regulations of 1864 and 1871 did limit the time that members could serve, yet did not ban re-election. By serving on one council for consecutive terms or by switching from the administrative council to the council of appeals and crime, certain local notables established an organic link between the administrative and judicial spheres of Ottoman provincial governance in Vidin. The judicio-administrative sphere in Vidin thereby reflected the power politics among the local notables as its offices and practices became domains of negotiation.

The publication in the provincial yearbooks of these members' continuous presence in Vidin's judicio-administrative sphere indicates that both the provincial and the imperial capital were aware of the connectedness of the organisations that were designed to function separately. Together with an official chronology of the empire, a timetable for prayers and a list of titles among the administrative ranks, the names of these notables became a part of the textually mediated organisation of the Ottoman state. Neither the Ottoman state nor the provincial society felt the need to conceal this obvious coexistence. It is in this openly announced symbiosis that we can see the boundaries of Ottoman governmentality operating in the provincial setting of nineteenth-century Vidin. As a theoretical framework, governmentality is useful because it avoids the presumed separation between state and society; nor does it assume homogeneity among the agents that are associated with state or society.

Contentious Dynamics

As domains of negotiation at the local level, these councils reflected the political balance and contentions among the provincial notables to a certain extent. Chapter 4 partially focused on a brief section in the copy register of Vidin's administrative council to analyse the participation patterns of members in the council's meetings. As the results indicate, getting elected did not necessarily mean that a member could, or had to, attend the meetings of the council. Conditions that we cannot fully understand from available evidence led to irregularities in the attendance patterns of these members. The lack of participation of the town's metropolitan can perhaps be explained by religious tension between different communities. However, there may have been different reasons behind other members' attendance at council meetings.

The participation patterns observed in the copy register help reveal that the yearbooks did not always accurately reflect the composition of the judicio-administrative sphere. Ironically, given their wide distribution and commitment to accuracy – as evidenced by the inclusion of encyclopedic information about almost everything regarding the province, from mountains and rivers to prayer times throughout the year – these books failed to note such details as when the *rüşdiye* school in the district was opened, and incorrectly identified some members of the administrative council. However, this does not change the value of these yearbooks as textual representations of Ottoman governance.

Despite some errors, provincial yearbooks are useful for understanding further details regarding the provincial administration. The names of people in different offices indicate that the judicio-administrative sphere was not limited to the administrative and judiciary councils. Several of those who served in these two more prominent offices of the judicio-administrative sphere served in other offices as well – such as the municipal council or the commercial court. When we take all these names into account, what emerges is a relatively consistent presence of a group of local notables in a contentious judicio-administrative sphere that provided

Conclusion

upward mobility. These notables were not significant enough to be well known at the imperial level; the archives do not seem to have a lot of information about them, aside from some petitions that were sent either directly from Vidin, or via the provincial capital in Ruse. This does not change the fact that they were rather prominent at the provinces. Understanding how they operated within the judicio-administrative sphere is essential for understanding how Ottoman local governance functioned.

Conniving Narratives

It is mostly through the reports of these councils that the imperial administration became aware of what was happening in the provinces. And it was these councils that the local populace mostly consulted in order to resolve issues regarding property and taxation.[8] To a certain extent, these councils 'translated' provincial life to the imperial centre and the imperial perspective to the locals and they took some liberties in this task. Chapter 5 focused on some examples to reveal the ways in which Vidin's administrative council investigated and reported the cases. What becomes clear is that Vidin's administrative council was able to report events in a particular way to achieve certain outcomes. Experienced members of the local government seem to be adept at explaining the events in the countryside in ways that would fit different groups' strategies.

When a complicated case was brought to the council, a member of the judicio-administrative sphere would be sent to investigate the matter and write a report for the council(s), which would meet to discuss the report. Neither the copy registers nor the interrogations allow us to understand the dynamics behind closed doors in these councils. The councils in Vidin did not keep their minutes (leaving no opportunity to assess the discussion environment inside the councils), and the interrogation files reveal little about how the actual questioning took place. The clerks of the judiciary council carried out the interrogations in a separate room, presenting the council members with the written testimonies. However, both the participation patterns examined in Chapter 4 and some of the cases analysed in Chapter 5 indicate that personal disputes among the members were an integral component of discussions in the councils and abuse of power was a persistent feature of local governance.

This is why we need to read the reports of these councils with caution. The council members were clearly aware of their power. Although they were not paid a salary, being at the centre of these organisations rendered them significant members of the judicio-administrative sphere. In this position, they engaged in strategic negotiations of power with the other members of this sphere and with the community in general. It is important to note that this was not a system where one person (such as the subgovernor or Zayko Ağa) or a group (such as the elected members) consistently dominated other Vidiners. My concern is not to paint a picture of oppressors vs the oppressed, because I do not wish to argue that one particular group consistently dominated the other even during the brief period under study here. Such an argument would fail to capture the complexity of power relations at the local level, which operated through an interweaving of the institutional structure and the agents utilising that structure. Local administration was a highly politicised process at this time of institutional restructuring, and the documents produced or edited by the offices of this textually mediated judicio-administrative sphere reflect the political nature of this process.

Politics of Liberalism

Ottoman provincial governance not only served as a negotiation platform for the politics of local administration but it also contributed to the problematisation of issues that were at the heart of the liberal-capitalist Ottoman social formation. As the provincial judicio-administrative sphere's treatment of the Circassian (and Tatar, Bulgarian and other) refugees reveals, issues pertaining to the 'dangers' created by the settlement process brought with it a necessary involvement by the Ottoman governance. The belief in the necessity to maintain a presumed spontaneous order of the market by providing security contributed to the *raison d'être* and the limits of Ottoman governmentality at the local level. Through its debates and actions, the offices and members of the single government of state and society in Vidin, however underfunded they were, contributed to the foundation of the liberal-capitalist order in the Ottoman Empire in the second half of the nineteenth century.

The focus of Ottoman biopolitics was not just the refugees. As part of multifaceted technologies of governance in the liberal-capitalist order, Ottoman refugee policies reflected similar concerns 'to rationalize the problems posed to governmental practice by phenomena characteristic of a set of living beings forming a population: health, hygiene, birth-rate, life expectancy, race' that are characteristic of many of the reforms in the eighteenth and nineteenth centuries (Foucault 2008: 317). The problematisation of refugee settlement in politics of local administration, however, provides a useful lens to explore the connections between politics and economics at the provincial level.

Conclusion

The shaping of a liberal-capitalist order in the Ottoman Empire was a process that began earlier and necessitated a shift of authority to networks of community notables involved in politics of local administration in the course of the long nineteenth century. The purpose of *Nineteenth-century Local Governance in Ottoman Bulgaria* was to reveal how this shift occurred. This was not the result of provincial reforms limited to the Tanzimat era, and imposed from the imperial centre. However, this shift could not have happened only in the provincial political sphere of post-1840s. Unfortunately, we know very little about the fiscal/financial organisational structure in the provinces prior to the elimination of the Janissary forces. Understanding the operation of provincial economies in the late eighteenth and early nineteenth centuries can help us extend the limits of studies of reform in the Ottoman Empire.

Notes

1. Abou-El-Haj also emphasised the significance of understanding the 'middle centuries' (1580–1800) in the first edition (1991) of his influential book where he was critical of the pre-1990s Ottoman historiography. While he elaborated more on this issue in the second edition (2005: 81–90), he did not refer to the works by scholars like Doumani (1995) or Khoury (1997) who do emphasise the middle centuries.
2. It is important to note that the Ottoman Empire's ability to incorporate local notables as part of its provincial rule predated the nineteenth century. This point is elaborated in Salzmann (1993). Cf. Hathaway (1997: 24–31) and Khoury (1997: 75–108).
3. Midhat (1903: 34–5).
4. Studies on Midhat Paşa's governorships show his sensitivity to the local socio-economic and political structure in introducing the reforms. For example, see Abu-Manneh 1998; Göyünç 1982; Todorova 1993; Petrov 2006. Midhat Paşa was not the only person who paid close attention to issues with provincial administration. The Ottoman grand vizier Kıbrıslı Mehmed Emin Paşa went on an inspection tour of the Balkans himself during the summer of 1860 to observe issues with provincial administration there (Köksal and Erkan 2007).
5. Meeker (2002: 224–5) gives a four-tiered stratification consisting of the imperial elite, regional elite, greater local elites and lesser local elites (see particularly his Table 2 on pp. 224–5). Cf. Zens (2004, 38–9); Khoury (2006, 153–5); and McGowan (1994: 662–3).
6. Here I am not referring to the rhetoric of decline that was prevalent among the Ottoman intellectuals during the long nineteenth century (Hathaway and Barbir 2008: 66). Rather, the term crisis applies to the complex institutional transformation involving not just organisations but the procedures and practices of governance and legitimacy I discussed in Chapter 2. This

transformation lasted for a couple centuries and was associated with the formation of the Ottoman liberal-capitalist social formation in which governance played a specific role of maintaining a market order.
7. The Tanzimat reforms were underfunded (Çakır 2001: 217–22; Findley 2010: 106–9, 159) and several bureaucrats and intellectuals criticised the imperial administration's financial policies (Çakır 2001: 141–216). Furthermore, the reforms also led to uprisings among the provincial populace (Uzun 2002; İnalcık 1993; Çadırcı 1994). In the face of such opposition and in an environment where the state's ability to closely monitor the application of the reforms was rather costly it would not be an exaggeration to claim that these councils were highly significant for efficient and effective application of the reforms.
8. I do not wish to presume that these offices were the only places that property disputes were resolved. In addition to the *shar'i* court that dealt with inheritance cases, there might have been other socially accepted but unofficial venues for dispute resolution that were not recorded by the organisations of the judicio-administrative sphere. On the transformation of *shar'i* courts in this period see Agmon (2006: 68–97). Property cases regarding foreigners in the Ottoman Empire were adjudicated at the council of appeals and crime after 1870. For more on the regulations regarding interaction of foreign nationals with the organisations of the judicio-administrative sphere see Twiss (1880: 12ff).

Select Bibliography

Archives

Başbakanlık Osmanlı Arşivi (BOA) – Prime Ministry Ottoman Archives
  A.MKT.MHM: Sadaret Mektubi Mühimme Kalemi Evrakı
  A.MKT.MVL: Sadaret Mektubi Kalemi Meclis-i Vala Evrakı
  A.MKT.NZD: Sadaret Mektubi Kalemi Nezaret ve Deva'ir Evrakı
  A.MKT.ŞD: Sadaret Mektubi Şura-yı Devlet Evrakı
  AMKT.UM: Sadaret Mektubi Kalemi Umum Vilayat Evrakı
  Ayniyat: Ayniyat Defterleri
  DH.HMŞ: Dahiliye Nezareti Hukuk Müşavirliği Evrakı
  DH. MKT: Dahiliye Nezareti Mektubi Kalemi
  DUİT: Dosya Usulü İrade Tasnifi
  İ. DH: İrade Dahiliye
  İ. HR: İrade Hariciye
  İ. MVL: İrade Meclis-i Vala
  Maliyeden Müdevver Defterler
  ŞD: Şura-yı Devlet Evrakı
  Y.PRK.KOMŞ: Yıldız Perakende Evrakı Komisyanlar Maruzatı
Narodna biblioteka 'Kiril i Metodiĭ' (NBKM) – Sts. Cyril and Methodius National Library, Oriental Section
  26: Fond 26 (Vidin)
  OAK: Fond OAK
  VD: Vidin pred-fond
Vidin State Archives
  ф. 17: Fond 17
National Archives, Kew
  FO 78
  FO 97
  FO 424
  FO 881

Encyclopedias and Dictionaries

Detrez, Raymond. 1997. *Historical Dictionary of Bulgaria.* Lanham, MD: Scarecrow Press.

Devellioğlu, Ferit. (1962) 1997. *Osmanlıca-Türkçe ansiklopedik lûgat*. 14th ed. Ankara: Aydın Kitabevi.
Encyclopaedia of Islam, Second Edition, edited by P. Bearman, Th. Bianquis, C. E. Bosworth, E. van Donzel and W. P. Heinrichs. Brill Online: Brill.
İslam ansiklopedisi. 1988–2013. Istanbul: Türkiye Diyanet Vakfı.
Loewe, Louis. 1854. *A Dictionary of the Circassian Language. In Two Parts: English Circassian Turkish, and Circassian English Turkish. Containing All the Most Necessary Words for the Traveller, the Soldier, and the Sailor; with the Exact Pronunciation of Each Word in the English Character*. London: G. Bell.
Redhouse, James W. 1890. *A Turkish and English Lexicon: Shewing in English the Signification of the Turkish Terms*. Beirut: Librarie du Liban.

Official Publications

1851. *Mecmu'a-yı kavanin (Düstur)*. Istanbul: Takvimhane-i 'Amire.
1863. *Düstur-ı atik*. 1st ed. Istanbul: Matba'a-yı 'Amire.
1866. *Düstur-ı atik*. 2nd ed. Istanbul: Matba'a-yı 'Amire.
1868–77. *Salname-i Vilayet-i Tuna*. 10 vols. Rusçuk (Ruse): Matba'a-i Vilayet-i Tuna.
1872a. *Düstur: I. Tertib*. Vol. 1. Istanbul: Matba'a-yı 'Amire.
1872b. *Düstur: I. Tertib*. Vol. 3. Istanbul: Matba'a-yı 'Amire.
1902. *Zemledelcheska statistika prez 1897 godina po nacelenie mecta*. Sofia: Durzhavna Pechatnitsa.
1945. *Spis'k na naselenite mesta*. Sofia: Durzhavna Pechatnitsa.
USOG (United States Office of Geography). 1959. *Bulgaria: Official Standard Names Approved by the United States Board on Geographic Names*. Washington, DC: Office of Geography.

Secondary Sources

Abou-El-Haj, Rifa'at 'Ali. 1991. *Formation of the Modern State: The Ottoman Empire, Sixteenth to Eighteenth Centuries*. Albany: State University of New York Press.
Abou-El-Haj, Rifa'at 'Ali. 1994. 'A Response to Linda Darling's Review of *Formation of the Modern State: the Ottoman Empire Sixteenth to Eighteenth Centuries*'. *IJMES* 26: 173–6.
Abou-El-Haj, Rifa'at 'Ali. 2005. *Formation of the Modern State: the Ottoman Empire, Sixteenth to Eighteenth Centuries*, 2nd ed. Syracuse: Syracuse University Press.
Abu-Manneh, Butrus. 1998. 'The Genesis of Midhat Pasha's Governorship in Syria 1878–1880'. In *The Syrian Land: Processes of Integration and Fragmentation in Bilad Al Sham from the 18th to the 20th Century*, edited by Thomas Philipp and Birgit Schäbler, 251–67. Stuttgart: Franz Steiner Verlag.

Select Bibliography

Adanır, Fikret. 2006. 'Semi-Autonomous Provincial Forces in the Balkans and Anatolia'. In *The Cambridge History of Turkey: the Later Ottoman Empire, 1603–1839*, edited by Suraiya Faroqhi, 157–87. New York: Cambridge University Press.

Adanır, Fikret, and Suraiya Faroqhi (eds). 2002. *The Ottomans and the Balkans: a Discussion of Historiography*. Boston: Brill.

Agmon, Iris. 2006. *Family and Court: Legal Culture and Modernity in Late Ottoman Palestine*. Syracuse: Syracuse University Press.

Akarlı, Engin. 2004. 'Gedik: a Bundle of Rights and Obligations for Istanbul Artisans and Traders, 1750–1840'. In *Law, Anthropology and the Constitution of the Social: Making Persons and Things*, edited by Alain Pottage and Martha Mundy, 166–200. Cambridge: Cambridge University Press.

Akgündüz, Ahmed. 2005. *Osmanlı Devleti'nde belediye teşkilatı ve belediye kanunları*. Istanbul: Osmanlı Araştırmaları Vakfı.

Akiba, Jun. 2005. 'From Kadi to Naib: Reorganisation of the Ottoman Sharia Judiciary in the Tanzimat Period'. In *Frontiers of Ottoman Studies: State, Province, and the West*, edited by Colin Imber, Keiko Kiyotaki and Rhoads Murphey, 43–60. London: I. B. Tauris.

Akiba, Jun. 2009. 'The Local Councils as the Origin of the Parliamentary System in the Ottoman Empire'. In *Development of Parliamentarism in the Modern Islamic World*, edited by Tsugitaka Sato, 176–204. Tokyo: The Toyo Bunko.

Anastasopoulos, Antonis and Yannis Spyropoulos. 2017. 'Soldiers on an Ottoman Island: the Janissaries of Crete, Eighteenth – Early Nineteenth Centuries'. *Turkish Historical Review* 8 (1): 1–33.

Anderson, Benedict R. O'G. 1983. *Imagined Communities: Reflections on the Origin and Spread of Nationalism*. London: Verso Editions.

Anderson, Lisa. 1987. 'The State in the Middle East and North Africa'. *Comparative Politics* 20 (1): 1–18.

Anscombe, Frederick F. (ed.). 2006. *The Ottoman Balkans, 1750–1830*. Princeton: Markus Wiener Publishers.

Anscombe, Frederick F. 2012. 'The Balkan Revolutionary Age'. *The Journal of Modern History* 84 (3): 572–606.

Anscombe, Frederick F. 2014. *State, Faith, and Nation in Ottoman and Post-Ottoman Lands*. Cambridge: Cambridge University Press.

Arıcanlı, Tosun. 1998. '19. Yüzılda Anadolu'da mülkiyet toprak ve emek'. In *Osmanlı'da toprak mülkiyeti ve ticari tarım*, edited by Çağlar Keyder and Faruk Tabak, 128–39. Istanbul: Türkiye Ekonomik ve Toplumsal Tarih Vakfı.

Asad, Talal. 2003. *Formations of the Secular: Christianity, Islam, Modernity*. Stanford: Stanford University Press.

Atabaki, Touraj and Gavin D. Brockett. 2009. 'Ottoman and Republican Turkish Labour History: an Introduction'. *International Review of Social History* 54: 1–17.

Ayalon, A. 'Na'ib'. *EI2*.
Aykan, Yavuz. Forthcoming. 'Property between Life and Death: a Legal Debate over the Property of a Missing Person (*Gâib*) in Eighteenth-Century Ottoman Amid'. In *Justice, Statecraft and Law: a New Ottoman Legal History*, edited by Huricihan İslamoğlu and M. Safa Saraçoğlu. Syracuse: Syracuse University Press.
Aymes, Marc. 2010. *Un grand progrès, sur le papier: histoire provinciale des réformes ottomanes à Chypre au XIXe siècle, Collection Turcica*. Leuven: Peeters.
Aymes, Marc. 2014. *A Provincial History of the Ottoman Empire: Cyprus and the Eastern Mediterranean in the 19th Century*. New York: Routledge.
Ayoub, Samy. 2015. 'The Mecelle, Sharia, and the Ottoman State: Fashioning and Refashioning of Islamic Law in the Nineteenth and Twentieth Centuries'. *JOTSA* 2 (1): 121–46.
Aytekin, E. Attila. 2006. 'Land, Rural Classes, and Law: Agrarian Conflict and State Regulation in the Ottoman Empire, 1830s–1860s'. PhD Dissertation, History, State University of New York, Binghamton.
Aytekin, E. Attila. 2012. 'Peasant Protest in the Late Ottoman Empire: Moral Economy, Revolt, and the Tanzimat Reforms'. *International Review of Social History* 57 (2): 191–227.
Aytekin, E. Attila. 2013. 'Tax Revolts During the Tanzimat Period (1839–1876) and before the Young Turk Revolution (1904–1908): Popular Protest and State Formation in the Late Ottoman Empire'. *Journal of Policy History* 25 (3): 308–33.
Bajraktarević, F. 'Paswanoghlu'. *EI2*.
Baker, James. 1877. *Turkey*. New York: H. Holt & Co.
Bakhtin, M. M. 1981. *The Dialogic Imagination: Four Essays*. Translated by Michael Holquist and Caryl Emerson. Austin: University of Texas Press.
Barakat, Nora Elizabeth. 2015. 'An Empty Land? Nomads and Property Administration in Hamidian Syria'. PhD Dissertation, History, University of California, Berkeley.
Barkan, Ömer Lütfi. 1999. 'Türk toprak hukuku tarihinde Tanzimat ve 1274 (1858) tarihli arazi kanunnamesi'. In *Tanzimat*. Vol. 1, 321–421. Istanbul: Milli Eğitim Bakanlığı.
Barkley, Henry C. 1877. *Bulgaria before the War during Seven Years' Experience of European Turkey and Its Inhabitants*. London: J. Murray.
Bartov, Omer and Eric D. Witz. 2013. *Shatterzone of Empires: Coexistence and Violence in the German, Habsburg, Russian, and Ottoman Borderlands*. Bloomington: Indiana University Press.
Ben-Bassat, Yuval. 2013. *Petitioning the Sultan: Protests and Justice in Late Ottoman Palestine, 1865–1908*. New York: I. B. Tauris.
Berki, Ali Himmet. 1938. *Eski hâdiselerde tatbiki lâzımgelen irs ve intikal*. Ankara: Hapishane Matbaası.

Select Bibliography

Bingöl, Sedat. 2002. *Hırsova kaza deavi meclisi tutanakları: nizamiye mahkemesi tutanaklarından bir örnek*. Eskişehir: Anadolu Üniversitesi Yayınları.

Bingöl, Sedat. 2004. *Tanzimat devrinde Osmanlı'da yargı reformu: nizamiyye mahkemeleri'nin kuruluşu ve işleyişi 1840–1876*. Eskişehir: Anadolu Üniversitesi Yayınları.

Birdal, Murat. 2010. *The Political Economy of Ottoman Public Debt: Insolvency and European Financial Control in the Late 19th Century*. New York: I. B. Tauris.

Blumi, Isa. 2011. *Reinstating the Ottomans: Alternative Balkan Modernities, 1800–1912*. New York: Palgrave Macmillan.

Blumi, Isa. 2012. *Foundations of Modernity: Human Agency and the Imperial State, Routledge Studies in Modern History*. New York: Routledge.

Blumi, Isa. 2013. *Ottoman Refugees, 1878–1939: Migration in a Post-Imperial World*. New York: Bloomsbury.

Bowen, H. 'Ahmad Djevdet Pasha'. *EI2*.

Bowen, H. 'A'yan'. *EI2*.

Braudel, Fernand. 1992. *The Perspective of the World: Civilization and Capitalism 15th–18th Century*. Berkeley: University of California Press.

Buchanan, Donna A. 2007. '"Oh, Those Turks!" Music, Politics, and Interculturality in the Balkans and Beyond'. In *Balkan Popular Culture and the Ottoman Ecumene: Music, Image, and Regional Political Discourse*, edited by Donna A. Buchanan, 3–57. Lanham, MD: Scarecrow Press.

Burbank, Jane and Frederick Cooper. 2010. *Empires in World History: Power and the Politics of Difference*. Princeton: Princeton University Press.

Çadırcı, Musa. 1994. 'Tanzimat'ın uygulanmasında karşılaşılan bazı güçlükler'. In *Tanzimatın 150. yıldönümü uluslararası sempozyumu: Ankara, 31 Ekim – 3 Kasım 1989*, edited by Türk Tarih Kurumu, 295–300. Ankara: Türk Tarih Kurumu.

Çadırcı, Musa. 1997. *Tanzimat döneminde anadolu kentleri'nin sosyal ve ekonomik yapısı*. Ankara: Türk Tarih Kurumu.

Çakır, Coşkun. 2001. *Tanzimat dönemi Osmanlı maliyesi*. Istanbul: Küre Yayınları.

Casale, Giancarlo. 2010. *The Ottoman Age of Exploration*. New York: Oxford University Press.

Cevdet Paşa, Ahmed [1869?]. 'Mahkeme-i temyizin hukuk şubesinin vazifesi'. *Atatürk Library, Muallim Cevdet Yazmaları* (O.0006).

Ceylan, Ebubekir. 2011. *The Ottoman Origins of Modern Iraq: Political Reform, Modernization and Development in the 19th Century Middle East*. New York: I. B. Tauris.

Cezar, Yavuz. 1986. *Osmanlı maliyesinde bunalım ve değişim dönemi: 18. yüzyıldan Tanzimat'a mali tarih*. Istanbul: Alan Yayıncılık.

Chatterjee, Partha. 1993. *The Nation and Its Fragments: Colonial and Postcolonial Histories*. Princeton: Princeton University Press.

Chatty, Dawn. 2010. *Displacement and Dispossession in the Modern Middle East*. New York: Cambridge University Press.
Cin, Halil. 1987. *Miri arazi ve bu arazinin özel mülkiyete dönüşümü*. Konya: Selçuk Üniversitesi.
Clark, Hyde. 1890. 'The Right of Property in Trees on the Land of Another, as an Ancient Institution'. *The Journal of the Anthropological Institute of Great Britain and Ireland* 19: 199–211.
Crampton, R. J. 2005. *A Concise History of Bulgaria*. 2nd ed. New York: Cambridge University Press.
Cuno, Kenneth M. 1992. *The Pasha's Peasants: Land, Society, and Economy in Lower Egypt, 1740–1858*. New York: Cambridge University Press.
Cuthell, David Cameron (Jr). 2005. 'The Muhacirin Komisyonu: an Agent in the Transformation of Ottoman Anatolia'. PhD Dissertation, History, Columbia University.
Daskalov, Rumen. 2004. *The Making of a Nation in the Balkans: Historiography of the Bulgarian Revival*. Budapest: Central European University Press.
Davison, Roderic H. 1963. *Reform in the Ottoman Empire, 1856–1876*. Princeton: Princeton University Press.
Davison, Roderic H. 1993. 'Effect of the Electric Telegraph on the Conduct of Ottoman Foreign Relations'. In *Decision-Making and Change in the Ottoman Empire*, edited by Caesar E. Farah, 53–66. Kirksville: Thomas Jefferson University Press.
De Kay, James E. 1833. *Sketches of Turkey in 1831 and 1832*. New York: J. & J. Harper.
Deguilhem, Randi. 2005. 'Shared Space or Contested Space: Religious Mixity, Infrastructural Hierarchy and the Builders' Guild in Mid-Nineteenth Century Damascus'. In *Crafts and Craftsmen of the Middle East: Fashioning the Individual in the Muslim Mediterranean*, edited by Suraiya Faroqhi and Randi Deguilhem, 261–80. London: I. B. Tauris.
Demirel, Fatmagül. 2003. 'Adliye nezaretinin kuruluşu ve faaliyetleri (1876–1914)'. PhD Dissertation, History, Istanbul University.
Deny, J. 2007. 'Ahmad Wafik Pasha'. *EI2*.
Dimitrov, Strashimir. 1972. *Vustanieto ot 1850 godina v Bulgariia*. Sofia: BAN.
Dimitrova-Grajzl, Valentina P. 2007. 'The Ottoman Economic Legacy on the Balkans'. *SSRN*. 2 January. <http://ssrn.com/paper=986265>.
Doumani, Beshara. 1995. *Rediscovering Palestine: Merchants and Peasants in Jabal Nablus, 1700–1900*. Berkeley: University of California Press.
Doumani, Beshara. 1998. 'Endowing Family: Waqf, Property Devolution, and Gender in Greater Syria, 1800 to 1860'. *Comparative Studies in Society and History* 40 (2): 3–41.
Duara, Prasenjit. 1995. *Rescuing History from the Nation: Questioning Narratives of Modern China*. Chicago: University of Chicago Press.
Duman, Hasan. 2000. *Osmanlı salnameleri ve nevsalleri*. 2 vols. Vol. 1. Ankara: Enformasyon ve Dokümantasyon Hizmetleri Vakfı.

Select Bibliography

Efe, Ayla. 2002. 'Muhassıllık teşkilatı'. PhD Dissertation, Tarih Bölümü, Eskişehir Anadolu Üniversitesi.

Ekinci, Ekrem Buğra. 2000. 'Tanzimat devri Osmanlı mahkemeleri'. *Yeni Türkiye* 31: 764–73.

Engelhardt, Edouard Philippe. (1882) 1999. *Tanzimat ve Türkiye*. Translated by Ali Reşat. Istanbul: Kaknüs Yayınları.

Ergene, Boğaç A. 2001. 'On Ottoman Justice: Interpretations in Conflict (1600–1800)'. *Islamic Law and Society* 8 (1): 52–87.

Ergene, Boğaç A. 2003. *Local Court, Provincial Society and Justice in the Ottoman Empire: Legal Practice and Dispute Resolution in Çankırı and Kastamonu (1652–1744)*. Leiden: Brill.

Ergin, Osman. 1939. *İstanbul mektepleri ve ilim, terbiye ve sanat müesseseleri dolayısıyla Türkiye maarif tarihi*. 5 vols. Istanbul: Osmanbey Matbaası.

Ergin, Osman Nuri. 1995. *Mecelle-i umur-ı belediyye*. Vol. 1. İstanbul: İstanbul Büyükşehir Belediyesi Kültür İşleri Daire Başkanlığı.

Evered, Emine Önhan. 2012. *Empire and Education under the Ottomans: Politics, Reform and Resistance from the Tanzimat to the Young Turks*. New York: I. B. Tauris.

Faroqhi, Suraiya. 1994. 'Crisis and Change, 1590–1699'. In *An Economic and Social History of the Ottoman Empire 1600–1914*. Vol. 2, edited by Suraiya Faroqhi, Bruce McGowan, Donald Quataert, Sevket Pamuk, 411–636. New York: Cambridge University Press.

Faroqhi, Suraiya. 2002. 'Coping with the Central State, Coping with Local Power: Ottoman Regions and Notables from Sixteenth to the Early Nineteenth Century'. In *The Ottomans and the Balkans: a Discussion of Historiography*, edited by Fikret Adanır and Suraiya Faroqhi, 351–82. Boston: Brill.

Faroqhi, Suraiya. 2006a. 'Guildsmen and Handicraft Producers'. In *The Cambridge History of Turkey: the Later Ottoman Empire, 1603–1839*, edited by Suraiya Faroqhi, 336–55. New York: Cambridge University Press.

Faroqhi, Suraiya. 2006b. 'Introduction'. In *The Cambridge History of Turkey: the Later Ottoman Empire, 1603–1839*, edited by Suraiya Faroqhi, 3–18. New York: Cambridge University Press.

Faroqhi, Suraiya (ed.). 2006c. *The Later Ottoman Empire, 1603–1839*. Vol. 3, *The Cambridge History of Turkey*. New York: Cambridge University Press.

Faroqhi, Suraiya. 2006d. 'Rural Life'. In *The Cambridge History of Turkey: the Later Ottoman Empire, 1603–1839*, edited by Suraiya Faroqhi, 376–90. New York: Cambridge University Press.

Faroqhi, Suraiya. 2009. *Artisans of Empire: Crafts and Craftspeople under the Ottomans*. London: I. B. Tauris.

Faroqhi, Suraiya and Fikret Adanır. 2002. 'Introduction'. In *The Ottomans and the Balkans: a Discussion of Historiography*, edited by Fikret Adanır and Suraiya Faroqhi, 1–57. Boston: Brill.

Findley, Carter V. 1980. *Bureaucratic Reform in the Ottoman Empire: the Sublime Porte, 1789–1922*. Princeton: Princeton University Press.

Findley, Carter V. 1989. *Ottoman Civil Officialdom: a Social History*. Princeton: Princeton University Press.

Findley, Carter V. 2008. 'Tanzimat'. In the *Cambridge History of Turkey*. Vol. 4. *Turkey in the Modern World*, edited by Reşat Kasaba, 11–37. New York: Cambridge University Press.

Findley, Carter V. 2010. *Turkey, Islam, Nationalism, and Modernity: a History, 1789–2007*. New Haven: Yale University Press.

Findley, Carter V. 'Muhassıl'. *EI2*.

Fortna, Benjamin C. 2002. *Imperial Classroom: Islam, the State, and Education in the Late Ottoman Empire*. New York: Oxford University Press.

Foucault, Michel. 1980. 'Truth and Strategies'. In *Power/Knowledge: Selected Interviews and Other Writings, 1972–1977*, edited by Colin Gordon, 134–46. New York: Pantheon Books.

Foucault, Michel. 1982. *The Archaeology of Knowledge and the Discourse on Language*. New York: Pantheon Books.

Foucault, Michel. 1984. 'Polemics, Politics, and Problematizations: an Interview with Michel Foucault'. In *The Foucault Reader*, 1st edition, edited by Paul Rabinow, 382–90. New York: Pantheon Books.

Foucault, Michel. 1991. 'Governmentality'. In *The Foucault Effect: Studies in Governmentality*, edited by G. Burchell, C. Gordon and P. Miller, 87–104. Chicago: University of Chicago Press.

Foucault, Michel. 1997a. 'The Birth of Biopolitics'. In *Ethics: Subjectivity and Truth*, edited by Paul Rabinow, 73–80. New York: The New Press.

Foucault, Michel. 1997b. 'On the Government of the Living'. In *Ethics: Subjectivity and Truth*, edited by Paul Rabinow, 81–5. New York: The New Press.

Foucault, Michel. 2000. 'The Political Technology of Individuals'. In *Power*, edited by James D. Faubion, 403–17. New York: The New Press.

Foucault, Michel. 2007. *Security, Territory, Population: Lectures at the Collège De France, 1977–78*. Translated by Graham Burchell. Edited by Michel Senellart. New York: Palgrave Macmillan.

Foucault, Michel. 2008. *The Birth of Biopolitics: Lectures at the Collège De France, 1978–79*. Translated by Graham Burchell. Edited by Michel Senellart. New York: Palgrave Macmillan.

Foucault, Michel and Colin Gordon. 1980. *Power/Knowledge: Selected Interviews and Other Writings, 1972–1977*. New York: Pantheon Books.

Foucault, Michel and Frédéric Gros (eds). 2005. *The Hermeneutics of the Subject: Lectures at the Collège de France, 1981–1982*. New York: Palgrave Macmillan.

Genç, Mehmet. 2000. 'Osmanlı maliyesinde malikane sistemi'. In *Osmanlı İmparatorluğu'nda devlet ve ekonomi*, edited by Mehmet Genç, 99–152. Istanbul: Ötüken Neşriyat.

Gerber, Haim. 1985. *Ottoman Rule in Jerusalem, 1890–1914*. Berlin: K. Schwarz.

Gerber, Haim. 1987. *The Social Origins of the Modern Middle East*. Boulder, CO: Lynne Rienner.

Select Bibliography

Ghazaleh, Pascale. 2005. 'Organising Labour: Professional Classifications in Late Eighteenth to Early Nineteenth Century Cairo'. In *Crafts and Craftsmen of the Middle East: Fashioning the Individual in the Muslim Mediterranean*, edited by Suraiya Faroqhi and Randi Deguilhem, 235–60, London: I. B. Tauris.

Giddens, Anthony. 1985. *The Nation-State and Violence: Volume Two of a Contemporary Critique of Historical Materialism*. Cambridge: Polity Press.

Glenny, Misha. 2000. *The Balkans: Nationalism, War, and the Great Powers, 1804–1999*. New York: Viking.

Gölen, Zafer. 2010. *Tanzîmât döneminde Bosna Hersek: siyasî, idarî, sosyal ve ekonomik durum*. Ankara: Türk Tarih Kurumu.

Goody, Jack. 2000. *The Power of the Written Tradition*. Washington: Smithsonian Institution Press.

Göyünç, Nejat. 1982. 'Midhat Paşa'nın Niş valiliği hakkında notlar ve belgeler'. *İstanbul Üniversitesi Edebiyat Fakültesi Tarih Enstitüsü Dergisi* 12: 279–316.

Gradeva, Rossitsa. 2006. 'Osman Pazvantoğlu of Vidin: Between Old and New'. In *The Ottoman Balkans, 1750–1830*, edited by Frederick F. Anscombe, 115–62. Princeton: Markus Wiener Publishers.

Gramsci, Antonio. 1971. *Selections from the Prison Notebooks*. Translated by Q. Hoare and G. N. Smith. New York: International Publishers.

Grigsby, W. E. 1895. *The Medjellè or Ottoman Civil Law*. Nicosia: Herbert E. Clarke.

Gros, Frédéric. 2005. 'Course Context'. In *The Hermeneutics of the Subject: Lectures at the Collège de France, 1981–1982*, edited by Michel Foucault and Frédéric Gros, 507–50. New York: Palgrave Macmillan.

Güran, Tevfik. 1989. *Tanzimat döneminde Osmanlı maliyesi: bütçeler ve hazine hesapları, (1841–1861)*. Ankara: Türk Tarih Kurumu.

Güran, Tevfik. 1998. *19. yüzyıl Osmanlı tarımı üzerine araştırmalar*. Istanbul: Eren Yayıncılık.

Gutting, Gary. 2006. *The Cambridge Companion to Foucault*. New York: Cambridge University Press.

Habermas, Jürgen. 1975. *Legitimation Crisis*. Boston: Beacon Press.

Habiçoğlu, Bedri. 1993. *Kafkasya'dan Anadolu'ya göçler ve iskanları*. Istanbul: Nart Yayıncılık.

Hanssen, Jens. 2005. *Fin De Siècle Beirut: the Making of an Ottoman Provincial Capital*. New York: Oxford University Press.

Hathaway, Jane. 1997. *The Politics of Households in Ottoman Egypt: the Rise of the Qazdağlıs*. New York: Cambridge University Press.

Hathaway, Jane. 1998. 'Egypt in the Seventeenth Century'. In *Modern Egypt, from 1517 to the End of the Twentieth Century*, 34–58. New York: Cambridge University Press.

Hathaway, Jane and Karl K. Barbir. 2008. *The Arab Lands under Ottoman Rule, 1516–1800*. Harlow: Longman.

Hershlag, Zvi Yehuda. 1995. 'Attempts at Land Reform in the Ottoman Empire, 1789–1858'. In *Türkische Wirtschafts- und Sozialgeschichte (1071–1920): Akten des IV. Internationalen Kongresses, München 1986*, edited by Hans Georg Majer and Raoul Motika. Wiesbaden: Harrassowitz.

Hertslet, Edward. 1874. *The Foreign Office List: Forming a Complete British Diplomatic and Consular Handbook*. London: Harrison.

Hertslet, Edward. 1877. *The Foreign Office List: Forming a Complete British Diplomatic and Consular Handbook*. London: Harrison.

Hupchick, Dennis P. 2002. *The Balkans: from Constantinople to Communism*. New York: Palgrave.

Imber, Colin. 1982. 'The Status of Orchards and Fruit Trees in Ottoman Law'. *Tarih Enstitüsü Dergisi* 12: 763–74.

Imber, Colin. 1997. *Ebu's-su'ud: the Islamic Legal Tradition*. Stanford: Stanford University Press.

İnalcık, Halil. (1943) 1992. *Tanzimat ve Bulgar meselesi: Doktora tezinin 50. yılı*. Istanbul: Eren.

İnalcık, Halil. 1993. 'Tanzimat'ın uygulanması ve sosyal tepkiler'. In *Osmanlı İmparatorluğu: toplum ve ekonomi üzerinde arşiv çalışmaları, incelemeler*, 361–424. Istanbul: Eren Yayıncılık.

İnalcık, Halil. 1998. 'Islamization of Ottoman Laws on Land and Land Tax'. In *Essays in Ottoman History*, 155–74. Istanbul: Eren Yayıncılık.

İnalcık, Halil and Donald Quataert. 1994. *An Economic and Social History of the Ottoman Empire*. 2 vols. Vol. 1 *(1300–1600)*. New York: Cambridge University Press.

İslamoğlu-İnan, Huri. 1987. 'State and Peasants in the Ottoman Empire: a Study of Peasant Economy in North–Central Anatolia during the Sixteenth Century'. In *The Ottoman Empire and the World Economy*, edited by Huri İslamoğlu-İnan, 101–59. New York: Cambridge University Press.

İslamoğlu, Huricihan. 2000. 'Property as a Contested Domain: a Reevaluation of the Ottoman Land Code of 1858'. In *New Perspectives on Property and Land in the Middle East*, edited by Roger Owen, 3–62. Cambridge, MA: Harvard University Press.

İslamoğlu, Huricihan. 2004a. 'Politics of Administering Property: Law and Statistics in the Nineteenth-Century Ottoman Empire'. In *Constituting Modernity: Private Property in the East and West*, edited by Huricihan İslamoğlu, 276–320. New York: I. B. Tauris.

İslamoğlu, Huricihan. 2004b. 'Towards a Political Economy of Legal and Administrative Constitutions of Individual Property'. In *Constituting Modernity: Private Property in the East and West*, edited by Huricihan İslamoğlu, 3–34. New York: I. B. Tauris.

İslamoğlu, Huricihan, and Çağlar Keyder. 1977. 'Agenda for Ottoman History'. *Review* 1 (1): 31–55.

İslamoğlu, Huricihan and Peter C. Perdue. 2001. 'Introduction'. *Journal of Early Modern History* 5 (4): 271–81.

Select Bibliography

Ivanova, Svetlana. 'Widin'. *EI2*.
Jelavich, Barbara. 1983. *History of the Balkans*. Vol. 1. *Eighteenth and Nineteenth Centuries*. New York: Cambridge University Press.
Joseph, Sabrina. 2007. 'The Legal Status of Tenants and Sharecroppers in Seventeenth and Eighteenth-Century France and Ottoman Syria'. *Rural History* 18 (1): 23–46.
Kalkan, Ibrahim Halil. 2017. 'Between Medicine and Honor: the Legal Ban on Torture in the Ottoman Empire, 1840–1858'. *JOTSA* 4 (1): 31–53.
Kanitz, Felix Philipp. 1865. 'Die Tscherkessen Emigration nach der Donau'. *Österreichische Revue* 3 (1): 227–43.
Kanitz, Felix Philipp. 1875. *Donau-Bulgarien und der Balkan: historisch-geographisch-ethnographische reisestudien aus den Jahren 1860–1875*. 3 vols. Vol. 1. Leipzig: H. Fries.
Kanitz, Felix Philipp. 1882a. *Donau-Bulgarien und der Balkan: historisch-geographisch-ethnographische reisestudien aus den Jahren 1860–1879*. 2nd ed. 3 vols. Vol. 2. Leipzig: Renger'sche Buchhandlung.
Kanitz, Felix Philipp. 1882b. *La Bulgarie danubienne et le Balkan, études de voyage (1860–1880)*. Paris: Hachette.
Karakışla, Yavuz Selim. 1995. 'The Emergence of the Ottoman Industrial Working Class'. In *Workers and the Working Class in the Ottoman Empire and the Turkish Republic, 1839–1950*, edited by Donald Quataert and Erik Jan Zürcher, 19–34. New York: Tauris Academic Studies in Association with the International Institute of Social History.
Karakoç, Sarkis. 2006. *Külliyât-ı kavânîn: kavânîn ve nizâmât ve ferâmîn ve berevât ve irâdât-ı seniyye ile muâhedât ve umûma ait mukâvelâtı muhtevidir*. 2 vols. Ankara: Türk Tarih Kurumu.
Karakoç, Sarkiz. 1924. *Arâzi kanunu ve tapu nizamnamesi (tahşiyeli)*. Istanbul: Kitaphane-i Cihan.
Karpat, K. H. 2002. *Studies on Ottoman Social and Political History: Selected Articles and Essays*. Leiden: Brill.
Karpat, Kemal H. 1972. 'The Transformation of the Ottoman State, 1789–1908'. *IJMES* 3 (3): 243–81.
Karpat, Kemal H. 1985. *Ottoman Population, 1830–1914: Demographic and Social Characteristics*. Madison: University of Wisconsin Press.
Kasaba, Reşat (ed.). 2008. *Turkey in the Modern World*. Vol. 4, *The Cambridge History of Turkey*. New York: Cambridge University Press.
Kasaba, Reşat. 2009. *A Movable Empire: Ottoman Nomads, Migrants, and Refugees*. Seattle: University of Washington Press.
Kaynar, Reşat. 1985. *Mustafa Reşid Paşa ve Tanzimat*. 2nd ed. Ankara: Türk Tarih Kurumu.
Khoury, Dina Rizk. 1997. *State and Provincial Society in the Ottoman Empire: Mosul, 1540–1834*. New York: Cambridge University Press.
Khoury, Dina Rizk. 2006. 'The Ottoman Centre versus Provincial Power-Holders: an Analysis of the Historiography'. In *The Cambridge History of Turkey: the*

Later Ottoman Empire, 1603–1839, edited by Suraiya Faroqhi, 135–56. New York: Cambridge University Press.

Köksal, Yonca and Davut Erkan. 2007. *Sadrazam Kıbrıslı Mehmet Emin Paşa'nın Rumeli teftişi*. Istanbul: Boğaziçi Üniversitesi Yayınevi.

Kostova, Ludmilla. 1997. *Tales of Periphery: the Balkans in Nineteenth-Century British Writing*. Veliko Turnovo: Sts. Cyril and Methodius University Press.

Kuneralp, Sinan. 1999. *Son dönem Osmanlı erkan ve ricali, 1839–1922: Prosopografik rehber*. Istanbul: Isis.

Kütükoğlu, Mübahat S. 1974. *Osmanlı-İngiliz iktisadi münasebetleri*. Ankara: Türk Kültürünü Araştırma Enstitüsü.

Kütükoğlu, Mübahat. 'Mühür'. *IA*.

Kütükoğlu, Mübahat S. 1994. *Osmanlı belgelerinin dili: diplomatik*. Istanbul: Kubbealtı Akademisi Kültür ve San'at Vakfı.

Lafi, Nora. 2011. 'Petitions and Accommodating Urban Change in the Ottoman Empire'. In *Istanbul As Seen from a Distance*, edited by Elisabeth Ozdalga, Sait Ozervarlı and Feryal Tansug, 73–82. Istanbul: Swedish Research Institute in Istanbul.

Latham, J. D. 'Salam'. *EI2*.

Lemke, Thomas. 2011. *Biopolitics: an Advanced Introduction*. New York: New York University Press.

Leonhard, Jörn and Ulrike von Hirschhausen. 2011. *Comparing Empires: Encounters and Transfers in the Long Nineteenth Century*. Göttingen: Vandenhoeck and Ruprecht.

Lewis, Bernard. 'Bab-ı Mashikhat'. *EI2*.

Lockman, Zachary. 2004. *Contending Visions of the Middle East: the History and Politics of Orientalism*. New York: Cambridge University Press.

Long, Kaylene Ann Gebert. 1980. 'A Rhetorical Analysis of the 1876 Bulgarian Atrocities Agitation in England: a Study of Victorian Argument'. PhD Dissertation, Department of Speech Communication, Indiana University.

Mallon, Florencia E. 1995. *Peasant and Nation: the Making of Postcolonial Mexico and Peru*. Berkeley and London: University of California Press.

Mardin, Şerif. 1961. 'Some Notes on an Early Phase in the Modernization of Communications in Turkey'. *Comparative Studies in Society and History* 3 (3): 250–71.

McGowan, Bruce. 1981. *Economic Life in Ottoman Europe: Taxation, Trade, and the Struggle for Land, 1600–1800*. New York: Cambridge University Press.

McGowan, Bruce. 1994. 'The Age of the Ayans, 1699–1812'. In *An Economic and Social History of the Ottoman Empire 1600–1914*. Vol. 2, edited by Suraiya Faroqhi, Bruce McGowan, Donald Quataert, Sevket Pamuk, 637–758. New York: Cambridge University Press.

Meeker, Michael E. 2002. *A Nation of Empire: the Ottoman Legacy of Turkish Modernity*. Berkeley: University of California Press.

Meriwether, Margaret Lee. 1999. *The Kin Who Count: Family and Society in Ottoman Aleppo, 1770–1840*. Austin: University of Texas Press.

Select Bibliography

Messick, Brinkley Morris. 1993. *The Calligraphic State: Textual Domination and History in a Muslim Society.* Berkeley: University of California Press.

Michelsen, Edward Henry. 1854. *The Ottoman Empire and Its Resources; with Statistical Tables . . . Drawn from the Consular Reports . . . Returns of the Board of Trade, and Various Foreign Documents . . . Preceded by an Historical Sketch of the Events in Connection with the Foreign and Domestic Relations of the Country, during the Last 20 Years.* 2nd ed. London: W. Spooner.

Midhat, Ahmet. (1877–8) 2004. *Üss-i inkilap.* 2 vols. Vol. 1. Istanbul: Selis Kitaplar.

Midhat, Ali Haydar. 1903. *The Life of Midhat Pasha: a Record of His Services, Political Reforms, Banishment, and Judicial Murder.* London: J. Murray.

Midhat, Ali Haydar. 1997. *Midhat Paşa'nın hatıraları.* Edited by Osman S. Kocahanoğlu. 2 vols. Vol. 1. Istanbul: Temel Yayınları.

Mikhail, Alan. 2013. 'Unleashing the Beast: Animals, Energy, and the Economy of Labour in Ottoman Egypt'. *American Historical Review* 118 (2): 317–48.

Mitchell, Timothy. 1999. 'Society, Economy, and the State Effect'. In *State/Culture: State Formation after the Cultural Turn*, edited by George Steinmetz, 76–97. Ithaca: Cornell University Press.

Mundy, Martha. 2000. 'Village Authority and the Legal Order of Property (the Southern Hawran, 1876–1922)'. In *New Perspectives on Property and Land in the Middle East*, edited by Roger Owen, 63–92. Cambridge, MA: Harvard University Press.

Nacar, Can. 2014. 'The Régie Monopoly and Tobacco Workers in Late Ottoman Istanbul'. *Comparative Studies of South Asia, Africa and the Middle East* 34 (1): 206–19.

Newton, Charles Thomas and Dominic E. Colnaghi. 1865. *Travels & Discoveries in the Levant.* London: Day & Son.

North, Douglass Cecil. 1997. 'Economic Performance through Time'. In *Economic Sciences, 1991–1995: Nobel Lectures, Including Presentation Speeches and Laureates' Biographies*, edited by Torsten Persson, 112–27. River Edge, NJ: World Scientific.

North, Douglass Cecil. 2005. *Understanding the Process of Economic Change.* Princeton: Princeton University Press.

Nuri, Mustafa. 1992. *Netayic ül-vukuat: kurumları ve örgütleriyle Osmanlı tarihi.* Edited by Neşet Çağatay. 2 vols. Vol. 2. Ankara: Türk Tarih Kurumu.

Ökçün, A. Gündüz. 1996. *Ta'til-i eşgal kanunu, 1909: belgeler, yorumlar.* 2nd ed. Ankara: Sermaye Piyasası Kurulu.

Ortaylı, İlber. 2000. *Tanzimat devrinde Osmanlı mahalli idareleri (1840–1880).* Ankara: Türk Tarih Kurumu.

Ostrorog, Léon. 1979. *The Angora Reform: Three Lectures Delivered at the Centenary Celebrations of University College on June 27, 28 & 29, 1927.* Westport, CT: Hyperion Press.

Palairet, M. R. 1997. *The Balkan Economies, 1800–1914: Evolution without Development.* New York: Cambridge University Press.

Palalı, Ilhan. 2010. 'Osmanlı salnameleri ve tarih araştırmalarındaki kaynak olarak önemi'. *Harran Üniversitesi İlahiyat Fakültesi Dergisi* 23: 1–14.

Paras, Eric. 2006. *Foucault 2.0: Beyond Power and Knowledge*. New York: Other Press.

Parker, Geoffrey. 2013. *Global Crisis: War, Climate Change and Catastrophe in the Seventeenth Century*. New Haven: Yale University Press.

Parry, V. J. 1970. 'Materials of War in the Ottoman Empire'. In *Studies in the Economic History of the Middle East: from the Rise of Islam to the Present Day*, edited by M. A. Cook, 218–29. London: Oxford University Press.

Paz, Omri. 2015. 'The Usual Suspect: Worker Migration and Law Enforcement in Mid-Nineteenth-Century Anatolia'. *Continuity and Change* 30 (2): 223–49.

Perry, Duncan M. 1993. *Stefan Stambolov and the Emergence of Modern Bulgaria, 1870–1895*. Durham, NC: Duke University Press.

Petrov, Milen V. 2006. 'Tanzimat for the Countryside: Midhat Paşa and the Vilayet of Danube, 1864–1868'. PhD Dissertation, Near Eastern Studies, Princeton University.

Philliou, Christine May. 2011. *Biography of an Empire: Governing Ottomans in an Age of Revolution*. Berkeley: University of California Press.

Pinson, Mark. 1970. 'Demographic Warfare: an Aspect of Ottoman and Russian Policy, 1854–1866'. PhD Dissertation, History, Harvard University.

Pinson, Mark. 1972. 'Ottoman Colonisation of the Circassians in Rumili after the Crimean War'. *Etudes Balkaniques* 3: 71–85.

Popovic, Alexandre. 1991. 'The Cherkess on Yugoslav Territory (a Supplement to the Article "Cherkess" in the Encyclopaedia of Islam)'. *Central Asian Survey* 10 (1–2): 65–79.

Porter, James and G. G. de Hochepied Larpent. 1854. *Turkey: Its History and Progress*. 2 vols. Vol. 2. London: Hurst & Blackett.

Quataert, Donald. 1987. 'The Silk Industry of Bursa, 1880–1914'. In *The Ottoman Empire and the World-Economy*, edited by Huricihan İslamoğlu, 284–300. Cambridge: Cambridge University Press.

Quataert, Donald. 1997. 'The Age of Reforms, 1812–1914'. In *An Economic and Social History of the Ottoman Empire*, edited by Halil Inalcık, Suraiya Faroqhi, Bruce McGowan, Donald Quataert and Şevket Pamuk, 759–946. Cambridge: Cambridge University Press.

Quataert, Donald. 2001. 'Labour History and the Ottoman Empire, c.1700–1922'. *International Labour and Working-Class History* (60): 93–109.

Quataert, Donald. 2005. *The Ottoman Empire, 1700–1922*. 2nd ed. New York: Cambridge University Press.

Reed, H. A. 'Agha Husayn Pasha'. *EI2*.

Rogan, Eugene L. 1999. *Frontiers of the State in the Late Ottoman Empire: Transjordan, 1850–1921*. Cambridge: Cambridge University Press.

Rose, Nikolas and Peter Miller. 1992. 'Political Power beyond the State: Problematics of Government'. *British Journal of Sociology* 43 (2): 173–205.

Select Bibliography

Rosser-Owen, Sarah A. S. Isla. 2007. 'The First "Circassian Exodus" to the Ottoman Empire (1858–1867), and the Ottoman Response, Based on the Accounts of Contemporary British Observers'. MA Thesis, Near and Middle Eastern Studies of the School of Oriental and African Studies, University of London.

Rubin, Avi. 2009. 'Ottoman Judicial Change in the Age of Modernity: a Reappraisal'. *History Compass* 7 (1): 119–40.

Rubin, Avi. 2011. *Ottoman Nizamiye Courts: Law and Modernity*. New York: Palgrave Macmillan.

Rubin, Avi. 2012. 'British Perceptions of Ottoman Judicial Reform in the Late Nineteenth Century: Some Preliminary Insights'. *Law and Social Inquiry* 37: 991.

Rubin, Avi. 2016. 'Modernity as a Code: the Ottoman Empire and the Global Movement of Codification'. *Journal of the Economic and Social History of the Orient* 59 (5): 828–56.

Sahillioğlu, Halil. 1970. '*Sıvış* Year Crises'. In *Studies in the Economic History of the Middle East: from the Rise of Islam to the Present Day*, edited by M. A. Cook, 230–52. London: Oxford University Press.

Salzmann, Ariel. 1993. 'An Ancien Régime Revisited: "Privatization" and Political Economy in the 18th Century Ottoman Empire'. *Politics and Society* 21 (4): 393–423.

Saraçoğlu, M. Safa. 1998. 'A Snapshot of the County of Kafirni through the Surveys of 1845'. MA Thesis, Department of Economics, Middle East Technical University.

Saraçoğlu, M. Safa. 2015. 'Economic Interventionism, Islamic Law and Provincial Government in the Ottoman Empire'. *JOTSA* 2 (1): 59–84.

Saydam, Abdullah. 1997. *Kırım ve Kafkas göçleri, 1856–1876*. Ankara: Türk Tarih Kurumu.

Sayın, Abdurrahman Vefik. (1910–11) 1999. *Tekalif kavaidi: Osmanlı vergi sistemi*. Ankara: T. C. Maliye Bakanlığı.

Scott, James C. 1998. *Seeing Like a State: How Certain Schemes to Improve the Human Condition Have Failed*. New Haven: Yale University Press.

Şener, Abdüllatif. 1990. *Tanzimat dönemi Osmanlı vergi sistemi*. Istanbul: İşaret.

Şentürk, Hüdai. 1992. *Osmanlı Devleti'nde Bulgar meselesi (1850–1875)*. Ankara: Türk Tarih Kurumu.

Seyitdanlıoğlu, Mehmed. 1999. *Tanzimat devrinde meclis-i vala (1838–1868)*. Ankara: Türk Tarih Kurumu.

Shaham, R. 'Yatim'. *EI2*.

Shami, Seteney Khalid. 2000. 'Prehistories of Globalization: Circassian Identity in Motion'. *Public Culture* 12 (1): 177–204.

Shannon, Richard. 1975. *Gladstone and the Bulgarian Agitation 1876*. Hamden, CT: Harvester Press.

Shaw, Stanford Jay and Ezel Kural Shaw. 1978. *Reform, Revolution and Republic*. Vol. 2, *History of the Ottoman Empire and Modern Turkey*. Cambridge: Cambridge University Press.
Sherry, Dana. 2009. 'Social Alchemy on the Black Sea Coast, 1860–65'. *Kritika* 10 (1): 7–30.
Singer, Amy. 2000. 'A Note on Land and Identity: From Ze'amet to Waqf'. In *New Perspectives on Property and Land in the Middle East*, edited by Roger Owen, 161–73. Cambridge, MA: Harvard University Press.
Somel, Selçuk Akşin. 2000. 'Osmanlı modernleşme döneminde kız eğitimi'. *Kebikeç* 5 (10): 223–38.
Somel, Selçuk Akşin. 2001. *The Modernization of Public Education in the Ottoman Empire, 1839–1908: Islamization, Autocracy, and Discipline*. Boston: Brill.
Spencer, Edmund. 1839. *Travels in Circassia, Krim Tartary, etc., Including a Steam Voyage down the Danube, from Vienna to Constantinople, and Round the Black Sea*. 2 vols. Vol. 2. London: Colburn.
Spencer, Edmund. 1851. *Travels in European Turkey, in 1850; through Bosnia, Servia, Bulgaria, Macedonia, Thrace, Albania, and Epirus; with a Visit to Greece and the Ionian Isles*. 2 vols. Vol. 1. London: Colburn.
St Clair, S. G. B. and C. A. Brophy. 1869. *A Residence in Bulgaria; or, Notes on the Resources and Administration of Turkey*. London: John Murray.
Stavrianos, Leften Stavros. 2000. *The Balkans since 1453*. New York: New York University Press.
Stefanova, Milena Christova. 1998. *Kniga za Bulgarskite chorbadzii*. Sofia: Univ. Izdat. Sv. Kliment Ohridski.
Sûdi, Süleyman. 1888 (1306). *Defter-i muktesid*. 3 vols. Vol. 1. Istanbul: Mahmudbey Matbaası.
Teplov, V. 1877. *Materialy dlia statistiki Bolgarii, Frakii i Makedonii*. St Petersburg: n.p.
Tezcan, Baki. 2012. *The Second Ottoman Empire: Political and Social Transformation in the Early Modern World*. New York: Cambridge University Press.
Todorov, Nikolai. 1983. 'Données démographiques sur la population urbaine de la province Danubienne (Tuna Vilâyeti) en 1866'. In *Économie et sociétés dans l'Empire ottoman (fin du XVIIIe-début du XXe siècle): actes du colloque de Strasbourg (1er-5 Juillet 1980)*, edited by Jean-Louis Bacqué-Grammont and Paul Dumont. Paris: Éditions du centre national de la recherché scientifique.
Todorova, Mariia Nikolaeva. 1980. *Angliia, Rusiia i Tanzimatut*. Sofia: Nauka i Izkustvo.
Todorova, Mariia Nikolaeva. 1993. 'Midhat Paşa's Governorship of the Danube Province'. In *Decision Making and Change in the Ottoman Empire*, edited by Caesar E. Farah, 115–28. Kirksville: Thomas Jefferson University Press.

Select Bibliography

Todorova, Mariia Nikolaeva. 1996. 'The Ottoman Legacy in the Balkans'. In *Imperial Legacy: the Ottoman Imprint on the Balkans and the Middle East*, edited by Carl Brown, 45–77. New York: Columbia University Press.

Todorova, Mariia Nikolaeva. 1997. *Imagining the Balkans*. New York: Oxford University Press.

Toledano, Ehud. 1997. 'The Emergence of Ottoman–Local Elites (1700–1900): a Framework for Research'. In *Middle Eastern Politics and Ideas: A History from Within*, edited by Ilan Pappe, Moshe Ma'oz, 145–62. New York: Tauris Academic Studies.

Toledano, Ehud R. 2007. *As If Silent and Absent: Bonds of Enslavement in the Islamic Middle East*. New Haven: Yale University Press.

Tsukhlev, Dimitr N. 1932. *Istoriia na grada Vidin i negovata oblast*. Sofia: Pechatnitsa P. Glushkov.

Twiss, Sir Travers. 1880. *On Consular Jurisdiction in the Levant and the Status of Foreigners in the Ottoman Law Courts (Read at the Eighth Annual Conference of the Association for the Reform and Codification of the Law of Nations held in the Hall of the National Council at Berne)*. London: William Clowes and Sons Ltd.

Ubicini, Jean Henri Abdolonyme. 1856. *Letters on Turkey: an Account of the Religious, Political, Social, and Commercial Conditions of the Ottoman Empire*. Translated by Elizabeth Easthope. London: J. Murray.

Uzun, Ahmet. 2002. *Tanzimat ve sosyal direnişler: Niş isyanı üzerine ayrıntılı bir inceleme (1841)*. Istanbul: Eren Yayıncılık.

Vulchev, Genadi. 2001. *Vidinskite rodove*. Vol. 1. Vidin: n.p.

Vulchev, Genadi. 2003. *Deputatite ot Vidinski Oblast*. Vidin: n.p.

Vulchev, Genadi. 2006. *Vidni Vlasi ot Vidinskiya krai*. Vidin: SD Ekspres.

Wagner, William G. 1991. 'Ideology, Identity, and the Emergence of a Middle Class'. In *Between Czar and People: Educated Society and the Quest for Public Identity in Late Imperial Russia*, edited by Edith W. Clowes, Samuel D. Kassow and James L. West, 149–63. Princeton: Princeton University Press.

Waldron, Jeremy. 1988. *The Right to Private Property*. New York: Oxford University Press.

White, Sam. 2011. *The Climate of Rebellion in the Early Modern Ottoman Empire*. New York: Cambridge University Press.

Wixman, Ronald. 1984. *The Peoples of the USSR: an Ethnographic Handbook*. Armonk, NY: M. E. Sharpe.

Yaycioglu, Ali. 2016. *Partners of the Empire: the Crisis of the Ottoman Order in the Age of Revolutions*. Stanford: Stanford University Press.

Yazbak, Mahmoud. 1997. 'Nabulsi Ulama in the Late Ottoman Period, 1864–1914'. *IJMES* 29 (1): 71–91.

Yazbak, Mahmoud. 1998. *Haifa in the Late Ottoman Period, 1864–1914: a Muslim Town in Transition*. Leiden: Brill.

Yildirim, Kadir. 2015. 'Proletarianization by Dispossession: Companies, Technology Transfer and Porters in the Late Ottoman Empire'. *International Journal of Turcologia* 10 (19): 61–80.

Yildirim, Onur. 2001. 'Transformation of the Craft Guilds in Istanbul (1650–1860)'. *Islamic Studies* 40 (1): 49–66.

Zens, Robert W. 2004. 'The *Ayanlık* and Pasvanoğlu Osman Paşa of Vidin in the Age of Ottoman Social Change, 1791–1815'. PhD Dissertation, History, University of Wisconsin.

Index

abuse of power, 84, 119–20
Ağa Hüseyin Paşa, governor of Vidin, 131, 132, 145n18

Bab-ı Meşihat, 87, 113n11
biopolitics *see* technologies of Ottoman governmentality (or governance)
Bulgarian Exarchate, 121, 124, 143n4, 143n7

Cevdet Paşa, 42n37, 75n18, 75n19
church
   as a proprietor, 122–4, 138–40
Circassians *see* refugees
circle of justice, 144n13
commercial code (of 1850), 27, 51
conversion, 51, 88, 97
copy registers of the administrative council, 3–5, 9, 78n40
   abstract nature of, 82, 84–5, 87, 90
   and politics of local administration, 55–6, 82, 111, 171
   recording procedures of, 96, 130
corruption, 53, 120, 128
corvée labour, 28, 120, 151
council members
   absence from the meetings, 82, 84, 86, 89, 96
   accountant (*muhasebeci*), 49, 85, 103, 105
   candidate lists, 59–63, 66, 69–70, 78n36, 79n44, 79n47, 90, 96–7, 113n19
   change in the numbers of, 50, 65, 78n39
   chief rabbi (*hahambaşı*), 49, 75n12, 86, 88, 90
   Christian religious leader (*metropolitan* or *despot*), 24, 49, 75n12, 86–91, 96–7, 99, 113n13, 118, 120–1, 124, 126, 142n4, 143, 170

deputy metropolitan, 94–5, 97
deputy subgovernor, 86–7, 90–4, 99, 101, 103
director of correspondence (*müdür-i tahrirat*), 49, 85–6, 103, 105
divisional general (*ferik*), 24
elected members (*a'za*), 24, 49, 51–2, 85, 112n10
elections of, 51–2, 60–2, 65–70, 73, 76n22, 77n34, 79n48, 81–2, 90, 96–7, 101, 105–6, 110, 113n19
examining clerk (*mümeyyiz*), 49, 62, 65, 70, 78n41, 103, 118, 137, 142n2
field marshal (*müşir*), 24
finance office director (*mal müdürü*), 120
governor (*vali*), 48–9, 52–3, 60–2, 65, 68, 75n11, 97
head secretary (*tahrirat katibi*), 120
hierarchy among, 58, 81–2, 84
imam, 134, 159
incompetence of, 74n10, 83, 120–2, 125, 126
and interrogations (*istintak*), 161
interrogators (*müstantık*), 103
land registrar (*arazi katibi*), 53, 139
land registry clerk (*tahrir-i emlak katibi*), 53
mobility within the judicio-administrative sphere, 53, 62, 105–6, 109, 169
Muslim religious leader (*mufti*), 24, 49, 69, 85, 87–8, 91, 99, 112n10, 142n4
and nominating committees (*meclis-i tefrik*), 51–2, 60–1, 65, 68, 86
participation of, 82, 84, 97–8, 101
prominence within the judicio-administrative sphere, 62, 69–70, 73, 101, 127–9, 136

council members (cont.)
  registrar of title deeds (tapu katibi), 53
  and reports, 5, 117–30, 141, 171
  resignation of, 53, 60–1, 68, 77n34, 90, 97
  and Russians, 153
  salaries of, 68, 78n43, 82, 103, 171
  shar'i judge (hakim el-şer' or na'ib el-şer'), 24, 49–50, 85, 87, 90, 96, 103, 106, 108, 120–1, 143n4
  strategies and negotiations among, 9, 36, 55, 61, 81–2, 84, 118, 120–1, 124–6, 161, 171
  subgovernor (mutasarrıf), 46, 49, 52, 60, 75n11, 85–6, 88, 90, 96–7, 101, 103, 106, 108–9, 112n10
  term limits and re-election, 52, 58, 60, 67–8, 70, 73, 78n41, 87, 96–7, 103, 106, 125, 161, 166, 169
council of appeals and crime
  duties of, 47–50
  and foreigners' property disputes, 174n8
  and limits of legal authority over disputes, 75n18
  as part of the nizamiye court system, 50, 72, 80n54
  see also provincial councils
Council of Judicial Ordinances (Divân-ı Ahkâm-ı 'Adliye), 11n8, 42n37, 75n19
Council of State (Şura-yı Devlet), 11n8, 29, 42n31, 75n19, 84, 112n9, 130–2, 134, 136
county administrative council
  duties of, 47–50
  see also provincial councils
county, as an administrative unit (liva or sancak), 44–8, 74n3

Dalyell, Sir R. A. O. (British consul), 148, 162n4
Danube province (vilayet), 1, 47
  formation of, 1, 162n3
  governors of, 4, 47, 78n42
  involvement with counties, 134, 135, 139
  Nish county (liva), 47, 149
  as a prototype, 5, 46–7
  Ruse, provincial capital, 30, 34, 45–6, 60, 68, 78n40, 79n44, 84, 96, 116, 130, 134, 139, 149
  Silistra county (liva), 47
  Sofia county (liva), 47
  Tarnovo county (liva), 47
  Tulcha county (liva), 47
  Varna county (liva), 47
district head official (ka'imakam), 48–9, 63, 88, 109, 113n22, 116–21, 124–8, 137–8, 140–1, 143n4, 146, 157, 161
drunkenness, 83, 120, 126, 128
Düstur (imperial legal corpora), 32–4

educational reforms, 114n28

forest, 18, 26, 78n38, 102, 110, 122–4, 139–40, 156
Foucault, Michel
  biopolitics, 77n30, 144n12, 146, 154
  economy as a spontaneous mechanism, 154
  governmental reason, 35, 114n24, 146, 154, 158, 160, 163n12, 164n14
  governmentality, 12n17, 117, 154, 163n11
  liberalism, 146, 154
  liberalism and a culture of danger, 160
  markets as a site of verification-falsification of government practice, 146, 154, 158
  police, 77n30
  political economy, 154, 163n12
  political knowledge/arithmetic, 35–7
  population, 35, 146, 154
  power, 136, 137
  problematisation, 116, 138, 146
  social structuration, 136
  strategies, 136, 137

Giddens, Anthony
  dialectic of control, 55, 57–8, 126
  sphere of the political, 31, 102, 125
  textually mediated organisation, 34, 125
gospodars see local notables
Great Britain, 112n2
guilds, 27–8

Index

Gülhane imperial decree, 14, 17–18, 21–2, 32, 36, 38n8, 42n37

Habermas, Jürgen
   legitimation crisis, 16, 21, 25, 38n6
   and liberal capitalist social formation, 10n1, 21, 34
   and means of production, 16
   social formation, 16, 31, 38n4, 38n5
   structural prerequisites of production, 26, 30–1
   and traditional social formation, 16, 21
hegemony (as a process), 16, 77n31
homo juridicus, 128, 142
   and *homo economicus*, 128

ihtisab see market order

Janissaries
   abolishment of, 17, 41n23, 114n26, 145n18
   involvement with provincial economy, 7, 114n26, 173
   and the local elite, 6–7, 168
judicio-administrative sphere, 8
   and Agricultural Credit Funds (*Menafi'-i 'Umumiye Sandığı*), 28–9, 41n28, 110
   authorial language in, 141
   clerks within, 52–4, 66, 76n20, 85, 96, 103, 114n25, 114n28, 130, 171
   council members within, 136, 161, 171
   as a domain of hegemonic negotiations, 15, 82, 105, 109, 111, 117, 130, 141, 142, 158, 169
   false accusations and inaccuracy of reports within, 54, 111, 122
   and governmental reason, 147, 157
   guarantors (for clerks) within, 53
   hierarchy among offices within, 45–6, 48–9, 51, 80n54, 82, 102–3, 111
   institutions of, 101, 174n8
   interaction among councils within, 51, 75n19, 96, 101, 111, 122, 127–30, 138, 170
   local notables' presence within, 4, 8, 54, 71, 73, 82, 111, 166, 170
   office of land registry (*defter-i hakani*), 139
   and Orphans' Funds (*Emval-ı Eytam Sandığı*), 29, 42n31, 110
   and property surveys/registrations, 23, 39n15 40n18, 135
   and the provincial regulation of 1864, 50, 72, 87, 169; *see also* provincial regulation(s)
   and the provincial regulation of 1871, 72, 169; *see also* provincial regulation(s)
   and *şehremaneti*, 105, 114n26
   and separation of judicial and administrative functions, 8, 47–51, 72, 74n8, 74n10, 80n54, 118, 127–9
   and *shar'i* court, 46, 51, 74n7, 75n15, 103, 114n25
   shift of power within, 106, 108
   and social mobility, 169, 171
   textual representation of, 141, 172

Kanitz, Felix, 123, 124, 148, 153, 163n5, 163n10

land registrar (*arazi katibi*) *see* council members
legitimation crisis, 15, 24–6, 135, 166, 168
liberal-capitalist social formation, 26
   and a culture of danger, 160
   in the Ottoman Empire, 1, 8–9, 15, 21, 26, 31, 36–7, 73, 130, 135, 162, 168, 172, 173, 174n6
   and refugee settlement process, 147, 160
   and textually mediated organisation, 37
liberalism *see* liberal-capitalist social formation
local notables
   *ayan*s, 6, 11n6, 12n11, 12n12, 28
   chorbadzhia, 72
   elite networks, 3, 56–7, 141, 167
   establishing a connection among councils, 72
   gospodars, 7–8, 12n14, 72
   higher-tier, 17, 165, 167
   intergenerational continuity in the prominence of, 72
   involvement with provincial governance prior to the 1864 provincial regulation, 17, 23, 36, 49, 72, 173n2

local notables (*cont.*)
  and Janissary forces, 168
  within judicio-administrative sphere, 25, 36, 44–5, 49, 58, 72–3, 74n10, 82, 111n1, 166, 170
  lower-tier, 165, 167
  and political influence after the end of the Ottoman rule, 44–5, 71–2
Longworth, John A. (British consul), 1, 10, 148, 153, 162

market order
  and government intervention, 158, 160
  ihtisab, 114n26
  narh, 114n26
  refugees as a threat to, 160
  spontaneous (or self-regulative), 9, 26, 31, 142, 162, 168, 172
  see also liberal-capitalist social formation
Mecelle, 42n37
Mehmed Emin Paşa, Kıbrıslı, 173n4
Midhat Paşa, 1, 4, 5, 9, 30, 47, 75n19, 78n42, 79n49, 112n6, 114n26, 152, 156, 166, 173n4
modernity, 10n3
municipal councils *see* provincial councils

na'ib, 87; *see also* council members, shari judge
narh see market order
negligence,125, 118–19, 116

office of land registry (*defter-i hakani*) *see* judicio-administrative sphere
official titles and honorifics, 33, 41n23, 77n33, 84, 88, 97, 102, 111, 115n29
Ottoman governmentality (or governance), 1, 114n24
  and Bulgarian governance, 73
  and cattle theft, 156–7
  challenging, 55–7, 117, 140
  difference with Ottoman government, 76n26
  and governmental reason, 35–7, 156–7
  as a hegemonic domain, 57, 116, 136, 137, 141
  institutions of, 57, 130, 142
  and legitimation, 34

and liberal capitalist social formation, 37, 147, 158
limits to, boundaries of, 142, 147, 160
and local economy, 105
and means of production, 18–22, 24–6, 31, 37, 116, 135, 138, 162, 166
omnipresence of, 158
and politics of local administration, 4
and power relations, 172
and refugee settlement, 9, 146, 150, 156, 157
refusing to be a part of, 140
and textually mediated information, 31–2, 37, 126, 130
see also technologies of Ottoman governmentality (or governance)
Ottoman institutional transformation, 1–2, 11n4, 14
  in the 17th century, 15–16, 19, 40n17, 165–7
  in the 18th century, 15, 17, 19, 165–7
  in the 19th century, 3, 5, 15, 17, 20–7, 31, 33, 46, 50, 57, 74n7, 74n10, 79n49, 87, 124, 165–8
  and provincial councils, 47, 169
  see also Tanzimat
Ottoman property regime
  and the land code of 1858, 7, 18–20, 38n10, 131, 133, 134, 168
  miri lands, 39n11, 39n13
  piror to the land code of 1858, 7, 16, 18–20
  and *waqf*, 19, 39n12
Ottoman social formation
  and means of production, 14, 18–22
  transformation of, 15, 24, 31, 36–7
  see also liberal capitalist social formation; traditional social formation

pastureland, 122, 130–5, 139, 140–1
Pasvanoğlu Osman Paşa, 6, 7, 8, 12n12, 17, 167
penal code, 21, 142n3
police (*zaptiye*), 106, 116, 119–21, 125–6
politics of local administration, 2, 4–5, 9–10, 14–15, 25, 37, 44–5, 54, 57–8, 66, 70, 73, 77n28, 82, 101, 110–11, 116, 126, 130, 142, 168, 173

Index

provincial councils, 1, 3, 49
  of 1849 (sing *eyalet meclisi*), 49, 72
  and application of Tanzimat, 24, 73n2, 174n7
  changes in the composition over time, 90–8, 132, 152
  commercial court, 27, 50–1, 78n43, 104
  commission of surveys (*tahrir komisyonu*), 70–1, 105–6, 108, 114n27
  and commissions, 135, 137, 139
  council of elders, 83, 159
  disputes within, 83–4, 122, 136, 171
  district administrative council, 51–2, 68, 116–17, 127–9, 143n4, 161
  district litigation council, 51, 68, 75n18
  editing/drafting of reports in, 9, 57, 78n40, 96; *see also* copy registers of the administrative council
  elected *vs ex officio* members within, 44, 47, 49, 51, 56, 58, 68, 74n9, 78n43, 103, 112n4
  election procedures for, 45, 51, 55, 62, 66–70, 67, 73, 76n22, 81, 116, 159, 169; *see also* council members, elections of
  hegemony within, 45, 68, 70, 87, 90, 101
  and interactions with the church, 138, 139
  and interrogations, 116, 121, 127, 128, 129, 171
  and investigations, 54, 118, 127, 128, 129, 130, 137
  land office (*arazi kalemi*), 105
  members' participation in, 9, 110
  municipal councils (*meclis-i da'ire-i belediye*), 44, 48, 71, 78n43, 81, 97, 102, 105–7, 111, 114n26, 124, 143n10, 170
  municipal councils, after the end of Ottoman rule, 44, 71
  and other offices within the judicio-administrative sphere, 9, 45, 111, 169
  and Ottoman institutional transformation, 15, 23–5, 169
  people circumventing, 117, 132
  and property appropriation/sale, 132, 133, 134, 139
  and property surveys/registrations, 24, 135
  record-keeping procedures of, 84, 96; *see also* copy registers of the administrative council
  and refugee settlement, 151, 153, 156–7, 160
  silencing resistance, 140, 141
  and a single government of state officials and local elites, 82, 108, 142, 169
  survey office (*tahrir kalemi*), 105
  tax collection councils (*muhassıllık meclisi*), 15, 23–6, 40n22, 70, 84, 87, 168
  and taxation, 49, 51, 88, 119–21, 126, 137, 138, 168, 171
  and transfer of information, 15, 54, 57, 66, 77n27, 111, 142, 171
provincial economy
  and credit availability, 28–9, 105, 168
  growth in the 19th century, 5, 150
  and influx of cattle, 147, 152, 168
  and Janissaries, 168
  and Ottoman treasury bonds, 105
  and refugees, 155, 160
  and taxes, 23, 168
provincial governance *see* Ottoman governmentality (or governance)
provincial regulation(s)
  of 1849, 49, 72
  of 1864, 1, 8–9, 15, 40n22, 44–51, 58, 68, 70–3, 74n8, 75n13, 84, 87, 166, 168, 169, ix
  of 1871, 9, 34, 42n36, 45, 47–9, 58, 68, 72, 73, 74n8, 74n9, 78n39, 169
  of the Danube Province, 47, 49–50, 74n4, 75n13, 78n43
  and the judicio-administrative sphere, 48–51, 169
provincial treasury
  and allocation of tax revenues, 155
public sphere of state administration, 102, 169

Refugee Commission, 11n8, 149, 150, 151
refugees
  allowances for, 155

197

refugees (*cont.*)
   and buffer-zone building/Islamicisation, 149, 150
   Bulgarian, 150, 157, 172
   and cattle theft, 143n6, 147, 156, 158, 160
   cattle for, 150, 155
   Circassian, 121, 137–9, 146–7, 149, 150–4, 160, 161, 162n3, 172
   compensation for lost property of, 151
   differences in settlement patterns of, 152
   different waves of migration, 148
   diversity among, 149, 150
   housing for, 39n15, 151
   impact on local economy, 152, 155
   interaction with locals and other groups, 138, 149, 151, 153, 154, 157, 159, 160
   and Islam, 163n7
   keeping records of, 151
   land for, 155
   leaving Russia, 148, 155
   local populace helping, 151, 157, 172
   medical help for, 149, 151
   mobility of, 160
   narratives and stereotypes about, 149, 152, 153
   number of, 147, 148, 149
   post-1877 wave, 163n7
   problematisation of, 147, 160
   and provincial councils, 160
   resettlement in Anatolia, 149
   and right to bear arms, 159
   and Russian influence, 153
   from Serbia, 151, 154
   and settlement process, 9, 142, 146, 149, 152, 157, 162n3
   staying in others' homes, 149, 150
   Tatar, 137–9, 146, 149, 150–4, 157, 172
   tax exemptions for, 150
   and travel permits, 158, 159
   villages for, 151, 152, 156, 157, 159
   wealth of, 163n8
roads/railways, 23, 30
rule of law, 125, 133
Ruse *see* Danube province

salaries, 53, 76n23, 78n43, 109, 114n23, 114n28; *see also* council members
schools, 30–1, 34, 109, 114n28
seals
   engraving/lettering of, 87–8, 98, 101, 112n8, 113n20
   theft of, 101, 128
   use for collecting payments, 101, 112n8, 113n21
   use for identification, 85, 101, 112n8, 113n22, 159
   use for marking participation, 84, 97, 101, 112n5
   use for proving authenticity of documents, 85
   use on provincial records, 85–98, 101, 109–10
   of Vidin's administrative council members (images), 99–100
selem money-lending contracts, 21, 30, 39n16, 119–21, 143n5
17th-century crisis, 16
silk production, 123, 143n9
social integration, 168; *see also* system integration
sodomy, 116, 119
state
   as a hegemonic environment, 56–7
   as monolith, 4, 58, 105, 158
   vs society as a dichotomy, 3, 9, 11n6, 36, 117, 125, 126, 136
state–society relations, 2
   in Ottoman Empire and in Europe, 2–3, 165
   a single government of state officials and local elites, 4, 9, 15, 82, 117, 136, 166
subgovernors
   duties of, 48
   see also council members
Supreme Council (*Meclis-i Vala*), 40n20, 75n19
Supreme Council of Judicial Ordinances (*Meclis-i Vala-yı Ahkam-ı Adliye*), 8, 12n14, 23, 51, 75n19, 84, 112n6, 155
survey (imperial) of population, property and income (*temettuat*), 20–1, 23, 40n19, 106
Svoboda (Bulgarian-language weekly published in Bucharest), 71, 79n49

Index

system crisis, 168
system integration, 168; *see also* social integration

Tanzimat reforms, 18, 32
  conventional historiography on, 2, 4, 10n3, 21–2, 36, 37n2
  provincial reaction to, 24, 79n49, 147n7
Tarnovo (Veliko) Constitution of 1879, 72
Tatars *see* refugees
taxation
  abuse of power in, 54, 126
  communal tax (*ancemaatin virgü*), 22–3, 40n21, 167
  reforms in, 22–6, 46
  tax collection councils (*muhassıllık meclisi*) *see* provincial councils
  tax collectors (sing. *muhassıl*), 22–5, 40n22
  tax farming (*mukata'a*), 22, 24, 26, 40n17, 40n22, 167
teachers, 109, 114n28
technologies of Ottoman governmentality (or governance)
  biopolitics, 105, 147, 152, 154, 157–8, 160–1, 162n1, 163n11, 164n13, 172
  and civil society, 147, 158
  problematisation, 9, 138, 146, 147, 152, 154, 158, 160, 161, 172
  refugee settlement, 147, 152, 154, 160–2, 172
  report writing, 55–8, 82, 140
  textually mediated organisation, 35
theft, 83, 128, 159
torture, 118–19, 121, 126, 142n3
traditional social formation
  crisis of, 15, 18–19, 24–6, 31, 36–7
  in the Ottoman Empire, 15, 73, 135, 168
  see also legitimation crisis

Vidin county (*liva*), 1, 5–6, 47
  'Adliye (Kula) district (*kaza*), 7, 47, 137, 140, 142, 154, 157, 161
  Belgradcık (Belogradchik) district (*kaza*), 1, 7, 47, 114n28

Berkofça (Bergovitsa) district (*kaza*), 1, 47, 89, 92, 113n14, 114n28, 116–19, 121–4, 127–9, 137–8, 141–2, 143n4, 143n9, 149
  Bregova (Briagovo) village, 69, 79n48
  Chernamasnice village, 157
  Draganiçe (Draganitse) village, 117–19, 121–4, 127
  1849 uprising in, 6–8
  Gradets village, 156
  Gumzovo village, 71
  Helvacı (Maior Uzunovo) village, 69–70, 79n48
  İvraca (Vratsa) district (*kaza*), 1, 47, 53, 88, 114n28, 138
  Kerkenez island, 135–6, 141
  Lom district (*kaza*), 1, 7, 47, 53, 114n28, 149
  Midhat Paşa village, 156, 157
  Müşriye pasture, 130, 133–4, 141
  number of villages within, 7, 79n46
  population of, 6
  Rabrovo village, 157
  Rahova (Rahovo) district (*kaza*), 1, 47, 54, 96, 114n28
  Roman village, 138, 140–2
  Slanatruna (Slanotrŭn) village, 69–70, 79n48
  Yukarı Ova pasture, 133–6, 141
village headmen, 118, 134, 159

yearbooks (sing. *salname*), 101–10
  accuracy of, 34, 65–7, 87, 97, 102–3, 106, 125, 170
  choice of information to include in, 33–4, 102, 109
  and council members' names, 78n38, 97, 144n11, 162
  and demographic information, 110, 156
  design of, 33–4, 102
  price of, 33–4
  and tables and statistics on the provinces, 78n38, 102, 110
  as textual representations of governance, 34, 66, 103, 105, 109–11, 114n24, 124, 143n4, 170

EU representative:
Easy Access System Europe
Mustamäe tee 50, 10621 Tallinn, Estonia
Gpsr.requests@easproject.com

www.ingramcontent.com/pod-product-compliance
Lightning Source LLC
Chambersburg PA
CBHW051058230426
43667CB00013B/2357